TRIAL OF
STRENGTH

TRIAL OF STRENGTH

Adventures and Misadventures on the Wild and Remote Subantarctic Islands

Shona Riddell

EXISLE
PUBLISHING

'I have seen nothing to surpass, or even equal, the grandeur, the savage majesty of its grim storm-beaten sea walls; standing up bold and defiant, sullenly challenging old Ocean to a trial of strength.'

— *New Zealand government representative Henry Armstrong, describing his first impressions of the Auckland Islands during a voyage on the* Amherst *in 1868 to establish castaway depots and search for shipwreck survivors.*

First published 2018

Exisle Publishing Pty Ltd
226 High Street, Dunedin, 9016, New Zealand
PO Box 864, Chatswood, NSW 2057, Australia
www.exislepublishing.com

A CiP record for this book is available from the National Library of New Zealand.

ISBN 978-1-77559-356-0

Designed by Nick Turzynski of redinc. Book Design
Typeset in Minion Pro 12/15
Printed in China

This book uses paper sourced under ISO 14001 guidelines from well-managed forests and other controlled sources.

10 9 8 7 6 5 4 3 2 1

For Sarah Ann Cripps (1822–92), my great-great-great grandmother and a reluctant seafarer with a heart of gold.

CONTENTS

A young elephant seal among king penguins on Macquarie Island.

INTRODUCTION

THEY'RE NOT COVERED IN ICE, but they can be brutally cold. Despite our globalized, 21st-century world of frequent flying, they are rarely visited. Most of them are uninhabited by humans, yet they are teeming with wildlife. They are forbidding and fragile, bleak and beautiful. They are the world's subantarctic islands.

The subantarctic islands circle the lower part of the globe, below the southern tips of Australia, New Zealand, South America and Africa, forming a 'ring of tiny stepping stones'[1] in the Roaring Forties and Furious Fifties latitudes encountered by those heading to Antarctica. But the subantarctic islands have no permanent ice on them and are warmer than their Antarctic neighbours, with plenty of wind, fog and rain caused by the colder Antarctic seas colliding with the warmer waters of the north.

Geographically and politically, the subantarctic is defined as the area north of the Antarctic Circle (the grey circle on the map on page 2) — in other words, the islands that lie between 47° and 60° latitude south of the Equator. But because of the subantarctic region's unique climate and environment, it's generally considered to be the area outside the Antarctic Convergence (the area outside the wavy blue line).

For the purposes of this book, 'subantarctic' follows the second definition and therefore excludes South Georgia Island and the Kerguelen Islands (considered 'Antarctic islands north of 60°S')[2]. What's more, the focus will be on New Zealand's and Australia's subantarctic islands in the Southern Ocean with the occasional leap across the globe to, say, the Falkland Islands in the South Atlantic Ocean, or the Crozet Islands in the Indian Ocean.

The 20-odd island groups in the subantarctic region appear on a world map as a series of tiny specks, surrounded and protected by vast, powerful oceans. Most of them are the remnants of ancient volcanic eruptions, and have been shaped over many centuries by glaciation and ocean currents. They contain some of the world's few remaining unspoiled environments, and are filled with unique wildlife and plants.

The human history of the islands

Despite their isolation and wild climates, these far-flung islands have been visited by countless people over the past two centuries — not always intentionally. Their stories feature births, deaths, greed, fear, triumph (sometimes) and endurance. The early arrivals hunted seals and whales; dozens of ships were wrecked there, leaving castaways to battle against the elements for survival; curious scientists and explorers ventured south with great enthusiasm; optimistic farmers leased the land; and wartime coastwatchers were ordered to keep a lookout for enemy ships.

There were even young families who sailed all the way from England to live there: the Hardwicke settlers of the mid-1800s. Two of them were my great-great-great grandparents, Isaac and Sarah Cripps. Their fourth child, my great-great grandmother Harriet, was born on Auckland Island, 465 kilometres (290 miles) south of New Zealand. It was, and still is, a very unusual birthplace.

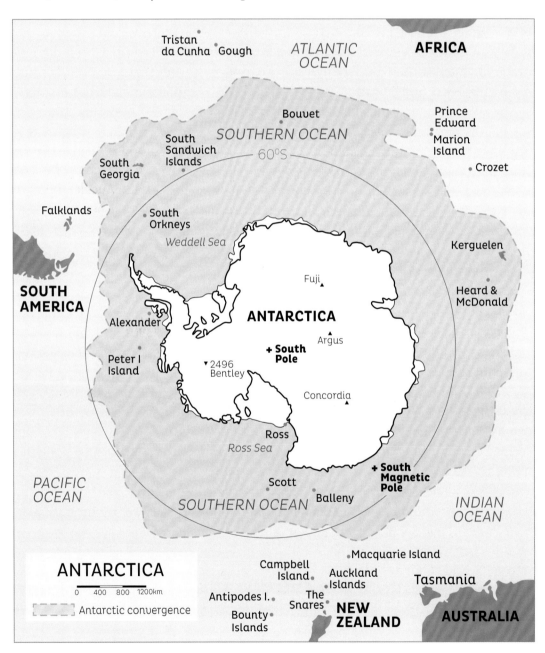

For four generations the tale of the short-lived, ill-fated Hardwicke township has been passed down through my family. As a child, I was unmoved by the story; I assumed that the Auckland Islands were somewhere near Auckland City and hence not very exotic (at least, not to a New Zealander). But once I grew up and studied a world map, I wondered: *What on earth were they thinking?*

After all, what could possibly possess a British couple to sail halfway around the world in 1849 with their three young children, along with just 55 other people, to live in a place so utterly hostile, remote and (they thought) uninhabited? Their motives are explained, and their story is told, in Chapter 4.

A personal pilgrimage

Today, all of New Zealand's subantarctic islands are uninhabited (Macquarie Island is Australian territory and still has an occupied research station), although they continue to attract small numbers of tourists, scientists and conservationists from around the world.

I felt drawn to the islands too, even though the idea of sailing over storm-tossed seas seemed rather nightmarish. The titles of books I'd read on the subject weren't reassuring: *Island of the Lost, Forgotten Islands, Islands of Despair …* One of the Auckland Islands is even called Disappointment Island! Perhaps curiosity simply got the better of me, or perhaps it's in my blood, but at the end of 2016 I took a deep breath and headed south to The Snares, the Auckland Islands, and Campbell Island.

I got there by ship, like my forbearers, and despite the modern comforts of warm, waterproof clothing and hot showers, riding the rolling waves of the Southern Ocean was far from a cocktail cruise (but that's part of the adventure). The experience changed me, but not in the way I'd anticipated; instead of feeling despair, I felt awed and inspired.

The otherworldly plants and curious wildlife were like nothing I had ever encountered before. The frothing surf pounding against jagged cliffs, and the fierce, stinging wind on my face were exhilarating. It was like travelling back in time to a pre-human era, with no crowds, no TVs, no Facebook, no cars, no cafes … and I was surprised to find that I loved it.

Visiting the subantarctic islands was a life-changing experience for me, but I certainly wasn't the first person to feel as I did. As one interviewee for this book put it: 'The islands stay with you. It's like an invisible cord always tugging, making you want to go back. I think about them every day.' This is particularly true for the small but dedicated group of people who have spent significant portions of their lives working there, often in challenging conditions. When you're thrown together to sink or swim in a remote location (literally, in the more historic cases), bonds form pretty quickly. Mention the sea lions, the albatrosses, the penguins, or the giant megaherb plants, and there's an instant spark, regardless of whether people were there one year ago or 60 years ago.

Forgotten books on forgotten islands

I returned home talking constantly about the subantarctic islands, reading every book and article that I could find on the topic, and connecting with other people who had been there too, either for scientific or meteorological work or simply for an unusual holiday. There is a growing awareness of the subantarctic islands thanks to mainstream media coverage, nature documentaries, and social media photos and hashtags, although most people would probably still struggle to point them out on a world map.

But I soon realized that most books on the subject were out of print and filled with outdated information. Even the more enduring history books from the 20th century are now several decades old. Fergus McLaren wrote about the history of the Auckland Islands (originally a PhD thesis) 80 years ago, and Conon Fraser's classic, *Beyond the Roaring Forties*, was published in 1986 — more than 30 years ago.

Since the 1980s, the Campbell Island Meteorological Station has become fully automated and there have been large-scale pest eradications on most of the islands, which have caused dramatic changes. There have been accidents and world-first helicopter rescues, as well as the ground-breaking use of new technology, such as drones and GPS, to study wildlife in tricky-to-reach locations.

The growth of the internet also means that many old documents, articles and photos, once buried in dusty corners of libraries, have been digitized and are now accessible from anywhere in the world with a few clicks. From the comfort of our homes we can read 19th-century shipwreck reports, experience the life of a subantarctic shepherd from his 100-year-old diary, or view high-quality footage of a stranger's journey to one of the most remote parts of the world. Still, not everything is online. Many precious documents are still buried in descendants' attics or boxed away in archives, and nothing on screen or paper compares with listening to the first-person accounts of people who have lived and worked on the islands over the years.

During my research I also noticed that women's stories were few and far between, either mentioned in passing or not at all. There were certainly men-only eras, but plenty of women have visited, worked on, or even lived on the subantarctic islands — my ancestors among them — and continue to do so in the case of Macquarie Island. Where were their stories? I had to dig a bit deeper to find them and have included several in this book.

An intertwining of narratives

Because the islands are so small, it's probably not a surprise that the different stories and eras tend to overlap. Macquarie Island penguin harvester Joseph Hatch's illegal sealing gang rescued the *Derry Castle* castaways from the Auckland Islands in the 1880s; Campbell Island conservationists camped in the old World War II coastwatching hut in the 1970s; German astronomers enjoyed Christmas dinner with the Auckland Island farmers in the 1870s; everyone stumbled across old shipwreck remains; and a tourist (me) visited her ancestors' long-abandoned, 19th-century home in the new millennium.

Despite the islands' location in the Southern Hemisphere, these stories span the globe. British, American and French explorers, Shetland farmers, New Zealand Māori, Chatham Island Moriori, Australian gold miners, European astronomers, a Scottish princess (albeit a mythical one) … it's a cast of thousands. But to manage expectations (and keep the book light enough to pick up), this book does not include a list of every single person, ship, and event related to the subantarctic islands. Instead, it offers snapshots of some of the livelier stories involving people who made it there — and sometimes, like Frodo, back again.

I may well have omitted a significant figure or left out a story that's close to someone's heart, and many events are only summarized (especially the ongoing conservation work, which could easily fill a book in itself), but these stories are intended to enlighten those who may have never heard of the subantarctic islands, or who have heard something about them and want to know more. There's a list of resources included at the back for those who would like to learn more about a particular island, person, or era. The subantarctic islands are an often-overlooked part of our planet and they deserve to be studied in more depth for their incredible history and unique environments (New Zealand's and Australia's subantarctic islands are all UNESCO World Heritage sites, a sign of their global importance).

People vs. Nature

Initially I'd thought that, as a non-scientist, I should focus on the human history and leave nature in the background, but I soon realized that was foolish and also impossible. Nature is the main character in all of these stories, featuring as the protagonist or antagonist (and sometimes both). After all, over the past two centuries nature has either drawn people to the subantarctic islands or driven them away. These days it forms a protective bubble around the islands, with lashing rain, fierce gales, and ferocious seas guarding their fragile ecosystems from long-term intrusion.

However, we still have a responsibility to protect and care for them. The subantarctic islands are vital breeding grounds for millions of seabirds and thousands of seals. But shifting air and water temperatures, introduced pests, diseases and fisheries all pose a threat to the rare and endemic wildlife, which depend on the islands' unique environments for their ongoing survival.

The subantarctic islands are beautiful, dramatic, remote and fascinating specks in the ocean that have so far managed to outlast their ephemeral human history. To mangle a line from Shakespeare: people make their entrances and their exits, but ultimately Mother Nature takes centre stage.

Shona Riddell, 2018

Te Reo Māori

A note on the pronunciation of Te Reo Māori (Māori language) words in this book: Longer vowel sounds are indicated by a macron (a straight bar) above the vowel. Vowels are pronounced a 'ɒ' (as in 'apart'), e 'ɛ' (as in 'entry'), i (as in 'eat'), o 'ɔ' (as in 'pork') and u 'ʉ' (as in 'loot').[3]

1. DISCOVERY
The sealing captain, the 'ship's wife', and the lonely ghost (1780–1830)

IMAGINE THE EUPHORIA OF BEING the first person in the world to officially discover an island. Now, imagine that excitement doubled when you discover two islands within six months of each other — both of them covered in seals, and right in the middle of a sealing boom.

It's a tale of rampant exploitation that today makes conservationists shudder, but in 1810 it was a jackpot of top-division lottery proportions for British–Australian captain Frederick Hasselburg of Sydney, who had sailed south through the Roaring Forties to seek his fortune.

But wait … was it Hasselburg, Hasselbourg, Hazelburg, or Hasselborough? These days no one seems quite sure how the intrepid captain's last name was spelled. The transcription of surnames was not an exact science in the early 19th century, and even the captain himself altered the spelling at least once.[1] If he'd named one of the two islands he discovered after himself, his surname may have been more accurately recorded for posterity. Instead, he claimed them both for Britain and dutifully named one 'Campbell's Island' after Campbell & Co., the Sydney sealing company that employed him, and the other 'Macquarie's Island', after the governor of New South Wales.

There's no surviving portrait of Captain Hasselburg, so let's imagine him for a moment as a 19th-century, subantarctic Chris Hemsworth, standing proud, legs astride, at the helm of his two-masted ship, clad in long sea boots and a heavy cloak. His dark hair ripples in the wind, and his expression is determined as he peers through a brass telescope and clutches a sextant.

The ship under his command, aptly named the *Perseverance*, pitches and rolls over the swells, its square sails cracking and rope rigging shuddering in the strong winds. On either side, giant petrels and wandering albatrosses surf the breeze, while frigid grey waves crash over the slippery wooden decks. Even today, the turbulent Southern Ocean is not for the faint-hearted. Waves regularly surge up 5 to 10 metres, or 15 to 30 feet — 23.8 metres (78 feet) is the highest on record, off Campbell Island in 2018.[2] The captain's

A Campbell albatross soars over the stormy Southern Ocean.

small, wooden-masted sailing ship would have bobbed along like a cork at the mercy of the gale-force winds that are so prevalent in the southern latitudes.

Captain Hasselburg was desperately seeking new sealing grounds because things hadn't been going well for him. His reports to Campbell & Co., his employer, were 'the reverse of cheerful'[3] because his sealing endeavours around the coasts of Australia and New Zealand hadn't amounted to much — there was simply too much competition and he was barely covering the costs of running his ship.

According to J.S. Cumpston's meticulously researched 1968 book, *Macquarie Island*, at the end of 1809 Campbell & Co. sent the *Perseverance* south with Hasselburg and a gang of sealers on a search for new sealing grounds.[4] However, journalist Robert Carrick, who was known for his entertaining but not always reliable historical accounts in the late 19th century, writes that the captain was visited in his dreams by an angel who whispered some coordinates in his ear.[5]

Cumpston's version seems more plausible, but either way the captain was about to go where no European man had gone before. He departed from Sydney in late October on an exploratory voyage deep into the Southern Ocean and, on 4 January 1810, he stumbled across his holy grail.

Captivated by Campbell

Campbell Island today, looking much as it would have when Captain Hasselburg discovered it in 1810 (apart from the Tucker Cove farm site), with a view over Perseverance Harbour.

Campbell Island (Motu Ihupuku in Māori) is the eroded remains of a shield (domed) volcano lying almost 700 kilometres (435 miles) south of New Zealand's South Island.

As Captain Hasselburg's ship approached, the crew's first glimpse of the island would have been of mist-shrouded, tussock-covered hills up to 550 metres (1800 feet) tall, rising abruptly out of the sea. It was probably raining, because it rains there at least 320 days a year.

The island extends over 112 square kilometres (43 square miles) and is covered in low dracophyllum scrub, often blown horizontal by the sharp, incessant winds. The captain arrived in January, so he would have seen the flowering of the giant-leafed megaherb plants that bloom yellow and purple in the subantarctic summer, adding a surprisingly tropical touch to a bleak landscape. A light falling of snow is not unusual at any time of the year.

Great albatrosses nest on the misty plateaus, stretching out their 3-metre (10-foot) wings and soaring over the clifftops

CAMPBELL ISLAND

0   1   2   3   4   5km

169°00'E   05°   10°   15°

52°30'S

35°

towards the open sea. The coastlines are peppered with seals, as well as yellow-eyed and rockhopper penguins. But the sight of these peaceful creatures in January 1810 would not have evoked a tender response in the captain. Instead, he would have had multiple pound signs flashing in a thought bubble over his head as soon as he saw the fur seals.

After sailing into the main harbour, which is 1 kilometre (0.6 miles) wide and cuts 8 kilometres (5 miles) deep into the middle of the island from the east, he and his crew quickly got to work and eventually filled the *Perseverance* with 15,000 fur-seal skins. (He was apparently less interested in what were later

described as the 'worthless and obnoxious' sea lions.[6])

The captain then departed on the *Perseverance*, leaving behind his gang of seven sealers with some empty casks for collecting seal oil and a few months' worth of provisions. He returned to Sydney at a leisurely pace to pick up more equipment, and somehow managed to keep his discovery of Campbell Island a secret. But while making his way back in July to pick up his sealing gang as promised, the captain stumbled across an even better prospect: Macquarie Island.

Mesmerized by Macquarie

Macquarie Island (now fondly known to the resident staff as 'Macca') is a narrow, rocky stretch of land, about 35 kilometres long and up to 5 kilometres wide (22 x 3 miles). Highly unusually, it consists of a portion of the earth's mantle that has risen above sea level in one of the roughest parts of the Southern Ocean. It is constantly blasted by gale-force westerly winds, and its nearest neighbour, Auckland Island, is more than 600 kilometres (373 miles) away. Rain lashes its coastline for most of the year and the mean annual temperature is 4.5° Celsius (40° Fahrenheit).

There is no harbour, so sealing ships had to take their chances and hurriedly land their crews and supplies before the weather turned and they either got dragged onto the rocks or blown back out to sea.

The island was uninhabited on Captain Hasselburg's arrival in 1810. However, the first thing he noticed on the shingle beach was the broken-up ruin of an old ship that he described as being 'of ancient design'.[7] It was an ominous welcome and proved that he wasn't technically the *first* visitor to Macquarie, but he would perhaps be the first to leave the island in one piece.

Despite the bleak conditions, Macquarie Island was a hugely exciting discovery for Captain Hasselburg, even more so than Campbell had been. In peak season the island's narrow beaches are filled with hundreds of thousands of fur seals, as well as tens of thousands of elephant seals. Millions of penguins also crowd onto its shores in the springtime — kings, royals (which are endemic to Macquarie), rockhoppers and gentoos — although penguins would not be exploited for another 80 years.

If only he could have kept the big news of his discovery to himself! Alas, the captain hurried back to Sydney and behaved in a highly suspicious manner.[8] His sealing peers, most of them ex-convicts and more than a little savvy, knew immediately that something was up; after all, the captain had arrived back so quickly. What's more, he had just ordered a suspiciously large volume of salt (used for curing sealskin), his employer Campbell & Co. was urgently advertising in the local paper for a dozen more sealers, and the captain was planning on heading straight back out to sea again. He might as well have put a giant notice in the paper announcing that he'd found a profitable sealing location.

That night, a few of the sealers invited Captain Hasselburg to dinner and filled him with rum. 'We already know where your precious island is,' they bluffed. 'Your discovery is not a new one. However, let's all have a wager of £20 and whoever writes down the most accurate coordinates will win the money.'

The captain, described in later testimony as 'more than half-seas over' from drinking (in other words, pretty far gone but still upright), eagerly scribbled Macquarie's longitude and latitude (55°S, 159°E) with a bit of chalk.

'That's the correct answer!' the men cried in feigned disappointment, after taking a good look at the numbers. 'You win £20.'

Captain Hasselburg happily collected his cash and went home. But the other men were set to gain a lot more than that, as they well knew.

Plunder in the South Seas

Within just a few years of discovery the seals had almost disappeared from both Macquarie and Campbell islands, hunted to near-extinction by sealing gangs from locations as far flung as the United States and England. Everyone was desperate to make their fortunes by selling the fur, which was in particular demand in Britain for hats and coats, as well as in China for trimming ceremonial robes.[9] The oil rendered from elephant-seal blubber also burned cleanly in lamps and was used for soaps and machine lubrication. (Penguins would become a target later in the 1800s for fur muffs and twine.)

Fur seals, elephant seals, leopard seals and sea lions were all there for the taking on the subantarctic islands, but there was little press about it at the time. Nobody wanted to disclose the seal-rich locations they found, and there were also laws in the early 1800s that prohibited vessels from operating too far south. As a result, there are few surviving records of such a hectic time in history.[10]

It was a brutal business. Sealers armed with clubs or knives would round up and slaughter tens of thousands of seals at a time — 100,000 skins are estimated to have been taken from Macquarie Island in just one season.[11]

Meanwhile, health and safety rules for the sealers themselves were non-existent. Small groups of men would sail south in wild seas, with the constant threat of being wrecked against the sharp rocks of remote islands that were mere specks in a vast ocean. The sealing gangs were dropped off with basic provisions in freezing, remote areas and told to expect a pick-up several months later. However, sealing employers were notoriously cavalier about returning at the agreed time and sometimes they didn't return at all.

The seal colonies weren't easy to locate. Sea lions on Auckland and Campbell islands frequent the bays during the summer months, but fur seals are shy animals that stick to remote, rocky areas on barely accessible coastlines. As a result, sealers would often be lowered from steep clifftops with ropes, armed with clubs and a week's provisions.[12]

Only the promise of good money and eventual respite must have sustained the sealers in such primitive conditions. The subantarctic climate was cold and exposed, and the men would sleep in caves for shelter, or make tussock or sod huts. Many died in accidents, from injuries, from exposure, or from starvation. In such wretched conditions, sealing and survival were the two priorities. As the *Mariner*'s Captain Douglass informed the *Sydney Gazette* after he visited Macquarie Island in 1822:

> 'The men employed in the [sealing] gangs appear to be the very refuse of the human species, so abandoned and lost to every sense of moral duty.'[13]

One of his contemporaries added more details to the grim picture:

> '... Their long beards, greasy seal-skin habiliments, and grim, fiend-like complexions, looked more like troops of demons from the infernal regions, than baptized Christian men, as they sallied forth with brandished clubs ...'

Of course, such callous slaughter wasn't sustainable in the long-term. Seal pups and mothers were also targeted, and within a few years barely a seal could be found. The subantarctic islands were abandoned once more.[14] The British explorer Benjamin Morrell didn't see a single fur seal in 1830 when he visited the Auckland Islands for a week,[15] and by the time the British Hardwicke settlers arrived in 1849 the few seals dotted around the coastlines provided a bit of sport for hunting and little else.[16] There was a short-lived sealing revival later in the 19th century, but nothing close to what it had been.

'His discovery proved to be his death-knell'

During the so-called 'fur rush' many sealing ships carried women, some of whom were collected for a fee from the New South Wales penal colony in exchange for their company. They were known euphemistically as 'ships' wives'. Travelling with sealing gangs across the open sea was a risky and sometimes perilous experience; some women died at sea from the rough conditions, while others were sold on to other ships or simply abandoned en route.[17]

One such woman (or girl, as we would now call her) was Elizabeth Farr, who was only 14 when she perished. Elizabeth came from the harshest penal colony of all, on Australia's Norfolk Island, so she may have been a convict or the daughter of a convict. She was on board the *Perseverance* with Captain Hasselburg when he discovered Campbell and Macquarie islands in 1810. (The captain was married to a woman named Catherine, but they had separated.[18])

By the time the captain finally got around to collecting his gang of sealers from Campbell Island, ten months after dropping them off, they were desperate for rescue, having run out of supplies many months earlier and surviving mainly on seal meat and albatrosses. Still, they were all alive and their barrels were successfully filled with seal oil, lined up on the shore for collection.

Transporting the barrels back to the *Perseverance* took several weeks, with progress hampered by bad weather. On one such day, 4 November, the captain leapt into a small boat with Elizabeth and five others to row to shore. On their way back to the ship they encountered a peculiar weather phenomenon known as a 'williwaw'.

Old whalers' slang for a sudden violent squall, a williwaw is a mini-tornado of rain and wind that swoops down the mountains at up to 240 kilometres (150 miles) an hour. The coldness of the high-altitude temperatures combined with the gravitational pull creates a mighty funnel that can overturn small boats and push ships backwards out of the harbour. Also known as katabatic winds, williwaws are common in the harbours of Campbell Island.[19]

A squall, caused by a williwaw, whips up the sea in Perseverance Harbour.

This particular williwaw was so ferocious that the jollyboat flipped over and all six of its occupants were instantly flung into the freezing water. Captain Hasselburg drowned almost immediately, weighed down by his heavy cloak and high sea-boots ('which must have baffled every personal exertion … necessary to his preservation' lamented the *Sydney Gazette*). The island he had so happily discovered almost a year earlier 'proved to be his death-knell'.[20]

Fortunately Elizabeth Farr could swim, so she started making for shore. Meanwhile the ship's carpenter, James Bloodworth, tried to save the captain, but quickly realized that it was too late. Instead he turned to help a 12-year-old cabin boy named George Allwright, the son of a Sydney baker, but he too had briefly flailed about before disappearing under the water. By then Elizabeth was struggling to stay afloat, so James swam across to her and headed with difficulty to shore while carrying her on his back. But once he had dragged himself out of the water, spluttering and hauling her out with him, he discovered to his horror that she was dead. Elizabeth was buried onshore the next day, but the captain's body was never found. He had, perhaps fittingly, been consigned to a watery grave. It was later revealed that, despite the distinction of discovering two islands, Captain Hasselburg died in debt to his employer, Campbell & Co.[21]

Even the *Perseverance* was destined to have the harbour as its final resting place. Twenty years later, the ship was wrecked in exactly the same spot, with more loss of life, in what is now known as Perseverance Harbour. It is the only recorded shipwreck on Campbell Island.

The world's loneliest ghost

Elizabeth Farr is not the only woman believed to have met her end on Campbell Island, although in the case of 'The Lady of the Heather', the rough reality of 'ships' wives' has morphed into a more romantic tale of aristocracy and betrayal.

From the early 19th century, sealers and whalers reported seeing a solitary woman roaming the shores of Perseverance Harbour, wearing a tartan shawl and a bonnet. Could the mystery lady have been the unwanted grand-daughter of Bonnie Prince Charlie, sent across the world to live in exile until her death?

This version of the 'Lady of the Heather' story claims that the 'Bonnie Prince', whose real name was Charles Stuart, had an affair with a woman called Clementina Walkinshaw who followed him from Scotland to France. Clementina and Charles had a love child named Charlotte (that part is true), who eventually had her own daughter named Marie (also true).

Marie, according to the legend, was eventually accused of spying on the Scottish Jacobites on behalf of the British government.[22] They wanted her gone yesterday, so Captain James Stewart (the source of Stewart Island's name in New Zealand) stepped up for the job. He'd always boasted of his close friendship with Charles Stuart, and was known to be somewhat of a rogue with loose morals.

In 1828 he dragged poor Marie onto his ship and set sail for New Zealand. However, he quickly decided that Stewart Island wasn't remote enough and carried on south for another 660 kilometres (400 miles) to Campbell Island, where he built the young woman a sod hut in Camp Cove and abandoned her to live in exile for the rest of her life.

Legend would have us believe that Marie tried to make the best of things. She created a white-pebbled path that led from her hut to the shoreline, planted some Scottish heather, and rang her Angelus bell each day (the Catholic call to prayer) as she waited in the vain hope of rescue. But poor Marie died within a year, and the ghostly form of the 'Lady of the Heather' now wanders (allegedly) over the lonely island in the moonlight, clad in her shawl of royal Stuart tartan and a Glengarry bonnet. If you listen carefully the next time you happen to be visiting Campbell Island, you might hear the faint ringing of the Angelus bell.

Sceptics will undoubtedly snort in derision and mutter that the whole thing is a farce ('That sound isn't the Angelus bell; it's the humming of my drone quadcopter!'). And it's true that the details don't quite add up — Charles Stuart's grand-daughter died in 1789, for one thing, before Campbell Island was even discovered. But there probably *was* a woman abandoned on Campbell Island, a non-princess who simply had some very bad luck. A female, subantarctic Robinson Crusoe who didn't fare quite as well.

After all, the British explorer James Clark Ross reported coming across a French woman's grave in 1840, although it might have been Elizabeth Farr's grave. Malcolm Fraser of the New Zealand government, who travelled to Campbell Island on the *Hinemoa* steamship in 1906 on the lookout for castaways, wrote of coming across a sod hut, the remains of a fireplace, and a pebble-lined path to the water. New Zealand surveyor and wartime coastwatcher Allan Eden also saw the same things when he visited Campbell Island in the early 1940s, and there are still signs of an old hut at Camp Cove.[23] The non-native heather plant was definitely there, too; some of it was brought back to New Zealand in the 1950s.[24]

Whatever the real story, journalist Robert Carrick picked up on the legend (or possibly invented it) and enthusiastically perpetuated it in a Sydney newspaper in the late 1800s. The romantic fable was then expanded in Will Lawson's rather soppy 1945 novel, *The Lady of the Heather*, which features a gentle, stoic woman who is cared for by shy, kind-hearted sailors. The opening page paints a vivid picture:

> *'The scene before her eyes was wild indeed … Above the little cove loomed bare slopes, surmounted by black basalt peaks, too smooth to hold the snow and reaching like fingers into the cloud-hidden skies. No more gloomy a place than this island fastness could be imagined in the light of the dying day …'*[25]

Invented or not, 'The Lady of the Heather' has become an indelible part of Campbell Island folklore and there is something quite compelling about a Scottish–French ghost princess wandering around a remote island in the moonlight. There have been no 'official' sightings recently; although, as one former resident put it, the odds of seeing her increase after a few glasses of brandy.

Living on The Snares

Women certainly weren't the only people abandoned on subantarctic islands in the early 1800s. Two hundred kilometres (125 miles) south of New Zealand lie The Snares (also known as Snares Islands, or Tini Heke in Māori), a small cluster of tiny islands named by British captain George Vancouver, who came across them in 1791 (Canada's Vancouver Island was named after him).

In his ship's log, Captain Vancouver described the islands matter-of-factly as 'craggy', and named them The Snares because of their potential to cause trouble for any ship that happened to be passing on its way from Australia to England. New Zealand Māori living on Stewart Island/Rakiura had already spotted The Snares lurking in the south and called the archipelago 'Te Taniwha' ('The Monster'). The islands are framed by forests of tree daisies and today are uninhabited apart from the wildlife, including Snares crested penguins, Buller's and Salvin's albatrosses, petrels, tomtits, fernbirds, and New Zealand fur seals.[26]

However, there was once a small group of very reluctant, long-term residents. In 1810 a group of four unfortunate men from the sealing ship *Adventure* were put ashore on The Snares and left there indefinitely. The captain had decided there weren't enough provisions on board to go around and the men, who are believed to have been ex-convicts from Norfolk Island, were shoved off the ship with their discharge papers. Perhaps the captain felt the islands' remoteness and emptiness made them a safer drop-off point than New Zealand. They were given a few handfuls of rice, half a bushel of potatoes and an iron pot, wished all the best of luck, and abandoned without a backward glance.[27]

What a miserable place to be left behind! These tiny islands in the middle of nowhere offered little chance of rescue, and constant wild weather. But in a cunning move that could have been inspired by the novel *The Martian* (if it had been published 200 years earlier), the men were smart enough to plant the potatoes, which fortunately managed to flourish during the *seven years* that they were forced to sit and wait for rescue. They also lived off the plentiful local birds and the seals.

An American whaling ship named the *Enterprise*, on a sealing voyage from Philadelphia to Sydney, sailed past The Snares in 1817 and discovered the stranded men. The ship's crew reported seeing an abundance of potatoes that covered at least half of the main island (the total area of The Snares is 3.5 square kilometres or 1.3 square miles). There were only three men left by that point. In the interim, the fourth man had apparently lost his mind from the isolation and discomfort. His odd behaviour unsettled the others, who dealt with the issue by pushing him off a cliff.[28] Given the unusual circumstances, they were eventually pardoned.

Today, The Snares are once again uninhabited. They are considered one of the world's least modified pieces of land and a special permit is required to set foot on them. There is no longer any sign of the potatoes.[29]

Snares crested penguins.

2. EXPLORATION
The polar explorers, the captain's wife, and the botanist with a secret (1760–1840)

CAPTAIN ABRAHAM BRISTOW did not have time for such frivolities as exploring new islands in August 1806. The whaling captain was making his way back to England after a southern voyage in his ship *Ocean*, owned by the British whaling and shipping empire Samuel Enderby & Sons. It had been a successful expedition and his vessel was laden with whale oil, a valued commodity for lighting at the time.

When he reached the 50th latitude south, a shadowy form emerged from the open sea. As he drew closer, Bristow saw that it was a group of islands, two large and many small, and previously unrecorded.[1] Bristow immediately pulled out his captain's log and scribbled:

> *'This place I should suppose abounds with seals, and sorry I am that the time and the lumbered state of my ship do not allow me to examine.'*[2]

He named them 'Lord Auckland's Groupe' after his father's friend William Eden, whose title was 1st Baron Auckland.

Bristow was the first European discoverer of the Auckland Islands. However, in 2003 archaeological evidence (including the remains of earth ovens, stone artefacts, and piles of bird, seal and fish bones) was found on Enderby Island, proving there was a short-lived settlement of Polynesians on the islands in the 13th or 14th century AD.[3]

The Auckland Islands (Motu Maha or Maungahuka in Māori) are the remnants of ancient volcanic rocks. There are two large islands, Auckland and Adams, separated by a strait of water called Carnley Harbour. Scattered around are a dozen smaller islands, including Disappointment Island (possibly named by an unimpressed Captain Bristow), Enderby Island, and Rose Island.

Auckland Island is by far the biggest of the group at 42 kilometres long and

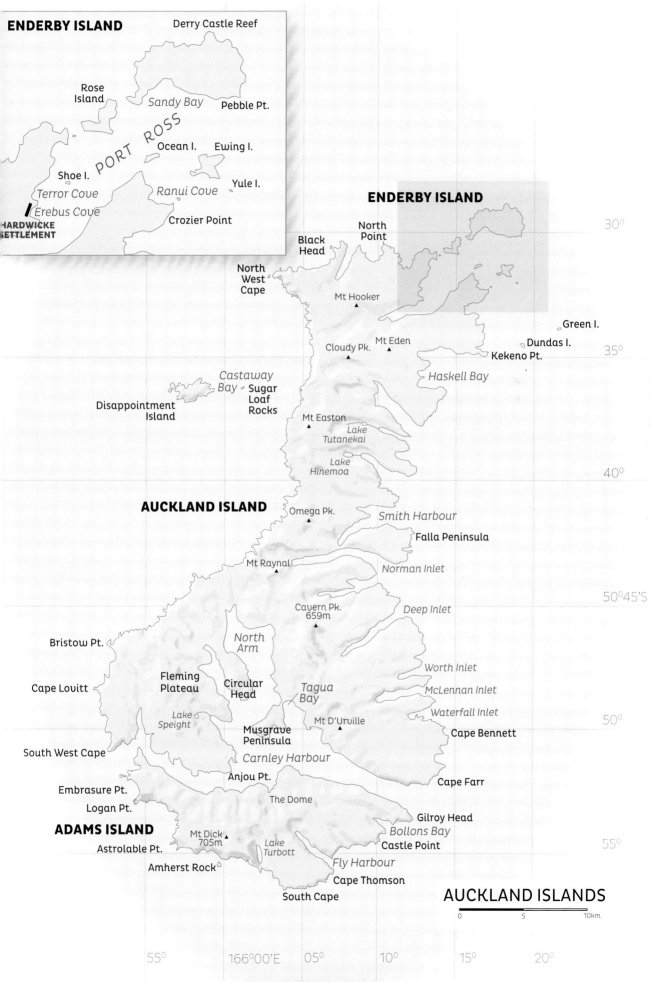

ENDERBY ISLAND

Derry Castle Reef

Rose Island

Sandy Bay

Pebble Pt.

PORT ROSS

Ocean I.

Ewing I.

Shoe I.

Terror Cove

Ranui Cove

Yule I.

Erebus Cove

HARDWICKE
SETTLEMENT

Crozier Point

ENDERBY ISLAND

North Point

Black Head

North West Cape

Mt Hooker

Green I.

Dundas I.

Cloudy Pk.

Mt Eden

Kekeno Pt.

Haskell Bay

Castaway Bay

Sugar Loaf Rocks

Disappointment Island

Mt Easton

Lake Tutanekai

Lake Hinemoa

AUCKLAND ISLAND

Omega Pk.

Smith Harbour

Falla Peninsula

Mt Raynal

Norman Inlet

Cavern Pk. 659m

Deep Inlet

Bristow Pt.

North Arm

Worth Inlet

Fleming Plateau

Circular Head

Tagua Bay

McLennan Inlet

Cape Louitt

Waterfall Inlet

Lake Speight

Mt D'Urville

Cape Bennett

South West Cape

Musgrave Peninsula

Carnley Harbour

Anjou Pt.

Cape Farr

Embrasure Pt.

The Dome

Logan Pt.

Gilroy Head

ADAMS ISLAND

Bollons Bay

Mt Dick 705m

Castle Point

Astrolable Pt.

Lake Turbott

Amherst Rock

Fly Harbour

Cape Thomson

South Cape

AUCKLAND ISLANDS

0   5   10km

30°

35°

40°

50°45'S

50°

55°

55°   166°00'E   05°   10°   15°   20°

15 kilometres wide (26 x 9 miles), with steep, mountainous terrain, low-hanging cloud and thick bush. It's also home to the last outpost of trees (southern rātā) en route to Antarctica. The island's western cliffs are tall and foreboding, eaten away by ferocious seas driven by gale-force westerly winds, while its eastern side, with its many undulating coves and inlets, is more sheltered and slightly more welcoming for visitors.

One year later, Bristow returned and spent several weeks exploring the islands. He visited during the winter so he missed the sea lions lounging on the sandy beach at Enderby Island, but he would have seen the bellbirds and parakeets flitting through the tangled rātā forests (*Metrosideros umbellata*), royal albatrosses soaring overhead, and white-capped and light-mantled sooty albatrosses nesting in the islands' rocky cliffs.

During his second visit, Bristow formally claimed the islands for Britain, naming Auckland Island's sheltered northern harbour 'Sarah's Bosom' after his ship the *Sarah* (the name was later changed to Port Ross in honour of the British explorer James Clark Ross). Bristow also released a number of pigs on the main island to feed any future visitors — a generous but short-sighted act that is still causing headaches for the New Zealand Department of Conservation more than 200 years later (see Chapter 12).

Not much else is known about Captain Abraham Bristow, except that in 1809 his ship the *Sarah* was snatched by a French privateering ship called the *Revenge*, which in turn was taken by a British privateering ship called the *Helena*, and then all three ships were claimed by yet another French privateering ship, called the *Enterprise*. Life at sea was a complicated, risky affair in the early 19th century.[4]

For a long time the visiting sealers disregarded the Auckland Islands' new name and simply called the islands 'Bristow's Land'. As with Macquarie and Campbell islands, they plundered the coastlines and slaughtered the seals for their skins and oil until there were barely any left.

Benjamin and Abby Morrell: the love boat

Between 1820 and 1840 the Auckland Islands were visited by several renowned explorers, a few of whom provided glowing accounts of the mild weather, excellent harbour and fertile soil, declaring the uninhabited islands to be an ideal location for a prospective settlement. Their naively optimistic reports would have consequences for decades to come.

At the time it was becoming more common for sea captains to take their wives along on expeditions, partly for company (voyages often lasted for two to three years) and also to maintain a sense of decorum on board. There were mixed feelings about this encroachment into men-only territory, and the ships with captain's wives on board were often known as 'hen frigates'.[5]

One such captain was Benjamin Morrell (1795–?1839). He not only took his wife Abby along on a two-year expedition to the Pacific, but they both published accounts of the journey. Morrell was a British explorer and trader, and already well-known

A white-capped albatross on a nest among megaherbs, Auckland Island.

An engraving of the adventurous but exaggeration-prone explorer Captain Benjamin Morrell.

for his daring Antarctic voyages by the time he visited the Auckland Islands in 1829. But he was also a braggart and somewhat delusional, penning wildly exaggerated accounts (19th-century 'fake news', perhaps?) of what he had seen and achieved during his expeditions. He eventually became a fugitive after wrecking his ship in Mozambique in the late 1830s, and is alleged to have staged his own death and secretly lived out his remaining years in South America.[6]

WIFE, MOTHER, EXPLORER

Benjamin Morrell was married twice, but his first wife's name is not recorded. After one of his early Antarctic voyages in the mid-1820s, he returned to England and discovered that she and his two children had died during his absence.

Within a year he had married his American second cousin Abby Jane, then aged just 15, in New York. Benjamin was 30. After a few short weeks of marital bliss, Benjamin announced that he was heading off on another expedition. He was gone for two years, from 1824 to 1826, and then he set off again for a year in 1828.

Abby missed him terribly during these long absences and worried for his safety. She resolved to accompany him on his next voyage and take care of him on the ship. When the possibility of a trading expedition to the Pacific came up in 1829 she suggested that she might go along too, declaring that she'd rather die at sea with him than risk becoming a widow at home.[7]

Benjamin replied with a firm no. After all, what would his employers think about his wife tagging along on a business trip? She would be a financial liability and a distraction on board. People might speculate on his leadership abilities, and what if something were to happen to her during the voyage?

To dissuade her, he tried to fill her mind with all the potential dangers of a long journey to explore strange lands: shipwrecks, 'savages', massacres, and more. However, Abby wouldn't have a bar of it. In her book, she wrote that she 'insisted … as far as affectionate obedience could insist' and that he 'reluctantly yielded'.[8] According to Benjamin's version, there were several weeks of tears, pleading and fasting before he finally relented.[9]

They travelled together from 1829 to 1831, sailing from New England to the South Pacific in the schooner *Antarctica*. They left their young son in New York in the care of Abby's mother, but Abby's brother accompanied them on the voyage. As the ship departed from New York, Abby apparently began to doubt her decision, fearing for her son's welfare in her absence and coming down almost instantly with terrible seasickness. The latter was 'a sensation that cannot be described, but which … reduces an adult to the baby'.[10] She eventually adjusted, but found she had to contend with endless free time to while away at sea. She was the only woman on board with 24 men, and with no fixed role or duties. Benjamin was distracted with running the ship. She never complained, as she'd promised to not be a burden, but at least she could vent in her journal: 'The nights are restless, the days endless.'[11]

After just over a month at sea many of the crew came down with a terrible fever, and so did Abby. It was so severe that she thought she might die, and dreaded the likelihood of her corpse being tossed overboard to be 'devoured by sharks'.[12] However, she bore her illness stoically, telling Benjamin to focus on the ship and his crew.

The wild seas didn't help matters. 'Fortitude … was much needed on our passage to Auckland's group,' she wrote, 'as we had no galley fire with the waves sweeping over us, while our sails were constantly splitting and our spars falling.'[13]

Southern rātā in bloom, Auckland Islands.

On arrival at the Auckland Islands, Abby, who was improving in health but still very weak, was carried off the ship by Benjamin and her brother. She records experiencing a sort of spiritual awakening when she found herself finally back on *terra firma*.

> *'I felt new life in the ecstasy of the moment … The very flowers seemed to open to receive me, while there came the sweet warblings of ten thousand beautiful birds … large paroquets [parakeets] and wood-pigeons … there is a green bird [probably a bellbird] whose melody and notes are so varied, that one might imagine himself regaled by a hundred different songsters all at once.'*[14]

Abby was amazed at the abundance of wildlife on the islands and their lack of interest in humans.

> *'The animals here are mostly strangers to man and have little fear, having seldom heard the murderous gun of a sportsman … the albatross and aquatic birds abound in the sea.'*[15]

However, she was less impressed by the chilly summer

A red-crowned parakeet (kākāriki), Auckland Islands.

temperatures: 'The thermometer here does not rise above 55 degrees [13° Celsius] at noon.'[16]

On her return to New York she published a vivid account of her two-year journey, named *Narrative of a Voyage to the Ethiopic and South Atlantic Ocean, Indian Ocean, Chinese Sea, North and South Pacific Oceans, in the Years 1829, 1830, 1831.*

In her book, she writes rather sanctimoniously of reforming wild seamen, taming the 'savages' on Pacific islands, and the natural right of British explorers to colonize whichever lands they visited. But she also provides vivid descriptions of the people and locations she encountered, and she apparently returned to America with a strong sense of injustice on behalf of the seamen, writing indignantly of the lack of comfort and education for the men who journeyed far from home on long expeditions.

Abby admits that as a woman her limited formal education may have made her less capable of analyzing everything she experienced, but 'the unstudied and unpractised mind … observes many things that escape the notice of the best educated'.[17] It was also a time of growth and self-discovery, and she learned that she was stronger than she'd anticipated: 'This little enterprise of mine … has taught me what my sex can do if called to act in the business of life.'[18]

'DEAR LITTLE ISLE'

Meanwhile, her husband's account of their time at the Auckland Islands was equally as joyful but also more than a little deluded. He spent just over a week there at the close of 1829, and perhaps he confused the islands with another destination, because many of the plants and geographical features he describes are not found there.

In his book *A Narrative of Four Voyages*, Benjamin Morrell comments favourably on Auckland Island's long stretch of

Abby Jane Morrell's book, *Narrative of a Voyage* ... , first published in 1833 after her husband Benjamin's book, *A Narrative of Four Voyages*.

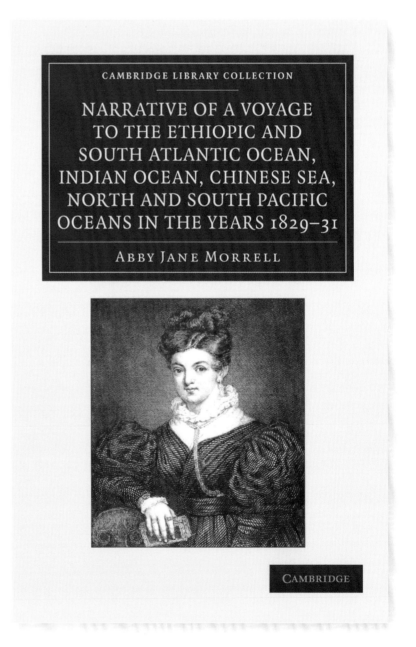

CAMBRIDGE LIBRARY COLLECTION

NARRATIVE OF A VOYAGE TO THE ETHIOPIC AND SOUTH ATLANTIC OCEAN, INDIAN OCEAN, CHINESE SEA, NORTH AND SOUTH PACIFIC OCEANS IN THE YEARS 1829–31

ABBY JANE MORRELL

CAMBRIDGE

'pebbly or sandy beach' and its 'extensive level plains covered with beautiful grass and refreshing verdure, extending back about five miles [8 kilometres]'. He also writes of its 'mild, temperate climate' and potential for 'excellent pasturage'. In reality, the island has mostly rough, uneven terrain, boggy soil, thick scrub and tangled forests; the climate is wild and unpredictable.

'Vegetables of all kinds could be made to flourish here,' he declares confidently, before concluding that it 'would form a delightful retreat to a few amiable families, who wish for a "dear little isle of their own" '.[19] The island's future residents probably came up with other, less printable adjectives.

Benjamin and Abby's narratives were published in 1832 and 1833 respectively by Harper Brothers. While probably ghostwritten, they were nevertheless based on the Morrells' journals and therefore provide extremely rare husband-and-wife accounts of a daring and lengthy voyage of exploration. Benjamin's book became an international bestseller; it was favourably reviewed, and was reprinted several times.[20] However, Abby's book apparently sold more copies, perhaps because a woman's perspective of a voyage was such a novelty.[21]

There was the odd matrimonial spat during their travels, as might be expected (he didn't take kindly to her bringing him a hat on deck when he was busy trying to prevent the ship from sinking, for example),[22] but they mostly remained on good terms. Just nine days after their return to New York, Abby gave birth to her second son and wrote that she hoped her narrative would be appreciated by the next generation: 'Perhaps his mother's Journal may in some future day be read by him.'[23]

Her seafaring days were behind her, but she had ventured into a world where very few women had gone before — and then published a book about it.

Three men and an island

Ten years after the Morrells' visit, there was an 'ice rush' of Antarctic expeditions that all made stop-overs at the Auckland Islands in the same year: the *Porpoise*, commanded by Charles Wilkes of the USA; the *Astrolabe* and the *Zélée*, commanded by Dumont D'Urville of France; and the HMS *Erebus* and HMS *Terror*, commanded by James Clark Ross of Britain. Wilkes didn't personally make it to the islands as the *Porpoise* was just one of seven ships under his command.[24]

Southern exploration was a competitive business, especially in 1840. The American *Porpoise* reached the Auckland Islands first, at the beginning of March, and took latitudinal and longitudinal measurements from the area Bristow had named Sarah's Bosom. After a few days, the ship departed just as the *Astrolabe* and the *Zélée* were arriving, which must have been a bit awkward for the two countries; did they wave as they passed or simply ignore each other?

The French expedition stayed on Auckland Island for ten days, setting up an observatory for magnetic observations (crucial for figuring out coordinates and

A painting by Louis Auguste Marie Le Breton (1818–64) from Dumont D'Urville's 1840 expedition to the Auckland Islands: *Vue de l'observatoire aux Îles Aukland*. Note the line for drying wet clothes, a recurring theme in images of subantarctic expeditions.

improving navigation), and the expedition artists also painted a prolific number of pictures that now serve as a record of the islands during that period.

Sir James Clark Ross: Antarctic royalty

Sir James Clark Ross (1800–62) was one of the world's most eminent explorers, visiting both the Arctic (he located the North Magnetic Pole in 1831) and Antarctica. Many regions and animals from the southern hemisphere are named for him: the Ross Sea and the Ross Ice Shelf in Antarctica, the Ross seal, the subantarctic Ross lily (*Bulbinella rossii*), Port Ross at Auckland Island … he even has his own crater on the Moon.[25]

He may not have made it quite that far, but he did visit the Auckland and Campbell islands in November–December 1840 in his ships HMS *Erebus* and *Terror* (hence the two cove names at Auckland Island's Port Ross, and also the two volcano names in Antarctica's Ross Sea). The British expedition stayed at Terror Cove for three weeks, setting up an observatory and taking magnetic observations. They also released sheep, rabbits

Commander James Clark Ross, painted by John R. Wildman in 1834.

and hens on the Auckland Islands, as well as some more pigs.

The British botanist Joseph Hooker was part of Ross's expedition, and he sketched many of the plants and animals they encountered on their voyage. He also planted a garden with turnips, cabbages, strawberry and raspberry plants, and gooseberry and currant bushes.[26] (None of these still exists on the islands.)

During their stay, Ross's officers found it very difficult scrambling through the thick scrub on Auckland Island and decided to clear some of it by lighting a fire. Apparently the fire got out of control, and viewed from the ships that night it appeared as if the entire island were ablaze. While his men found the spectacle entertaining, Ross was unimpressed by their 'thoughtless prank'.[27]

Ross was also rather piqued that Wilkes' and D'Urville's expeditions had both beaten him to the subantarctic islands and Antarctica in 1840, but he made up for it by eventually sailing further south than either of them.[28]

During their respective visits, both Ross and D'Urville were very impressed by the harbour at Sarah's Bosom/Port Ross. However, D'Urville was less enamoured of Auckland Island itself, writing of the 'miserable trees, twisted and stunted' and questioning Benjamin Morrell's glowing descriptions from a decade earlier.[29] D'Urville also rejected the local fish, which were 'riddled with huge worms of astonishing thickness and length'.[30]

Later, Ross wrote that the Auckland Islands had an excellent harbour and might be useful to the British government as a penal colony or a whaling location:

'In the whole range of the vast Southern Ocean, no spot could be found combining so completely the essential requisites for a fixed whaling station.'[31]

Before the decade was out, Ross's hearty and respectable endorsement would prove to be life-changing for a small group of British families.

William Bligh — The Bounty Islands

While most people are unfamiliar with the small but mighty Bounties, many will have heard the dramatic tale of the ill-fated ship that encountered them in the late 18th century. The Bounty Islands (Moutere Hauriri in Māori) were discovered in 1788 by Lieutenant William Bligh on the *Bounty,* while en route from England to Tahiti to collect breadfruit plants just before the infamous mutiny. A few months after passing the Bounty Islands, Bligh and 18 of his men were abandoned in the middle of the South Pacific Ocean and left to drift in a small boat. The mutineers, led by Acting Lieutenant Fletcher Christian, settled on Pitcairn Island and Tahiti. Meanwhile, Bligh managed to sail 6500 kilometres — 4000 miles — to land. Two hundred years later, Anthony Hopkins played him in the 1984 film *The Bounty.*[32]

The Bounties are 670 kilometres (416 miles) south-east of New Zealand's South Island and consist of 22 tiny islands, or granite rocks, with a combined area of 1.35 square kilometres (½ square mile). The largest, Depot Island, is just 700 metres long (750 yards).

While not a common holiday destination (in fact, they have been visited only a handful of times over the past two centuries), the Bounty Islands are packed full of wildlife, including Salvin's albatrosses, erect-crested penguins, New Zealand fur seals, and the Bounty Island shag, which all crowd onto the tiny rocks.[33] There is almost no vegetation and the rocks are covered in a slippery and polished covering of encrusted guano.

Portrait of William Bligh
by Alexander Huey,
painted in 1814.

Fur seal pups on Depot Island, Bounty Islands. The pups weren't spared during the sealing era, driving the subantarctic islands' seal populations almost to extinction.

Henry Waterhouse —
The Antipodes Islands

In 1800, Captain Henry Waterhouse discovered a small group of wild and mountainous islands on his way from Port Jackson to England, and named them 'Isle Penantipode' because they were almost directly opposite his homeland on the globe. Now called the Antipodes Islands (or Moutere Mahue in Māori), the 21-square-kilometre, or 8-square-mile, tussock-covered volcanic group lies about 870 kilometres (540 miles) south-east of New Zealand and is peppered with fur and elephant seals, as well as Antipodean, white-capped, black-browed, and light-mantled sooty albatrosses; Antipodes and Reischek's (red-crowned) parakeets; and erect-crested and eastern rockhopper penguins.[34] The main island, Antipodes, is about 7 kilometres long and 5 kilometres wide (4 x 3 miles) and is surrounded by six much smaller islands, The archipelago is lashed by storms, and 'the thunderous echo of waves breaking against the hollows of the jagged coastline never ceases'.[35]

Sealers descended on the islands in the early 19th century, and there have also been three known shipwrecks. However, in 1892 visiting journalist Robert Carrick dismissed the Antipodes Islands as having 'very little or no soil … and absolutely no history'.[36]

Jeanne Baret: globe-trotting botanist in disguise

On the other side of the globe, and more than half a century before Abby Morrell's journey to the Auckland Islands, another woman made it down to the Furious Fifties latitudes. But she wasn't a captain's wife, or even a so-called 'ship's wife'; she was there because she had a job to do, and she had to do it by stealth.

Jeanne Baret (or Baré, or Barrett, depending on the source) lived from 1740 to 1807. She worked as a botanist's assistant in the 1760s and is recognized today as the first woman to sail around the globe.[37] Sailing on the French naturalist Louis-Antoine de Bougainville's ships the *Boudeuse* and the *Étoile* on a journey that lasted from 1766 to 1769, she was forced to disguise herself as a man (named 'Jean') in order to be part of

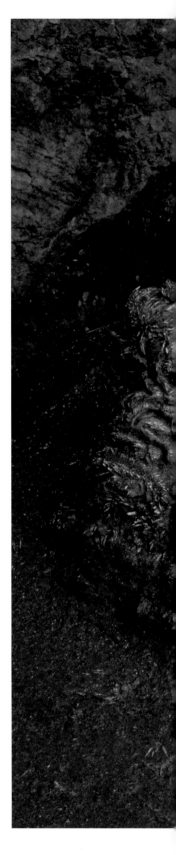

An abandoned cache of rolled-up penguin skins in a shallow cave on the Antipodes Islands. The skins were valuable for a short time in the late 1800s for making ladies' hand muffs in Britain.

MAD.^{LLA} BARE.

Dall'Acqua inc.

Portrait of Jeanne Baret painted in 1806 by Cristoforo Dall'Acqua, portraying her in 'men's clothing' for the Bougainville expedition.

the voyage. Women weren't allowed to travel on French naval ships at the time, and they certainly weren't encouraged to take up careers as scientists. But Bougainville was leading the first French expedition around the world, ordered by King Louis XV himself, and Baret didn't want to miss out on the opportunity to discover exotic plants previously unseen by the western world.

On board was also the celebrated natural scientist Philibert Commerson, whom Baret had first met when she was employed as his housekeeper in France. They were in a relationship, but Baret is confirmed by Bougainville's journals to have also been an experienced and talented botanist in her own right.[38]

To protect her true identity, Commerson and 'Jean' pretended not to know each other. She turned up at the port just as the *Étoile* was about to set sail from France, offering her services as Commerson's assistant. In the last-minute rush to leave, Baret was allowed to come on board. She and Commerson shared a cabin, and Baret wrapped linen bandages tightly around her chest day after day, wore men's clothing, and claimed to be a eunuch to offset any suspicion caused when she didn't undress or urinate in front of the ship's crew. There were 330 men on board the two ships, and later some reported becoming suspicious over 'Jean's' cagey behaviour and lack of facial hair.

One of Bougainville's stops in 1767 was at the Falkland Islands, which lie to the east of the bottom tip of South America, near Cape Horn. The Falklands must be some of the most contested islands in history. At the time Baret, Commerson and Bougainville visited, they were changing from French-owned to Spanish-owned islands, renamed from 'Îles Malouines' to 'Islas Malvinas'. Bougainville was reluctantly assisting with this transition and helping to evacuate French refugees from the islands. (Currently both Argentina and Britain claim ownership of the Falklands, although they are officially British territory.)

At the Falklands, Baret would have observed king penguins, black-browed albatrosses, southern elephant seals, the Falkland Islands wolf (known as the warrah, now extinct), and South American fur seals. The ocean would have been packed with southern right whales, humpback whales, sperm whales and blue whales, which would all be hunted almost to extinction in the following decades. The Falklands also have an abundance of native plants, including the national flower 'Pale Maiden' with its slender stem and white petals.

Baret was literate (which was rare at the time, especially for a woman from a working-class background), so she was able to document many of her discoveries from exotic locations such as Brazil, Patagonia and Tahiti, where she was finally exposed (figuratively, if not literally) as a woman. As Bougainville recorded in his ship's journal:

> 'Baret, with her face bathed in tears, owned to me that she was a woman … that she well knew … that we were going round the world, and that such a voyage had raised her curiosity. She will be the first woman that ever made it, and I must do her the justice to affirm that she has always behaved on board with the most scrupulous modesty. She is neither ugly nor pretty, and is no more than twenty-five.'[39]

Commerson pretended to be equally shocked by this turn of events, so Bougainville never knew of their shared history. Despite the duplicity, Bougainville allowed Baret to remain with the expedition, and as Commerson suffered from ongoing bad health, including a leg ulcer, Baret spent much of her time nursing him and doing chores on the ship, battling the scurvy, seasickness and dysentery that was prevalent on board, as well as lugging heavy equipment and specimens over rough and dangerous terrain whenever the ship was docked.

Baret and Commerson collected and documented thousands of plants during the expedition, including the well-known vine Bougainvillea, which was discovered in Brazil. But while 70 species of plants are named after Commerson, only one bears Baret's name: *Solanum baretiae*, a relatively new species of nightshade that grows in northern Peru and southern Ecuador. It was named in her honour in 2012, in recognition of her pioneering journey and her often overlooked contribution to botany.[40]

3. MAUNGAHUKA
The warriors and the slaves (1842–56)

JUST TWO YEARS AFTER THE FRENCH, American and British explorers had visited the Auckland Islands, a long-term settlement was formed. It wasn't government-funded, very few people knew of its existence, and only two-thirds of its residents had chosen to be there.

The Maungahuka colony existed for 14 years, from 1842–56, and is the longest-known human settlement on the Auckland Islands.[1] The remote colony consisted of 40 Ngāti Mutunga Māori and their 26 Moriori slaves, divided into two or three pā (villages) as well as a few 'independent' dwellings.

The story of how they came to be on the Auckland Islands starts in 1835, when about 900 Māori men, women and children of two hapū, or extended family groups, called Ngāti Mutunga and Ngāti Tama, voyaged from New Zealand to the Chatham Islands.[2] Inter-tribal warfare had displaced them from their ancestral home in Taranaki, and they had settled in Wellington. However, with tensions still simmering around them, they decided to migrate across the ocean to the Chatham Islands.[3] One of their chiefs, Tauru Matioro, had visited the Chathams two years earlier on a sealing voyage and seen their potential for Māori settlement.

The Chatham Islands are an archipelago of ten islands in the South Pacific, 830 kilometres (520 miles) east of New Zealand's South Island — they are one of the first parts of the world to greet the new day. They are not subantarctic islands, but the climate is cool, wet and windy. The Moriori, who are believed to be descended from the same Polynesian ancestors as New Zealand Māori, have lived there since at least 1500 AD.[4] The islands were visited by European explorers in the 1790s, with sealers arriving in the early 1800s. Since 1842 they have been part of New Zealand territory and are called 'Rēkohu' in Moriori and 'Wharekauri' in Māori. The largest island is Chatham Island, with a population today of about 600 people.

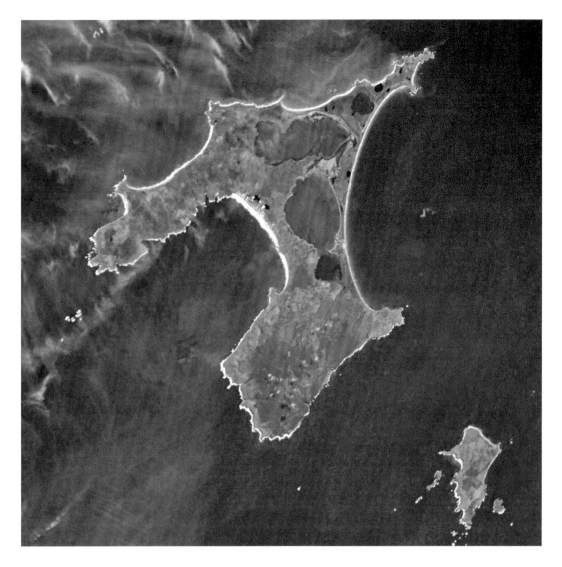

Colonization and enslavement

A Sydney brig named the *Rodney* carried the Māori migrants from New Zealand to the Chathams via two crowded journeys in November and December 1835 (there are conflicting accounts, but the *Rodney*'s captain may have ferried them under duress). After recovering from their cramped and arduous voyages, the new arrivals began to takahi (take possession of the land by walking over it), laying claim to the indigenous Moriori people and villages as they passed.

The Moriori held a meeting to plan their response. While they outnumbered the Māori on the island by almost two to one, Moriori refused to kill, even in self-defence; any hand-to-hand combat to resolve disputes had to cease the moment

The Chatham Islands, photographed by NASA. The two largest are Chatham Island and Pitt Island.

blood was drawn. Instead, the Moriori elders decided to offer the Māori newcomers peace and friendship, and to share their resources.[5]

This peaceful response (known to the Moriori as Nunuku's Law[6]) to a threat of invasion may well not have been expected by the Māori. They meanwhile had become suspicious of the private Moriori gathering, and decided to make a preemptive strike to retain the upper hand.

Led by several chiefs — including Tauru Matioro, a Ngāti Mutunga rangatira (chief) who would eventually lead his people and slaves to settle on the Auckland Islands (see below) — and armed with tomahawks, clubs and muskets, they took possession of the Chatham Islands. During 1835 and 1836 they killed at least 300 men, women and children — about 20 per cent of the Moriori population at the time. They claimed the remaining survivors as their slaves.

As historian Michael King notes in his book *Moriori* (1989), this process of using combat to claim or defend land was nothing new for New Zealand Māori, many of whom had been engaged in inter-tribal warfare for decades (as well as dealing with European migration to New Zealand from the late 18th century and the introduction of firearms).[7] Combat was often necessary for survival, and warriors who fought well in battle were admired for their mana (authority and prestige). As Matioro later put it, 'It was in accordance with our custom.'[8]

In contrast, Moriori customs had been formed over many centuries of isolation and their sacred law of peace made for a very one-sided battle. The half-a-dozen European settlers on the Chatham Islands at the time (mainly former whalers and sealers) appear to have stood by and done nothing during the invasion — possibly because they were vastly outnumbered.[9]

The destruction of the *Jean Bart*

A few years later, in 1838, a group of 40 Māori men had a violent altercation with some visiting French whalers on board the *Jean Bart* while attempting to trade goods.[10]

Tension had been brewing between Ngāti Mutunga and Ngāti Tama for a while as the two hapū competed for land and trading rights, and the *Jean Bart* crew witnessed one of their arguments. Not understanding the Māori language, they mistook the quarrel for a threat against them and attacked the Māori traders with flensing knives (used for cutting whale blubber).[11] As a result, there were multiple deaths on both sides (the 40 French crew either all died in the battle or some escaped but were never heard from again) and the *Jean Bart* was looted and burned.

Shortly afterwards, a French naval ship in New Zealand named the *Héroïne* heard about the incident and arrived at the Chathams to destroy three Māori villages in retaliation, resulting in more deaths and the taking of two Māori hostages to France.[12]

One of the men involved in the *Jean Bart* incident was Ngāti Mutunga chief Matioro, who in 1842 decided to sail with his extended family and their Moriori slaves to the

Auckland Islands. His reasons for choosing to relocate to the subantarctic islands aren't recorded; possibly he wanted to avoid further disputes with Ngāti Tama, or he may have feared more retaliatory attacks from the French. Perhaps he simply wanted to maintain his independence — the Chathams became part of New Zealand in 1842 and Christian missionaries were beginning to arrive and spread their religious message, quickly converting both Ngāti Mutunga and Ngāti Tama.[13] Although it would be another 20 years before slavery was formally abolished on the Chatham Islands, the early 1840s were a relatively peaceful time — at least, compared with the mid-to-late 1830s. Matioro may have simply grown weary of the Chathams, and felt it was time to seek more freedom and new opportunities elsewhere.

A new life in the subantarctic

Matioro had worked on whaling and sealing ships in the past, and had visited the Auckland Islands at least once in the years before he arrived at the Chathams.[14] Like Morrell, Ross and Bristow, he probably saw the sheltered harbour and the animals and thought only of the opportunity to fish and hunt, as well as grow vegetables. After all, the islands were uninhabited at the time and they can look deceptively attractive in calm weather.

At the end of 1842 the small community of 40 Ngāti Mutunga Māori and their 26 Moriori slaves reached the Auckland Islands on a chartered ship, a Sydney brig called the *Hannah* (hired for the price of 150 pigs). Their supplies included muskets, small boats, rum, tea, flour, bacon and potatoes. However, on arrival, two of the Ngāti Mutunga men apparently didn't take a fancy to their bleak new home and hurried back to the ship. The captain of the *Hannah* quickly set sail for the Chathams, leaving Matioro and the others behind while they were performing takahi, walking across Auckland Island to take possession of the land.[15]

The remaining settlers built huts from rātā wood and eventually split into two main hapū (groups), with one pā (village) headed by Matioro at Crozier Point on Auckland Island (later shifting to nearby Enderby Island) and another at Ocean Point with Matioro's distant cousin Ngatere as chief. The settlers called the Auckland Islands 'Maungahuka'; 'mauna' means mountain in Māori and 'huka' generally means snow, but it was also the 19th-century, southern Māori sealers' name for albatross down.[16]

The varied diet that Matioro had probably anticipated didn't eventuate; many of the local fish were filled with worms, and the wild descendants of the pigs introduced by Bristow and James Clark Ross tasted of fish because they ate seal meat and seabirds. Vegetables would have been difficult to cultivate in the peaty soil and wild climate. The settlers survived mostly on cabbages, turnips, small potatoes, megaherb leaves, seals, kuku (mussels), albatrosses and mutton birds.[17]

From their arrival in 1842 until 1849, little is known about the isolated Maungahuka colony. Historians have generally described the settlers as being stranded on the islands and living in miserable conditions, but more recently it has been argued that the

Dea's Head (formerly
known as Whale's Head)
at the northern end of
Auckland Island, near the
site of one of Matioro's
pā (villages).

recorded observations and opinions, almost entirely by males of European descent from the 19th and 20th centuries, don't necessarily provide a balanced or accurate perspective.[18]

After all, the Māori settlers in particular were nomadic and used to adapting to new locations. Ships would have passed through sporadically on whaling and sealing voyages, offering goods to trade and the potential to be transported elsewhere. The Maungahuka settlers were good at sealing, using the skins for clothing and blankets, and would prove to be much better than the British colonists (who arrived in 1849; see Chapter 4) at growing vegetables in the harsh climate, often sharing their supplies to prevent the Hardwicke settlers from starving.[19] There was also the (unrecorded) labour of two dozen slaves to maintain the Maungahuka colony.

Occasional arguments between hapū would erupt over land or possessions. In 1850, Toenga, a cousin of Matioro, stole and ate one of his pigs; fearing retaliation, Toenga then led an attack on Matioro's pā. A gunfight ensued with the French weapons taken from the *Jean Bart* at the Chatham Islands, and two of Matioro's slaves were killed.

Toenga had been temporarily defeated, but his spirit was not broken. Next, he planned an ambush on Matioro's father-in-law,

Patukumikumi, who lived independently on one of the smaller islands in the harbour. But Patukumikumi was prepared, as historian Archibald Shand (1893) describes:

'Patukumikumi loaded his gun, and lying flat on the floor of the house with the muzzle of his gun protruding, waited until the boat grounded. As Toenga was proceeding to land, Patukumikumi sent a bullet smashing through the boat, which so alarmed Toenga that he and his party beat a hasty retreat. Seeing this, Patukumikumi's daughter Ngawhanga [Matioro's wife], who also had her gun loaded, did not fire as she had been on the point of doing; they were quite satisfied with the retreat of the enemy.' [20]

Toenga had clearly had enough by that point, as shortly thereafter he and his wife managed to quickly escape on a passing ship and returned to the Chathams.[21]

The end of Maungahuka

Tauru Matioro of Ngāti Mutunga was one of two rangatira (chiefs) who lived at the Auckland Islands. Matioro is described as a large man, almost 1.8 metres tall (just under 6 feet) and weighing up to 160 kilograms (350 pounds), heavily tattooed and with a history of warfare.[22]

Despite his reputation, he peacefully welcomed the British settlers on their arrival in December 1849. He and his men were quickly employed to work for the new British colony, building houses and guiding ships into the harbour. For almost three years, the British and Māori–Moriori colonists coexisted amicably on the Auckland Islands.

In August 1852, when the last of the British residents departed, at least some of the Maungahuka settlers wanted to leave with them. Hardwicke's assistant commissioner William Mackworth recorded in his diary that the Maungahuka settlers had initially decided to stay (to Mackworth's amazement). They apparently changed their minds at the last minute, but were refused passage.[23]

Chiefs Matioro and Ngatere also wrote to New Zealand Governor George Grey in a joint letter in 1852, asking (in English) to be taken to New Zealand. 'Do not exile us!' commanded Matioro in the letter, while Ngatere asked Grey to 'Hasten here within the year'. The letter was accompanied by the mournful lyrics of a Māori waiata (song) that expressed their feelings of separation from their homeland: 'Longing for my people rises up within me.'[24]

There is no record of Grey's reply (if there was one), but he arranged for the Maungahuka settlers to be provided with a small boat and six sheep.[25]

Matioro and 30 of his people and slaves left the Auckland Islands in 1854 (almost half of the Maungahuka population), two years after the British settlers had departed, and lived for a while on Stewart Island/Rakiura in New Zealand before returning to the

Chathams. Matioro eventually died in Waikanae, on New Zealand's North Island.[26]

In 1856, the last of the Māori and Moriori settlers were picked up from the Auckland Islands in a boat chartered by Ngāti Mutunga relatives from the Chatham Islands, for the price of 100 tonnes (100,000 kilograms) of potatoes. Among those on the ship was Tangari Te Umu, one of the two men who had spontaneously sailed off in the *Hannah* 14 years earlier, leaving his family behind. He was not greeted with a warm welcome. Instead, his furious sister-in-law Ngapera whacked him over the head with a stick, drawing blood, and shouted that she refused to go with him after he'd abandoned them in 1842.[27] However, once threats of removal by force were made, she relented. The bones of their Ngāti Mutunga dead were exhumed for transferral back to the Chatham Islands, and they set sail.

The Auckland Islands were uninhabited once more.

There is no remaining sign of the Maungahuka villages on the Auckland Islands, but the New Zealand harakēkē flax they planted at the northern end of the main island to protect their garden sites has prospered.

Rohana (Tini Waihe)

Apart from a few sketchy accounts, very little is known about the 26 Moriori slaves who lived on the Auckland Islands, but they spent 12 to 14 years there with their captors and endured what must have been gruelling conditions. At least two slaves were murdered on the islands, while others died of natural causes.[28]

One young woman named Rohana (1820–1902) was captured as a teenage girl when the Māori took possession of the Chatham Islands in 1835.[29] When the Moriori were taken as slaves, husbands were separated from wives, and children were taken from their mothers and forced into work from a young age.

There was a high number of Moriori fatalities: according to the Native Land Court hearings in 1870 to verify land claims on the Chathams, at least 300 Moriori men, women and children were killed in 1835 and 1836.[30] Over the next 20 years, the population further dwindled by at least 1300 due to introduced diseases and the physical and psychological effects of slavery. By 1862, there were just over 100 Moriori left.[31]

Rohana was one of 26 Moriori slaves taken to the Auckland Islands in 1842, about 8 per cent of the surviving Chatham Islands Moriori population.[32] She would have been put to work, labouring over the wind-blasted cabbage, potato and turnip plots on Enderby Island, collecting seafood by the shore in cold and dangerous conditions, and carrying water uphill in bags made of thick sea-kelp.[33] (Rohana later described her time on the Auckland Islands as being the second-harshest experience of her life. The harshest was the 1835–36 attack on her people.[34])

When her 'owner', Chief Matioro, returned to the Chathams in the late 1850s she somehow managed to escape from him, although Matioro did try to abduct her again.[35] The local constable on the Chathams was apparently intimidated by Matioro and 'could

not, or would not venture to interfere.'[36] (Coincidentally, the constable in question was Toenga, Matioro's cousin, who had left the Auckland Islands after their battle in 1850.)

Slavery was finally abolished on the Chathams in the early 1860s and Rohana went on to marry Hirawanu Tapu, a respected Moriori leader. They had no children; she would have been in her forties by then, but infertility was also common for Moriori women who had been enslaved.[37] Rohana died in 1902, the last surviving Moriori slave of Maungahuka.

Former Moriori slave Rohana with her husband, Hirawanu Tapu, outside their Chatham Islands home in the 1890s. Rohana spent at least 12 years on the Auckland Islands, from 1842–54, as a slave.

4. HARDWICKE
The small town at the end of the world (1849–52)

ON 29 DECEMBER 1849, a worn-out old brig ironically named the *Fancy* limped into Port Ross. The 24 men, women and children on board had endured a gruelling four-and-a-half-month journey across the world from England, buffeted by heavy storms and squashed into clammy, dark steerage quarters. 'Crowded to excess and battling against the furies of the sea' was how one passenger described it.[1]

In the final days of the journey the ship had almost sailed right past the Auckland Islands due to a heavy fog, and on arrival at Port Ross, the *Fancy*'s inept captain was immediately dismissed for gross misconduct.[2]

Two other ships, the *Samuel Enderby* and the *Brisk*, had arrived several weeks earlier and the men were busy unpacking the prefabricated buildings from the ships and struggling to cut back the thick, tangled rātā trees around Erebus Cove. In all, there were 36 men, 16 women and 14 children who would be the first settlers of a new British whaling and agricultural colony to be named Hardwicke.[3]

Hardwicke was the brainchild of Charles Enderby, of the famous British whaling and shipping firm Samuel Enderby & Sons. His father's and grandfather's ships had carried some of the first Antarctic explorers as well as Abraham Bristow, who had discovered the Auckland Islands in 1806. Enderby had read the enthusiastic accounts of Benjamin Morrell and James Clark Ross, and wrote a lengthy proposal to the government about setting up a new whaling and agricultural colony on the other side of the world.[4]

At the time, the Auckland Islands were part-way along a common passage route from Australia to England that took advantage of the frequent westerly winds to blow ships in the right direction. The islands are the winter-time breeding ground of the southern right whale (so-called because it was the 'right' whale to catch for oil; they swam slowly, grew up to 18 metres or 60 feet long, and floated to the surface once killed), so it seemed like an ideal time and place to set up a new colony. Britain was lagging behind America in the whaling stakes and whale oil was in high demand for domestic and commercial lighting, as well as whalebone for riding crops, umbrella ribs and women's corsets.[5]

Charles Enderby's proposal was accepted by the British government. A 30-year lease was offered, a royal charter (letter of decree) was granted by Queen Victoria, and £100,000 (about £11 million in today's money) was raised in capital for the Enderby firm's new subsidiary, the Southern Whale Fishery Company. A few dozen young men were hand-picked to join the colony, including an accountant, labourers, farmers, a surveyor, a storekeeper, masons (stoneworkers), boatmen, blacksmiths, engineers, bricklayers, carpenters, coopers and two doctors.[6]

The whaling ship *Samuel Enderby* departing from England for the Auckland Islands, 1849.

Many of the men were married with young children, as the plan was to quickly create a thriving township, to be named Hardwicke in honour of the governor of the Southern Whale Fishery Company. Charles Enderby himself would live at Hardwicke as the chief commissioner and lieutenant governor.

Victorian London: Dickensian smog

Why on earth would anyone board a crowded ship with their young children and set off across the open sea for the great unknown, especially to live on a group of remote, uninhabited islands?

Well, life in late-1840s England wasn't exactly paradise. For one thing, London was in the middle of a cholera pandemic (caused by dirty drinking water) and no one at the time knew how to fix it. While some parts of London were wealthy and prosperous, there were strong class divisions and many areas were overcrowded and filthy, with slum dwellings. The population of London was over two million people by the late 1840s (later called the 'Hungry Forties' due to the European potato famine and economic depression). It was an age of progress and industrialization, but not cleanliness; water was collected from polluted wells, smoke poured out of factories, and raw sewage was pumped straight into the River Thames.

Unemployment was high, wages were low, and there were no work or health benefits. Infant mortality was high too, and a mother's death during childbirth was a real risk. There weren't many options for women; they had no property rights, and the British vote for women was still 70 years away. Many working-class women had jobs as domestic servants, took in washing or mending, or toiled in factories with poor conditions.[7]

The mostly working-class Hardwicke settlers, who all came from London or the surrounding countryside, were offered a chance to give their families a fresh start, with their own homes and secure, well-paying jobs (a five-year contract was offered), as well as clean air and water, and weekly food rations. They would be the first residents of a thriving, independent colony. It was sold to them as a kind of utopia.

But what they encountered when they arrived wasn't, figuratively speaking, in the advertising brochure. Benjamin Morrell's abundant pastures were nowhere to be seen; instead, there was thick scrub, barking sea lions, acidic soil and constant rain. It was hardly the 'dear little isle' they had sailed across the world for.

An unexpected welcome

When the *Samuel Enderby* glided into Port Ross on 4 December 1849, its passengers experienced the biggest shock of all: a small party of four Māori men and one woman, dressed in sealskin loincloths and with feathers in their hair, rowed out to greet them.[8]

One of the ship's crew was fluent in Te Reo Māori, so the British colonists quickly learned that the islands they'd thought to be uninhabited already had a settlement of 40 Māori and their 26 Moriori slaves, all of whom had arrived there from the Chatham Islands in 1842.

Once on land, Enderby immediately changed into his lieutenant-governor's Windsor uniform — dress sword, gold tassels and all — and 'read over his commission, the laws of the place, and his power over the people'.[9] It was very much an Anglo-centric approach and the Māori were firmly told they had no rights to the land or the animals, including the introduced pigs. They were given some form of financial compensation by Enderby and permitted to continue cultivating their gardens. However, the specifics of the agreement were not recorded, and with language difficulties there may well have been confusion on both sides as to who 'owned' the land and who was leasing it.[10] After all, the British Crown assumed ownership based on a paper trail in London, while the Maungahuka settlers had resided there for at least six years prior to Enderby's arrival.

Despite Enderby's authoritarian approach the moment he stepped ashore, the British and Maungahuka settlers coexisted mostly in harmony. The Māori and Moriori men were quickly employed to help with constructing the buildings and making roads, as well as working on the whaling ships and guiding vessels into the harbour.

There were certainly language and cultural barriers over the years, and the diary entries of Mackworth, the assistant commissioner, and Munce, the accountant, occasionally display frustration ('It is difficult to make any arrangement with these men'[11]) and contempt of cultural traditions ('Altogether the exhibition appeared a very hypocrisy of mourning,' commented Munce, after witnessing Māori women chanting and weeping during a child's tangi (funeral)[12]). However, there was also admiration ('I find much intelligence in … Mateoro [sic], the Chief of this district'[13]), and both Matioro and Ngatere were hired as special constables to help maintain order at Hardwicke.

The Moriori slaves are not mentioned in the Hardwicke officials' reports and diaries. Most likely they chose to turn a blind eye, as Enderby's Māori translator George Cook told him about Matioro's Chatham Islands history.[14]

A town is born

Charles Enderby soon moved into Government House, a 14-room mansion for use as his private residence and for accommodating visiting ships' captains and officers. His servants included a cook, a maid and a butler. Everyone else lived in one- to two-room cottages, although the officials had four-room cottages. There were also the single men's barracks, a cooperage for making barrels to store all the anticipated whale oil, a large warehouse that doubled as a store, a 'mangling house' for laundry, a jetty made out of rātā logs, a four-gun battery, and a flagpole to raise the British flag. A few roads and paths were made using shingle from the beach.

At its peak the settlement had 30 buildings and 150 residents (excluding whaling crews), but it never turned into the established town that was originally planned.

'Our greatest enemy … is the weather'

The first few weeks were hectic and productive, as everyone shrugged off their initial shock and got to work assembling the prefabricated buildings. Land was cleared on Auckland and Enderby islands for farming, while sheep and cattle were released. There were chickens too, but the few imported horses fared poorly in their new environment.

However, from day one the boisterous weather was the biggest challenge. Mackworth quickly described it as the colony's 'greatest enemy in this difficult undertaking'.[15] Typical entries during a week in March (autumn) 1850 read: 'Strong gales … Strong gales still with hail … Strong gales and rain hail snow.'[16] It wasn't uncommon for ships' arrivals or departures to be delayed for days or even weeks by poor weather. Drying laundry must have been impossible.

Watercolour painting of
Hardwicke, Port Ross,
possibly by Charles
Enderby, between
1850 and 1852.

At least the winters were relatively mild, but autumns and springs were filled with rain and gusty, cold winds. Hail in the summer was commonplace. Rare fine days — or even hours — must have been all the more appreciated.

The 'Antarctic Prince of Whales'[17]

Hardwicke was Charles Enderby's vision. He was part of the Samuel Enderby & Sons family whaling and shipping empire in London (Enderby ships get an honorable mention in the whaling novel *Moby-Dick*) and his proposal for the new colony was met with wholehearted government and Crown support. In his defence, he had been given inaccurate accounts of the islands' climate and agricultural potential by previous explorers (see Chapter 2).

As Hardwicke's first and only lieutenant governor, Enderby entertained many distinguished guests including the New Zealand governor (see p. 60) in his mansion on Auckland Island. But his ability to manage the colony quickly came into

question; he was described by the colonists as both 'law maker and law breaker',[18] overturning sentences on a whim. He was in his fifties at the time, much older than most of the Hardwicke settlers, so there would have been a noticeable generation gap. One historian has described him as a 'pompous, muddle-headed scion'.[19]

Charles Enderby (1798–1876). This photo was taken in England in the late 1850s, after the abandonment of Hardwicke.

After the demise of Hardwicke in 1852 Enderby continued to campaign for a settlement on the islands, volunteering his services to the British government. No one was interested. He eventually died alone and forgotten, in his late seventies, in London.

William Mackworth

William Augustus Mackworth was an earnest, practical man and only in his early twenties when he travelled to the Auckland Islands as assistant commissioner. The diary he kept during his time at Hardwicke was discovered in a descendant's attic in the 1970s and eventually published in New Zealand in 1999, along with the accountant William Munce's diary.[20] Mackworth's entries in particular reveal his constant frustration over the general lawlessness and heavy drinking at Hardwicke, while both diarists offer previously unknown glimpses into day-to-day life at the British colony.

Mackworth was practical and efficient, quickly taking over day-to-day management from Enderby on arrival after witnessing the confusion and slow progress.[21] He was also a leader when it came to religion, although not everyone shared his enthusiasm. He read 'Divine Service' most Sundays, but was constantly disappointed by low or non-attendance, and by mid-1852 he had all but given up.

After Enderby's reluctant departure in 1852, Mackworth was left to manage the breaking up of the colony, a responsibility which almost broke him completely: 'I am in very low spirits … My health too has suffered much latterly from anxiety of mind and exposure to the weather.'[22] He married quickly after leaving the Auckland Islands, to a young woman he had met in New Zealand during a business trip in 1850, but died of typhoid in Australia just a couple of years later and only months before the birth of his first child, a daughter named Wilhelmina in his honour.

Love and marriage

An official registry was kept of the four weddings, 16 births and four deaths that occurred during the Hardwicke era (Maungahuka events were not formally recorded, but a few deaths are mentioned in the officials' diaries).[23]

Two weddings were officiated almost the moment the brides stepped off their respective ships: George Cook, the *Brisk*'s first mate, married Matilda Fawkes, Enderby's maid, within a few weeks of their arrival at the islands in December 1849. The colony's second accountant, William Munce, married Elizabeth (Liz) McKenny, his first wife's sister, the day she arrived from Australia in December 1950 (his wife had died one year previously, leaving six children).[24]

Not every wedding was conducted on the islands. James Bromley, Hardwicke's butcher, travelled to Otago in 1850 to buy more sheep for the colony. He returned a few weeks later with 150 sheep — and also a new wife, Charlotte.[25]

Sarah and Isaac Cripps, photographed later in life in New Zealand.

Isaac and Sarah Cripps

Sixty men, women and children from Britain arrived at the Auckland Islands in 1849, and two of them were my great-great-great grandparents. Isaac was a former London constable who was employed by the Southern Whale Fishery Company as a 'general servant' (labourer) at the Auckland Islands for £50 per year. He was a tall, gruff, bearded man who carried a mahogany truncheon from his London Metropolitan Police days (history doesn't record if he used it on anyone).[26]

Sarah, who has been described as 'very short and very stout',[27] was aged 27 when she arrived at the Auckland Islands. Once a former seamstress who had started her own business, and now a mother to three children under the age of five, she hadn't been thrilled at the prospect of sailing across the world to a remote island.[28] But Isaac, 29, had landed a five-year contract, so off they went. Poor Sarah was bedridden for most of the four-and-a-half-month voyage due to acute seasickness, and repeatedly begged the captain to throw her overboard to end her misery. As a result, she developed a lifelong loathing of the ocean.[29]

Isaac's 1849 contract with the British Southern Whale Fishery Company has survived, and its terms reveal a great deal about the time in which it was written:

'He shall be subservient to and obey the orders and directions of the Court of Directors ... in all things; he shall devote the whole of his time and attention to the service of the said Company.'[30]

When the settlement crumbled in 1852, Isaac was left with a heavy box full of five pounds' worth of pennies, since Hardwicke's paper currency, which had been used to pay the colonists, wasn't legal tender anywhere else.[31]

Sarah became the colony's nurse and midwife (there were 16 births during the Hardwicke era) and, though the job may have been unofficial, she was paid for her work.[32] It was an important role; she assisted women through the ordeal of giving birth, often for the first time and enduring protracted labours in the middle of nowhere, with no pain relief, at a time when maternal and infant mortality was high, and with the local doctor probably intoxicated.[33] (As was typical at the time, spouses did not attend the birth; the accountant Munce reports getting a poor night's sleep in an armchair in another room, and also playing cribbage with the doctor to pass the time, while his wife spent 24 hours in labour with her first child — his seventh.[34])

In April 1851 it was Sarah's turn. She gave birth to her fourth child, Harriet Sophia, my great-great grandmother. There was no minister at Hardwicke to christen or baptize Harriet, but in 1852 the HMS *Calliope* was passing through and the ship's chaplain gathered together all the children born at Hardwicke and baptized them, scribbling a certificate for each child on a bit of notepaper.[35]

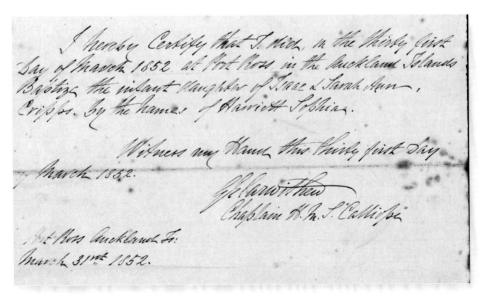

A copy of Harriet Sophia Cripps' hand-written baptism certificate from the Auckland Islands, 1852 (one year after her birth).

By all accounts, Sarah was a kind, cheerful and hospitable woman, and evidently full of energy — she went on to have ten children and continued her work as a midwife in the Wairarapa, New Zealand, where the Cripps family eventually settled. Sarah was also the hostess of a boarding house that she and Isaac set up called Sevenoaks, and was the local storekeeper and postmistress. Affectionately known as 'Granny Cripps' in her later years, Sarah died at the age of 70, in 1892. (Isaac died in 1904).[36]

Fun and games

The colonists did manage to enjoy the occasional bit of fun. Nearby Enderby Island offered more sunshine and a sandy beach, so families were sometimes sent there for a week of R&R, and some respite from the low cloud literally and figuratively hanging over the settlement on Auckland Island.

In his diary, Mackworth writes of picnics by the waterfalls at one of Auckland Island's many coves for the officials (Enderby, Mackworth, Munce, the various doctors, the sea-captains and their wives). Hunting was a favourite pastime for the officials, with birds, pigs and seals shot for sport, as well as evening card games and dinner parties. Munce seems to have enjoyed his time at Hardwicke a bit more than Mackworth: he took long walks, admired the views, attended social gatherings, chopped wood, did gardening, and enjoyed reading and hunting.[37]

It's clear from both Mackworth's and Munce's diary entries, however, that Hardwicke's officials and general servants didn't socialize together. There were still distinct British class divisions, even in such a tiny settlement on the other side of the world.

Farming in the wild

Twenty acres (8 hectares) of land were eventually burned and cleared for farming on Enderby and Auckland islands. Initially 300 sheep and 80 cattle were released on Enderby Island, and then sporadically topped up.[38] But many of the cows ran wild due to the lack of fencing and were difficult to catch. Sheep were a dietary staple, but many died en route from Australia or New Zealand.[39] The wild pigs were plentiful on Auckland Island thanks to Bristow and friends but, as noted earlier, often tasted fishy because they ate seaweed and dead seal flesh.[40] Most of the local fish (*Nothothenia,* a species of cod) was inedible, or at least extremely non-appetizing, due to a parasitic worm infestation.

Vegetables proved difficult to grow in the acidic soil, and cabbages were ripped out of the ground by wild winds.[41] R.E. Malone, a ship's official visiting in 1852, frowned at the pitiful results:

'The potatoes are an inch and a half in diameter [4 centimetres], and bad; and the turnips run down like miserable radishes … The Maories [sic], at a small pah

[sic] of theirs at Ocean Point, grew the best cabbages and turnips, but they were good for nothing.[42]

The lacklustre vegetables weren't enough to keep everyone fed, let alone make a profit from. Thus there were many expensive, capital-sapping trips to New Zealand and Australia to replenish supplies, and the labourers regularly went on strike over the lack of flour, meat or potatoes in their weekly rations.[43]

'A receptacle for culprits'[44]

Right from the start there was mutiny and insubordination among the ships' crews and settlers, and the most common reasons for incarceration were intoxication and refusal to perform duty.

'Culprits' were initially put in the custody of the two Māori chiefs, Matioro and Ngatere, but from February 1850 prisoners were banished to Shoe Island, a tiny, barren rock directly opposite the settlement, with only a barrel for shelter.

Shoe Island's most frequent occupant was Dr Rodd, the medical officer, who one night was fished out of the water by the jetty thrashing about 'so violent through intoxication that confinement for a short time was necessary'.[45] The island henceforth became known as 'Rodd's Castle' in his honour.[46] Perhaps he drank out of boredom — due to their isolation the settlers remained mainly in good health.

A small hut with restraining irons was eventually built on Shoe Island. However, in what could be viewed as self-defeating behaviour, the inmates burned it down one night. Prisoners were then sent to Adams Island, the southernmost island in the Aucklands group and far from the eyes of Hardwicke. They would be dropped off there with some rations and collected a few months later.

The demon drink

Boredom, frustration, depression and discomfort were all chased away by alcohol, resulting in what was described by Mackworth as 'a damning fountain of crime'.[47]

Drinking was an ongoing problem, especially among the returning crews of whaling ships. Early on, some of the married men were employed as 'special constables' to protect women from 'disturbance and insult' while they were temporarily housed in the single men's barracks.[48]

Social drinking was tolerated and there was a pub for the labourers and sailors, but things often went too far. The sale of spirits was soon regulated, to much complaining; Mackworth even proposed a Total Abstinence Society, which would allow no drinking on, or within sight of, the Auckland Islands, but only six people signed the pledge.[49] Enderby, in a fit of fury, once ordered the contents of every bottle to be tipped into the sea, but the men began distilling their own spirits.

Shoe Island, the town's first jail site.

The settlers are described by Munce as being 'often led into mischief through intoxication',[50] including Mrs Ewington, another doctor's wife, who seemed to succumb quite regularly to the bottle. 'She was so intoxicated I would not stop to tea …' Munce sniffily wrote in his diary, and on another occasion, 'Mrs E — seen this evening as a Lady ought <u>not</u> to be seen.'[51] Even her own husband tried to distance himself; when the settlement crumbled in 1852, Dr Ewington announced that he would rather leave his wife behind than pay for her passage to Sydney, but he was forced to take her with him.[52]

Chief Matioro's village was regularly visited after dark by drunken sailors when their whaling ships were in port,[53] and the sailors were later described by Thomas Younger, the colony's civil engineer, as having 'taken liquor and gone amongst the Maori girls'.[54] Younger also recalled that Matioro's wife Ngawhanga, nicknamed 'Kuini' (transliteration for 'Queen' due to her status as a chief's wife), tried to hang herself after her husband accused her of fraternizing with the sailors for money. Matioro later retracted the accusation.

Island sickness

A condition now known as 'island sickness' undoubtedly played a part in the unravelling of the colony. Months or years living in isolated conditions, far from civilization and with limited sunshine could make people lethargic, moody and unpredictable.[55]

One of the most dramatic events during the Hardwicke era was a murder–suicide attempt in November 1850. One night Hepzibah Hallett, the sister of the colony's chief medical officer, fired a gun at her brother through a door in their cottage, carefully reloaded it, and then shot herself in the head. Both survived the incident, although Hepzibah suffered terrible head lacerations. They were allowed to remain at Hardwicke after Dr Hallett promised Charles Enderby that it wouldn't happen again (presumably the gun was taken away), but the Halletts eventually moved on.[56]

There was also at least one reported incident of domestic violence: 'Mr George Cook … has been beating his wife, disturbing his neighbours, and refused to give up a supply of wine … His Wife rushed into my room today begging for protection,' wrote Mackworth, who quickly assembled a group of men to protect Mrs Cook. The next day her husband was reprimanded, but mainly for failing to hand over the wine as ordered.[57]

Mackworth's diary entries become increasingly despondent as time goes by in what he calls his 'miserable banishment'[58] on the Auckland Islands, especially once he is left in charge of breaking up the colony — a thankless task indeed. 'How my broken temper and debilitated health are to get through the next few months I cannot comprehend,' he wrote, and then crossed out of his diary, in May 1852.

Sir George and Lady Eliza Grey

New Zealand Governor Sir George Grey and his wife, Lady Eliza Grey, bravely headed south to celebrate Hardwicke's first anniversary in December 1850. According to newspaper reports of the time, Grey was impressed by how quickly the settlement had been established but was also concerned about the locally manufactured 'promissory notes' for payment of wages, which were not legal tender in New Zealand.[59]

The weather was unpleasant for most of their one-week stay, and most of the outdoor events on Anniversary Day had to be cancelled. A planned lunch was also quickly called off when it was discovered that Miss Hallett, who had tried to shoot her brother only weeks earlier, had been invited.[60] But during the Greys' visit there was still singing, dancing and pig hunting, and the sailors gave a theatrical performance that Munce wrote off in his diary as 'wretched'. Governor Grey also took a particular interest in Māori culture, and wrote down some of Chief Matioro's unique karakia, or prayers.[61]

Eliza Grey is not mentioned in the reports or diary entries of the time, other than that she was there with her husband. The Greys made a dashing couple, but their relationship was strained and she was deeply unhappy during her years in New Zealand (as recorded in letters she wrote to friends).[62] Grey reputedly had a fiery temper and a jealous streak, and was allegedly unfaithful. He abandoned Eliza in Rio de Janeiro in 1860, but they reconciled in England almost 40 years later.[63]

'No Oil'

Despite the initial confidence of the Southern Whale Fishery Company, whaling was not a profitable venture and the small amount of oil collected during long, challenging expeditions proved disappointing.

There were eventually eight whaling ships for use by the colony, but they were not built to the specifications recommended by Charles Enderby due to cost-cutting efforts by the Board of Directors in London. Very few whales were caught during the 17 voyages from 1850 to 1852 (ranging from the Balleny Islands, near the Antarctic continent, to the seas north of Japan), and sometimes expeditions would come back completely empty-handed. 'No Oil', wrote Mackworth with rare emphasis, after a disappointing early attempt by the *Brisk*.[64]

A few expeditions that ventured into the North Pacific fared better, but only about 2000 barrels of oil, and 10 tonnes of whalebone, were collected during the two and a half years of the colony — far short of expectations and requirements, as the colony depended on the sale of whale oil to sustain itself.[65]

Whales would occasionally be sighted in the bay, but as the whalers were out at sea, attempts to catch them were generally unsuccessful. Southern right whales had also been hunted almost to extinction in the previous decades, so their numbers were greatly reduced.

Whaling itself was a cruel, prolonged and dangerous business. Ships would be at sea for months or years, and when a whale was sighted, whalers with sharpened harpoons would lower small boats into choppy waters in pursuit. Once speared, a whale sometimes retaliated in fury, splitting the whaleboat in two with its tail or churning up the water so the whaleboat overturned. Even extracting the oil was stressful: the whale carcass was chained to the side of the ship, and the crew stood on slippery platforms over shark-infested waters with flensing knives to strip off the blubber, which was then boiled on deck in giant try pots for the valuable oil.[66]

It was a rough existence for all on board; Hardwicke's Captain Barton took his wife along on a whaling expedition in 1851, but poor Mrs Barton returned to Hardwicke in a weak condition and took months to recover.[67]

Isabel Younger: 'the silent spot where a little baby lies'

During the Hardwicke settlement there were four recorded deaths: two infants and two sailors. One of the infants was Isabel Younger, the 15-week-old daughter of civil engineer Thomas Younger. She died of a fever in November 1850, described by Munce as 'the first death of a Christian since the settlement of the island' (there was a tangi for an unnamed Māori infant on the same day as Isabel's funeral). Charles Enderby donated an unused grindstone, upon which her grieving father carved Isabel's initials and the date. He also carved his own initials, 'T.Y.', on the side.[68]

Sunrays illuminate the silhouette of a
southern right whale, Auckland Islands. The
whales proved elusive in the 1850s, having
already been hunted to near-extinction.

Isabel's gravestone, photographed in 1874. It looks much the same today.

The stone is still standing, a little lopsidedly, in the tiny, picket-fenced graveyard called Hardwicke Cemetery on Auckland Island. It is a poignant little symbol of the colony's failed dreams.

The cemetery is maintained as a historic site by the New Zealand Department of Conservation and there are six graves: Janet Stove, another Hardwicke infant who died at 14 weeks old in October 1851; an American sailor who died at Hardwicke in 1852; and three shipwreck victims and castaways from later years. Most of the graves have replacement wooden markings. The Maungahuka settlers had their own burial site, and the bones of the Māori (not Moriori) graves were exhumed when the last of the Maungahuka settlers departed in 1856.[69]

The downfall

With the wild weather, constant drinking, lack of decent crops and barely any whale oil, it was just a matter of time before Hardwicke fell apart.

The London Board of Directors had quickly grown concerned by the vague and unsatisfactory reports emerging from the colony (where was all the promised whale oil, and was the soil really 'everywhere rich beyond description', as Enderby had claimed in an early report?[70]). In 1852 they sent two special commissioners named Dundas and Preston to investigate. They were horrified by the state of things at Hardwicke and forced Enderby to resign.

Enderby threatened to shoot anyone who tried to remove him from Government House and eventually tried to have the commissioners arrested in New Zealand for gross misconduct, but nothing came of it.[71] At the time the Auckland Islands were considered British land that had been leased to the Southern Whale Fishery Company, and no one wanted to get involved.[72]

A few months after Enderby was escorted to New Zealand on the *Black Dog* by the special commissioners, Government House was pulled apart and taken to Sydney, where it was auctioned without its ill-fated origins being mentioned. But the New Zealand press certainly lamented the building's symbolic fall from grace: 'Alas, the mutability of fortune! So lately the residence of the representative of royalty — in a month or two, degraded to a gin shop, or a store for the sale of soap and candles!'[73]

The last of the disillusioned Hardwicke settlers departed in August 1852. Many had already left by then, driven away by the rough conditions or drawn to the promised riches of the Victorian goldrush in Australia. Most of the final settlers went on to Australia or returned to England, with just a couple of families settling in New Zealand.[74] Two Hardwicke employees decided to stay at Port Ross, having 'allied themselves with Maori women'.[75] One of Mackworth's final diary entries is memorably emphatic: 'The satisfaction I feel at this moment is beyond description. My miserable life at Port Ross will never be forgotten.'[76]

All the prefabricated buildings were taken apart and packed into the departing ships, leaving just one or two huts behind. Twenty years later, a German photographer named Hermann Krone (see Chapter 6) visited the abandoned and overgrown Hardwicke site:

Scattered bricks from the Hardwicke site.

'[It was] a garden gone wild ... where they constructed for themselves their miserable little huts ... The space inside most of them appeared to be about four square metres [43 square feet], with no kind of partitioning ... All around in between lay colourfully all kinds of remains, bricks, timber and kitchen utensils ... parts of ovens and cans ... rusty hooks ... bottles grown through with grass.'[77]

Clearly, it was a time before the 'leave only footprints' mantra.

Hardwicke was one of Britain's smallest, shortest-lived and most remote colonies.[78] Today, apart from the cemetery, only a few moss-covered bricks and broken bottles remain at the site.

5. SHIPWRECKS
The Grafton, the *Invercauld* and the
General Grant (1864–67)

HEAVY FOG, WILD SEAS, SHARP CLIFFS, STRONG WINDS, rudimentary
navigation techniques and frequent passages through the Roaring Forties and Furious
Fifties latitudes — together, these formed a deadly cocktail that resulted in at least
eight known shipwrecks on the Auckland Islands in the 19th and early-20th centuries.

'Destruction, death and desolation'[1] was how journalist Robert Carrick summed it
up in 1892 after he visited the islands on a government steamer looking for castaways.
(He went on to describe the Auckland Islands — poetically, if melodramatically — as
a 'hydra-headed monster of the deep'.)

The fact that the islands had been inaccurately mapped several times in the mid-
1800s (one often-used chart placed them 56 kilometres (35 miles) south of their actual
location, and another chart didn't include them at all) also confused matters no end.[2]
When ships did sight the islands, their crews often weren't sure which area they were
seeing; they would try to follow the coastline only to be driven into the jagged cliffs by
the strong ocean currents and westerly gales.

Passages from Australia to England involved travelling via what was known as the
'clipper route' in the 19th century. Ships sailed south of New Zealand to catch the
strong westerly winds that pushed them across the Southern and Pacific oceans and
below Cape Horn, at the southern tip of South America. It was an efficient yet risky
route and the Auckland Islands eventually became known as a 'graveyard for ships'.[3]

Wrecked and wretched

Of course, not every shipwreck had survivors and ships were known to sail off and
never be heard from again. But for those who did live to tell the tale, the isolated
location and hostile weather conditions didn't help matters. Rescue might be months
or even years away, if it came at all.

Finding ourselves in similar circumstances today, many of us would probably just
curl up, overcome by the lack of groceries, utilities and smartphones, and without
even a rudimentary hut to shelter in. After all, a bonafide 19th-century castaway

experience would make the TV show *Survivor* look like *Sesame Street*. Fortunately, many of the subantarctic castaways were tough, practical and resourceful; they came from the Victorian goldfields, or were sea-hardened sailors. Dozens of men (and one woman) managed to tough it out and tell the tale — and, in the case of three men, even managed to rescue themselves.

There is only one recorded shipwreck at Campbell Island, which was the *Perseverance* in 1828 (coincidentally, the same ship that had discovered the island 18 years earlier). Three wrecks are known to have occurred at the Antipodes Islands, in 1893, 1908, and in 1999 when a 10-metre (33-foot) yacht called the *Totorore* disappeared while supporting an albatross research study, with the loss of two lives.

The hostile climate of Macquarie Island, and its lack of a sheltered harbour, also caused a series of shipwrecks in the 1800s, including the *Eagle* in the 1860s. Nine men and a woman were washed ashore and spent two years shivering in a cave. The woman allegedly died in mysterious circumstances just one day before the men were rescued.

The majority of subantarctic shipwrecks, however, were on the Auckland Islands, which are further north and have steep cliffs that are often hidden by dense fog and would have surprised unsuspecting ship's captains. We can't know exactly how many shipwrecks there were, but the most infamous of the known wrecks on the Auckland Islands include the *Grafton* (1864), the *Invercauld* (1864), the *General Grant* (1866), the *Derry Castle* (1887), and the *Dundonald* (1907).

The *Grafton*

The story of the *Grafton* is one of (*warning: spoilers ahead*) triumph over adversity through strong leadership, resourcefulness and courage displayed against almost impossible odds.

In December 1863, the *Grafton* sailed south from Sydney to Campbell Island on the lookout for tin-mining and sealing opportunities. After not finding much of value on Campbell, they decided to sail on to the Aucklands, but on 3 January 1864, hurricane-level winds pushed the small ship onto a wall of rocks in Carnley Harbour, which separates Auckland and Adams islands.

The crew of five men, who were British, American, French, Portuguese and Norwegian, all managed to exit the small schooner. They rescued a few supplies from the ship and existed shiveringly for a few weeks under a leaking tent made of sailcloth. A box of wet matches was discovered in one of the men's pockets; they eventually managed to light a fire (after five heart-stopping broken matches) and made sure that it never went out.

After sourcing some food from the local pigs and sea lions, they built a decent-sized (7 x 4 metre, or 22 x 16 foot) hut, which they named Epigwaitt (according to Captain Thomas Musgrave, this was a Native American word meaning 'dwelling near the water'). It was very civilized for a castaway house, with a thatched roof, a stone

fireplace, beds, a table and desk, and wooden floorboards. There were even two glass windows that had been salvaged from the *Grafton*.

Musgrave's command continued on land — the men unanimously voted to keep him in charge, with the caveat that a re-election would happen if he let them down. Each

A rib of the *Grafton* wreck in Carnley Harbour.

man played to his strengths, and they lived as comfortably and amicably as they could for the next 18 months. They ran a 'school' in the evenings to share their knowledge with one another, divided the work fairly among themselves, read prayers on Sundays, kept endemic parakeets as pets that they trained to talk, and quickly resolved any grievances.

At the beginning, the men were quietly confident of imminent rescue. Before departing from Sydney, Musgrave had sensibly told several acquaintances about their journey, and said that if they weren't back in four months to send a government steamship to collect them. However, as the months dragged on, it became disappointingly obvious that their trusted acquaintances either hadn't followed up or didn't realize they were marooned on the Auckland Islands.

A 19TH-CENTURY FRENCH 'MACGYVER'

One of the castaways was François Raynal (1830–92), a French sailor who had become dangerously ill during their expedition to Campbell Island and was recovering, but still very weak, when the *Grafton* was wrecked. The others somehow managed to get him off the ship — at great personal risk — and he initially tended the campfire while they hunted for food and shelter. Left alone with his thoughts for hours on end, he tried very hard not to succumb to depression.

> 'Alone, and abandoned to myself, you may guess of what melancholy reflections I was soon the victim. I began to think of my family … I was separated from them by a whole hemisphere.'[4]

Raynal had been forced into self-sufficiency from a young age, when his parents came into financial difficulties. At the age of 14 he had abandoned his education in France and taken to the sea to seek his fortune, working on ships and in Australian goldmines, and was determined to return to his home country a rich man. While getting shipwrecked on a remote island mightn't have been part of the 33-year-old's life plan, the practical skills he had acquired over the years would come in very handy.

But during that first dreadful night, as he lay on the ground feeling cold and afraid, it was difficult to find a silver lining.

> 'How and when should I escape from this island, hidden in the midst of the seas, and lying beyond the limits of the inhabited world? Perhaps, never! A violent despair overmastered me … and I wept like a child.'[5]

He quickly pulled himself together for the sake of his fellow castaways, vowing to make himself useful to them. He began by filling a salvaged pot with some water to boil their tea. Once Raynal regained his strength, his talents and resourcefulness

The remains of Epigwaitt.

knew no bounds. First, he figured out how to make soap from the burnt ashes of seaweed, pounded shell fragments, and sea lion oil. Next, he taught himself how to tan sea-lion hide to make shoes, blankets and clothing for the five men. It was also Raynal's makeshift mortar, made from a mixture of calcified sea-shells and fine gravel, that cemented together the stones for Epigwaitt's chimney.[6]

To help while away the long evenings, when depression and frustration threatened to consume them, Raynal made some chess pieces and cards — although the cards were soon tossed into the fire when Musgrave turned out to be a bad sport.[7] He also whipped up an alcohol distillery, but wisely destroyed that as well after it occurred to him that plentiful booze could be their downfall.

Crucially, the men figured out how to salt-dry seal meat to keep themselves fed throughout the long winter, once they realized that most of the seals departed the islands in the colder months and became increasingly hard to find. They also discovered that they could fry up the local megaherb roots (*Stilbocarpa polaris*) as a vegetable, thereby warding off the dreaded scurvy. An ongoing lack of vitamin C could cause spots to form on the skin, bones to weaken and teeth to fall out.

MUSGRAVE: A TORMENTED LEADER

Captain Thomas Musgrave, who was only 32 when the *Grafton* was wrecked, had a calm and stoic presence that helped band the five men together on the island. However, he was also quietly battling an overwhelming depression (understandable, given the circumstances). He had a wife and kids in Sydney whom he worried about constantly, and in the privacy of his journal he occasionally succumbed to despair: 'The sad fate which may have befallen those I love wrings my soul with agony and remorse which is crushing me ...'[8]

The weather didn't help matters and its wildness came as a shock, even to the seafaring captain who previously thought he had seen it all.

> *'Never have I experienced, or read, or heard of anything in the shape of storms to equal this place. The sea booms, and the wind howls; these are the sounds which have been almost constantly ringing in my ears ... sometimes it makes my flesh creep to hear them.'*[9]

Meanwhile, the lack of sunshine was causing Raynal to suffer from what we now call Seasonal Affective Disorder: 'An eternal veil of gray, a dull arc of sinister clouds! Oh, for more blue! For more sky!'[10] After 12 months as castaways, their hopes of being rescued had faded and they dreaded facing another winter on the island.

Raynal suggested that they make a small boat and sail north to New Zealand. However, to do so they would need some nails and bolts, which they didn't have. *Pas de problème!* In typical Raynal-esque fashion, the enterprising Frenchman somehow managed to create a pair of forge bellows made from some ship's metal, sealskin and wood.

The men got to work, but after several months they found they lacked the right tools to successfully complete the job. Instead, they repurposed the small boat they'd salvaged from the *Grafton*, a job that took a few additional months. In June 1865 the boat was ready, but could only safely carry three of the men. So Musgrave, Raynal and Alick McLaren, the Norwegian sailor, set off without a map or compass to sail 400 kilometres (250 miles) north to Stewart Island, which was the closest piece of inhabited land.

A PERILOUS JOURNEY

For five days and five nights they were pummelled by what Raynal later described as hurricane-level winds, as well as rain, hail and snow.[11] Their boat overturned at least

La chaumière des naufragés.

once. The seal meat and shags they'd packed for food spoiled quickly and had to be tossed overboard. Musgrave also had to remain standing the entire time, pumping water out of the boat as large waves crashed over them. After the fifth night they made it — barely — to Stewart Island, where the locals stared at them in amazement as they staggered off the boat and collapsed on the beach. They were quickly taken to a nearby house and given food and shelter.

Musgrave was eager to return to the Auckland Islands and collect the other two men, but the New Zealand government was reluctant to pay for a ship to rescue them. However, the people of Invercargill heard of their predicament and everyone chipped in (an early example of crowdfunding?), eventually raising enough cash to hire a small ship. Keeping his promise, Musgrave then returned to the islands as soon as he could to rescue the men, who by then were in a bad way, fighting between themselves and resorting to eating mice. They were understandably delighted to be rescued, having almost given up hope.

The 'Epigwaitt' dwelling as illustrated by Alphonse Marie de Neuville in François Raynal's book *Les Naufragés ou Vingt Mois sur un Récif des Îles Auckland* (Hachette, Paris, 1860s).

But the story was not quite over. To their surprise, the rescue team in the *Flying Scud* came across the corpse of an unknown man who appeared to have died of starvation on the island. He was lying in the derelict ruins of a house at Port Ross (from the Hardwicke era, though they didn't know it at the time) and next to the body was a slate with some writing that they couldn't decipher. It later turned out that he was one of the crew from the *Invercauld,* James Mahoney (see below). The *Invercauld* castaways had been stranded on the island at the same time as the *Grafton* castaways, but the two groups never encountered one another.

The *Grafton* men later reported having seen smoke rising in the north while they were stranded on the island, but at the time they dismissed it as low fog. The lack of contact is understandable; Auckland Island is only 42 kilometres (26 miles) long but much of it is difficult terrain, with steep cliffs and impenetrable scrub, and shrouded by low cloud.

As for the *Grafton* survivors, both Musgrave and Raynal wrote books about their castaway experiences based on the journals they kept while stranded on the island (when they ran out of ink, they turned to sea-lion blood). Raynal's book was published anonymously in France in 1868. It became an international best-seller, was translated into several languages, and is still in print today: *Les Naufragés*, or *Wrecked on a Reef.*

Musgrave was reunited with his family in Sydney and promised them he'd never sail off again. But his love of the sea didn't wane; he became a lighthouse keeper, and died aged 59 after having 16 children, including three sets of twins.[12] He repeatedly urged the Australian and New Zealand governments to do something to help potential castaways on the subantarctic islands, which led to the eventual establishment of castaway depots as well as ongoing search and rescue missions by both countries for almost half a century (see Chapter 7).[13]

The *Invercauld*

While the *Grafton* men were living in a cosy hut, manufacturing tools and planning their escape, another group of castaways was dying off one by one from exposure and starvation, just 30 kilometres (18 miles) north on the same island.

The *Invercauld* was a Scottish ship sailing in ballast (i.e. weighted down on the journey to pick up cargo) from Melbourne to Peru in May 1864, when it encountered thick fog and a strong breeze — a deadly combination. The ship slammed into the steep western cliffs of Auckland Island, broke apart almost immediately and sank away in the darkness, taking the lives of six men.

Robert Holding, a young Scottish sailor, wrote an account of the wreck 60 years later to record the horror of that fateful night: 'It was now every man for himself with the most dismal outlook anyone could possibly imagine.'[14]

The 19 survivors made it to shore and were forced to camp on a narrow beach

A 1904 painting of the doomed *Invercauld* by T.G. Purvis.

for five cold, miserable days. No one seemed to know which island they had washed up on.[15] Instead of rallying his men and seeking food and shelter, the *Invercauld*'s Captain Dalgarno fell into a deep depression. Two men each found a box of matches in their pockets but both boxes were accidentally burned after a fire was started, with only a couple of matches rescued by Holding.

From the shore they were also forced to endure the ghastly sight of a shipwreck victim's corpse suspended in front of them:

> '... jammed amongst the wreckage was one of our poor shipmates hanging by one foot as naked as the day he was born. Although he was close to us we could not ... get near, as the waves were breaking high above him ... The poor fellow hung there all day.'[16]

With little food to nourish them, and scantily clothed — many were barefoot and without a coat — those with the strength to do so scaled the sharp, imposing cliffs, which were 600 metres (2000 feet) high, to reach the rest of the island.

CLIFF-CLIMBING FOR SURVIVAL

Robert Holding, who was just 23 years old at the time the *Invercauld* was wrecked, took the initiative to climb the steep cliffs to find some food. He also returned to help some of the other men. However, some weren't strong enough to make it or simply decided to remain on the beach, and for the others conditions weren't much better at the top, with howling winds, hail, snow and boggy soil. The bush was so thick that that some of the men found it easier to climb over it than to cut through the dense interior. Next came the tangled rātā forest, which was even more difficult to navigate.

By this point they were surviving on megaherb roots and a pig they had managed to catch. The men divided into small groups to see if they could find some decent shelter. One by one they began to die. Conditions on the island were harsh and food was scarce; seals at the time were few and far between, because in the winter they head out to sea. As a result, there was at least one incidence of cannibalism.[17] Most of the shipwreck survivors perished within the first few weeks of starvation and exposure.

Holding wisely suggested that they head to the more sheltered east coast, and they experienced some luck when they stumbled across the ruins of the Hardwicke settlement, including a derelict building and a few half-buried tools, as well as a plentiful supply of limpets on the nearby beaches. But even in such primitive conditions there was an attempt to maintain the ship's hierarchy. James Mahoney, the *Invercauld*'s second mate, had a bandaged foot and would order the others to fetch and carry for him while he lay by the fire in the semi-collapsed ruins of a Hardwicke house. At one stage he pulled a knife on Holding and told him to bring him some roots. But Mahoney's aggression backfired and he eventually starved to death, alone and abandoned, covered in the clothing he'd removed from the corpses of other *Invercauld* castaways for warmth.[18]

A year later, it was Mahoney's badly-decomposed body that a bemused Captain Thomas Musgrave discovered when he returned to the Auckland Islands in the *Flying Scud* to retrieve the final two *Grafton* castaways. Musgrave picked up a roof slate next to the corpse with a message that Holding had scratched many months earlier, after he had returned to check on Mahoney and found him dead ('James Mahoney. Wrecked. With the Ship Invercauld. May 10th 64.'). However, Musgrave couldn't decipher Holding's writing, which had been blurred by time and weather, and at that stage he'd never heard of the *Invercauld*. Musgrave then buried Mahoney and planted a wooden cross carved with the word 'Unknown'. (From Holding's 1919 account, published in 1997, it was revealed what he had written on the slate.[19])

THE FINAL FEW

By the time a Portuguese ship called the *Julian* arrived in May 1865 (the crew were looking to repair their vessel at the Hardwicke settlement, which had been abandoned more than a decade earlier[20]), it had been 12 months since the *Invercauld* was wrecked and there were only three emaciated men left: Holding, Captain Dalgarno, and the first mate, Andrew Smith.

Holding had built a small boat out of sealskin and twigs and they eventually moved to Rose Island, where they made a thatched sod hut, caught fish using some of Hardwicke's abandoned fencing wire,[21] and struggled to catch the local wiry and evasive rabbits for food.

The three men were collected and taken to Peru. The *Grafton* castaways were still at the southern end of Auckland Island at that point, but the *Julian* didn't bother exploring the rest of the island.

All three of the *Invercauld* survivors wrote accounts of their

The gravestone at Hardwicke Cemetery of James Mahoney (his surname is misspelled and his first name is incorrect on the grave; the ship's name is given as '*Inverauld*'). The stone was laid several decades after Mahoney's death.

time on the islands, but the captain's and first mate's versions were light on details and skipped over their personal failings. Holding's much more detailed account was written later in life, in 1919.

The predicament of the *Invercauld* castaways has been inevitably compared with that of the *Grafton* men, since both groups lived on the Auckland Islands at the same time. Why did one group handle things so well and the other so very badly? All five of the *Grafton* castaways survived, compared with just three out of 19 *Invercauld* men (25, if you count the ship's total before it sank), and they lived in much better conditions.

The *Grafton* men had several advantages: they were fortunate (well, relatively) to be stranded at the southern end of the island during the summer, close to an abundance of seals. They managed to salvage many useful items, including a hunting rifle and a small boat. Meanwhile, the *Invercauld* was wrecked in the middle of the night, during the winter, and against steep, exposed cliffs that quickly broke the ship to pieces before it sank.

But Raynal's resourcefulness and Musgrave's strong leadership skills also strongly contributed to their survival. Musgrave considered the group as a whole — for example, Raynal, who was weak from illness when they became shipwrecked, was taken off the ship and tended to until his health improved. They all stuck together from day one and shared what they had.

While the two outcomes were undoubtedly dependent to some extent on circumstance rather than strategy, both stories provide useful lessons on what to do, or not do, in the event of a shipwreck. (Rule number one: always carry a box of waterproof matches in your pocket.)

The *General Grant*

But what of 19th-century passenger ships — how did ordinary men, women and children fare in similar circumstances? Not very well, as you might expect.

The ill-fated *General Grant* was sailing to London from Melbourne in May 1866. Its cargo was mainly wool and hides, but according to the ship's manifest it was also carrying two boxes containing 2500 ounces of gold. In reality there was probably much more than that on board, since many of the passengers were prospectors from the Victorian goldfields and travelling back home to England.

The *General Grant* was a large ship for its time, about 55 metres (180 feet) long. It carried 83 people, including six women and 20 children. But near the beginning of its voyage, the ship drifted too far south; thick fog and no wind for days on end had interfered with its navigation.

On the night of 13 May 1866, the captain sighted what was probably Disappointment Island, but he assumed that it was Auckland Island and ordered the crew to continue east. It was only a matter of time before the ship was drawn towards the sharp western cliffs of Auckland Island. It struck the cliffs and then drifted into a large cave.

The passengers then spent a terrifying night in the pitch darkness, listening to the ship surge further forward, getting more and more wedged into the cave. The ship's masts slowly broke apart and were pushed down through the decks by the cave roof, which also rained rocks over the ship.

At first light, the crew lowered a 9-metre (30-foot) longboat and two 6-metre (20-foot) quarterboats into the water. One quarterboat took three men; they immediately exited the cave but failed to return to help anyone else. The other quarterboat took eight men and one woman. Forty others then escaped from the sinking ship into the longboat, but the wind had picked up overnight and the boat quickly capsized in the rough, churning waters near the cave entrance. Only three men managed to swim clear and haul themselves into the quarterboat, including sailor Billy Sanguilly. He later described the horror:

'The scene at this moment was one of such misery as few men ever see, and fewer still survive to tell of … Women

An illustration of the *General Grant* striking the western cliffs of Auckland Island in May 1866, published in *Harper's Weekly*, 1868.

clinging to their children, and crazy men to their gold, were seen washing to and fro as the water invaded the upper deck of the General Grant.[22]

There were 68 victims and just 15 survivors on that grim day: 14 men and one woman. Several of the men had simply abandoned their families to save themselves. A few had pleaded with their wives to leave the children behind and leap off the ship, but they'd refused. Other men had tried to take their gold with them as they jumped into the water, and were weighted down to meet their doom. Captain William Loughlin went down with his ship, standing on deck and waving his handkerchief as a final sign of encouragement to those who had escaped into the boats.[23]

MARRIED CASTAWAYS

One of the 14 men who survived was Joseph Jewell, a gold-miner who had left England in the 1850s to seek his fortune in the Victorian goldfields. He and his young wife, Mary Ann, had been on their way back to England to start a new chapter of their lives together. Instead, they had to face an unexpected and unwelcome period as married castaways.

When the *General Grant* started sinking, a rope was tied around Mary Ann's waist by her husband and she was quickly swung out and lowered feet-down from the stern, her long skirts billowing around her 'like a miniature parachute' as she descended.[24] The rope was difficult to manoeuvre and she sank into the cold, foaming water, but was quickly hauled back up to the surface by James Teer, an Irishman who had made it into the second quarterboat. However, he struggled to pull her out of the water with all her heavy clothing, so Joseph leapt off the ship and swam across to reach her. They both made it into the boat.[25]

Outside the cave was a wall of vertical cliffs, so the 15 survivors spent a cold, wet, miserable night sheltering in the two quarterboats behind the nearby Sugar Loaf Rocks, shivering in the snow and strong winds. Joseph later recalled: 'My wife, through being cramped up so much, did not get the use of her limbs for months afterwards.'[26]

The next morning they rowed further out to Disappointment Island, which lived up to its name when one of their boats capsized by the shore and they lost most of the food they had saved from the ship.

As soon as the wind died down, they rowed around the northern coast of Auckland Island to find shelter at Port Ross.

JAMES TEER'S FINAL MATCH

By then the survivors had only a few tins of soup left and a few damp matches that had been saved by James Teer, a tall sailor aged about 40 years old. Teer was a tough nut who had worked in the goldmines of Australia and New Zealand. He wasn't a ship's officer but he nevertheless became their unofficial leader, making the most of the islands' resources and rallying the group when they became despondent.[27]

Teer initially wanted to put the precious matches in his hair to dry them, but the others were impatient to quickly get a fire going. The first match burned out while they searched for something to light. Bart Brown, the ship's chief officer, then started to panic and tried to strike more matches, which all broke. Teer, driven to fury over Brown's potentially fatal stupidity, punched him in the face.[28]

Fortunately Teer had held onto one last match, and he waited until it was dry. William Sanguilly, who was only 18 years of age at the time, later described the unbearable tension.

'This was the most critical moment of our lives. If that last match failed starvation and perhaps cannibalism were to be our lot. The men were already talking of the probability of having to cast lots for a victim. Being the smallest of the party, I determined to keep out of the way until the question had been decided.'[29]

But Teer calmly struck the match and got a fire going, to everyone's relief, and they made sure the fire never went out during the 18 gruelling months that it took to be rescued.

Having endured several days with no food, they quickly cooked up some albatross broth and a few limpets. 'This was our first meal after three days and two nights of suffering, and never did sumptuous repast taste better to a king than this frugal meal to us,' Teer later recalled.[30]

They soon discovered a ruined old hut at the Hardwicke site — probably the one the *Invercauld*'s James Mahoney had died in two years earlier — and fixed it up as shelter. Eight men then decided to move to the Epigwaitt hut further south (which they must have known of from published accounts of the *Grafton* survivors), but fared no better there. The others found the abandoned hut of the three *Invercauld* survivors on Rose Island, but were disappointed upon finding the message carved on Auckland Island's 'Victoria Tree' (see Chapter 7) that no shelter had been provided for castaways and no visiting ship seemed to be imminent. It didn't help that they all came down with dysentery, and also struggled to find enough food to get through the harsh winter.

They eventually built a few huts on Enderby Island, keeping a constant daylight watch for passing ships. Thanks again to the creativity and resourcefulness of James Teer, they survived by fashioning clothing out of cured, softened sealskin to keep warm, using albatross bones for needles and New Zealand flax as thread. The impractical and flimsy clothes they were wearing when the ship wrecked were no match for the conditions.

They survived on the Auckland Islands' seals, goats, pigs (which were caught by using hooks on a pole), albatrosses and birds' eggs. They also discovered some discarded cast iron stoves at the Hardwicke site, enabling them to boil seawater and use the remaining salt to preserve seal meat. In a letter to his parents a few years later,

One of the castaway huts on Enderby Island, photographed in 1874.

Joseph Jewell described the castaways' diet:

'Sometimes we used to get rabbits and boil them, but they were very dry eating, especially without anything else with them. For eighteen months and seven days we never tasted bread, and we only had one potato each during the time … I should say that we killed over one thousand seals for our use while we were on the island, and sometimes we had to go a distance of ten or twelve miles [25 kilometres] to get them.'[31]

Due to the lack of vegetables, they inevitably came down with scurvy. They tried burying themselves in the sand, an act that was thought to relieve swollen limbs, but it didn't work. Vigorous exercise, however, seemed to help.

James Teer kept a castaway diary, using bleached seal skin as paper and scratching the words with a nail or using a bit of charcoal, and he also made weekly schedules for rostered duties. For amusement they fashioned playing cards out of some tin box lining and played football, although what passed as a football is not recorded.

'WANT RELIEF'

In the hope of eventual rescue, the *General Grant* castaways carved miniature wooden boats with tin sails and engraved messages saying 'Want relief', with details of the shipwreck, the date and their location. They also attached similar bits of wood to inflated pig and goat bladders, which they pushed out to sea in the hope that a passing ship would see them, or that they might wash up on the shore of a bigger piece of land.

One of the 'Want relief' messages, carved in rātā wood.

A few ships did pass by the islands after the castaways had been stranded for about six months, but either the crews failed to notice their desperate fire signals or they simply refused to stop. One can only imagine the bitter and overwhelming disappointment the castaways must have felt.

On one of those disappointing days, Joseph Jewell sighted a sail in the distance and leapt into one of their small boats to pursue it. He eventually returned, dejected, to his wife on shore. 'I found her careworn and depressed, and the few clothes she had on were torn to pieces while she was gathering bushes and grass to keep the fire alight.'[32]

Mary Ann was a lone woman stranded with 14 sailors and miners, most of whom were probably not used to being around females. There was some initial tension, with 'alarming interest' shown in Mary Ann by one man and with another recorded as making an 'insulting remark' to her. James Teer told him off, and when the man failed to apologize, Teer 'smashed [him] to the ground with a powerful punch to the head'.[33]

Mary Ann eventually became a 'governess' to the men, tending to the fire, preparing their meals, nursing the sick, and doing any sewing or mending. Using bird bones as needles, she sewed together blankets, skirts, trousers, jackets and even underwear from softened sealskin. Rabbit fur was used for scarves. In return, she was excused from lookout duty and heavy labour. She turned 23 while they were stranded, and was later remembered by the others for her uncomplaining hard work and her kind and patient nature — in other words, exactly the sort of person you'd want to be stranded with on a remote island.

Finally, the castaways were rescued by the New Zealand sealing brig *Amherst* in November 1867, after being stranded for 18 months. However, there were only ten of them left by then. A Scottish sailor named David McLelland had died of an infected wound, and four men had attempted to sail to New Zealand in one of the quarterboats, without a compass or map, and were never heard from again.[34]

The *Amherst*'s sealing expedition had only just got underway, so the castaways were asked if they wanted to stay on the brig and help out with the work. This they did, spending two months on board and delighting in the coffee and tobacco they had craved for so long. When the castaways arrived in New Zealand, en route to Melbourne, the sight of the survivors stepping off the boat caused a sensation. They were quickly required to give a testimony of their ordeal and the sinking of the *General Grant*.

The local press described their appearance on the day and explained their lack of suntans:

> '[The former castaways,] mustered outside the Court-House, awaiting their turn to give evidence, formed a picturesque group, with their Robinson Crusoe-looking dresses, and weather-beaten but not bronzed faces — the climate of the Aucklands has too little sunshine for that.'[35]

Mary Ann in particular was described as 'looking rosy', but amazingly there appears to have been no effort to interview her personally, even though:

1. she was the only surviving woman from a shipwreck carrying a large amount of gold
2. she had escaped from the sinking ship and spent 18 months stranded as a castaway in a very inhospitable location, and
3. she was *standing right there.*

Today, it would be another story. Mary Ann would most likely be surrounded by a throng of paparazzi and offered top dollar for a World Exclusive ('Being Shipwrecked Saved My Marriage … But Where's the Missing Gold?'). Passers-by would be taking selfies with her on the street and she'd have her own trending hashtag on Twitter (#girlfriday).

It was a different time, however. When the castaways finally arrived back in Melbourne, carrying nothing but some borrowed clothes, there was a reluctance from local government to help them. This was typical of the uncertainty at the time as to which country should take responsibility for shipwreck survivors on the Auckland Islands, and again, as with the *Grafton*, the general public had to chip in with donations. (Local organizations also helped: Melbourne's *The Age* newspaper got behind the fundraising, while Melbourne Hospital offered the castaways free health checks.[36])

As Joseph Jewell explained:

Joseph and Mary Ann, wearing their sealskin clothing, photographed in 1874 by Hewitt Bros.

'When we arrived in Melbourne the Government could do nothing for us as we were under the American flag. The General Grant *having belonged to Boston, United States, and the American Consul said he could do nothing for us as we were all foreigners, and as none of us were fit for work they made a subscription, and we received £5 11s. 5d. each. It was not enough to pay for our board, much less clothing that we were in need of …'[37]*

Mary Ann was illiterate, so she hadn't kept a diary and she didn't leave a written record of her experiences on the islands. But later in life she toured Australia in her sealskin clothes, making good money — up to £600, according to family legend — from sharing her shipwreck story with transfixed audiences. She and Joseph didn't (or couldn't) have children together, but a daughter was born in the 1880s using a surrogate, with Joseph listed as the father on the birth certificate.[38]

BUT WHAT OF THE GOLD?

The tragic tale of the *General Grant* shipwreck and its 68 victims was soon over-shadowed by the excitement of the lost gold. Since 1867 there have been dozens of attempts to find both the wreck and the gold, but to no avail.[39]

Even some of the original survivors returned to the Auckland Islands to find the gold. James Teer was unsuccessful in 1868 (he wasted no time, returning to the site just a few months after being rescued), a passenger named David Ashworth died (somewhat ironically, having survived first the shipwreck and then 18 months as a castaway) during his attempt in 1870, and a sailor named Cornelius Drew also had a look in 1876, but he failed as well.

More than 150 years have passed, and people are still sailing south in the hope of finding the missing gold. Did somebody already find it and quietly squirrel it away, was it found and then lost again in another shipwreck somewhere else, or is it still there for the taking? If you know, please get in touch.

The albatross messenger from the Crozet Islands

On a more distant part of the globe, another shipwreck story is particularly remarkable for an impressive feat of communication involving a message delivered *par avion*.

The Crozet Islands (Îles Crozet) are an archipelago of six large and 15 tiny French islands jutting out of the sea in the middle of the southern Indian Ocean. The largest island is Île de la Possession, or Possession Island, with a scientific research station usually consisting of 20 to 30 residents, depending on the season. Multitudes of penguins, including king and macaroni penguins, breed there each year. The temperature is cool but mild. The islands are buffeted by severe westerlies and heavy rain and, according to one 19th-century visitor, 'white mist like a virgin veil conceals their melancholy loveliness'.[40] Killer whales and Patagonian toothfish swim around the coastlines, while elephant seals lounge on the beaches. Wandering albatrosses nest above its rocky precipices and glide around its moss-covered hills.[41]

Perhaps unsurprisingly, shipwrecks also occurred rather frequently on the Crozet Islands in the 19th century. In March 1887, a French ship called the *Tamaris* was en route to New Caledonia when it was wrecked in the middle of the night on Île des Pingouins (Penguin Island), which is little more than a steep, fog-covered piece of rock. The 13 desperate crew managed to lower two small boats, along with a bag of biscuits and some water, and sailed to the nearby Île aux Cochons (Pig Island) where to their delight they discovered a hut with some clothing and provisions that had been placed there several years earlier by an English ship.

Five months later, with no sign of a rescue ship, they scratched a mayday (or *m'aidez* in French) note on a rusted tin band and attached it to the neck of a wandering albatross: '*13 naufragés sont réfugiés sur les îles Crozet, 4 août, 1887*' ('13 shipwreck victims are stranded on the Crozet Islands, 4 August, 1887'). The albatross soared off to the east and the men watched its departure, fearing for their lives as their provisions dwindled and winter approached.

In September the bird was discovered in Western Australia (5700 kilometres or 3500 miles east of Pig Island), lying dead on a beach in Fremantle with the castaways' note still attached to its neck. (Cause of death: the albatross had tried to swallow a mussel, but the metal ring prevented it from doing so and the bird choked.) As New Zealand's *Otago Daily Times* newspaper described it:

'It seemed almost as if in obedience to some unknown law of intercommunication of ideas and impressions, this message of life and death had passed from the anxious senders to a conscious messenger who flew over the vast extent of the ocean to the Southern Continent, and died in delivering its precious message.'[42]

There were initially doubts expressed that the message could have travelled so far as to possibly be genuine. A rescue ship was dispatched from Australia, but as no castaways were found the note was written off as a hoax. However, a few months later the French ship *Meurthe* visited the Crozet Islands to replenish supplies for the provisions hut on Pig Island. Under a pile of stones the crew came across a note written on a scrap of paper by the *Tamaris*'s captain back in September, explaining that he and his men had run out of supplies and were going to brave the strong ocean currents in their two small boats to reach Possession Island, which is just over 100 kilometres (62 miles) from Pig Island.

The men were never seen or heard from again. If only they had lingered on Pig Island for just a little while longer! They had left the island only eight days after their albatross delivered the message.

The ill-fated Frenchmen were later criticized for attempting to sail to Possession Island all at once, instead of sending just a couple of men as guinea pigs, and for carelessly using up all the provisions left in the hut on Pig Island rather than turning to the island's natural resources. 'Would British or American seamen have acted differently? I think so,' sniffed the *Otago Daily Times*.[43]

With unusually placed sympathy — or was it sarcasm? — the *Pall Mall Gazette* also lamented that the life of a 'noble bird' had been sacrificed in vain.[44]

Meanwhile, the French commanding officer of the *Meurthe* put the men's demise down to the threats of an otherworldly land teeming with strange wildlife.

'Truly this land is stranger than the enchanted lands of Sinbad the Sailor … Is it not a frightful country where the sea-weed is 300ft [100 metres] long, and where those gigantic birds, the albatrosses, nest in meadows of great mosses?'[45]

6. TRANSIT OF VENUS
The astronomers, the photographers, and the epic poem (1874–75)

ON 9 DECEMBER 1874, at 1pm New Zealand Standard Time (GMT+12), something extraordinary yet predictable happened: the planet Venus began to pass across the face of the sun.

The transit of Venus was, and still is, an extremely rare astronomical event. The transit occurs in eight-year pairs, but each pair is separated by more than a century; for example, it happened in 1874 and 1882, and then again, most recently, in 2004 and 2012. (An earlier transit in 1769 brought James Cook to the Pacific and resulted in his discovery of New Zealand.)

A burning question

The question of the sun's distance from Earth had interested humans since the 3rd century BC, but it was Edmond Halley (discoverer of Halley's Comet) who first realized in the 1600s that the transit of Venus was an opportunity to calculate the distance by measuring the angle of the transit from different locations on earth. Crucially, the answer would also reveal the relative distance of other planets in the solar system.[1]

The subsequent 1761 and 1769 calculation attempts during the transits came in close, but were imprecise. However, with new inventions and more modern equipment available by the 1870s, the 1874 transit was finally the astronomers' chance to get it right … or so they hoped.

By December 1874 the world's top astronomers, including those from Britain, Europe, Russia and America, had all eagerly stationed themselves at various points around the globe, in locations as diverse as Egypt, Hawaii, China, Auckland Island and Campbell Island, to record significant measurements from the transit that would reveal the earth's distance from the sun. It was, as one scholar has described it, 'the first internationally co-ordinated assault on a major astronomical problem using the emerging technology of photography'.[2]

The German expedition at Terror Cove

The Auckland Islands expedition involved eight men, who formed the first scientific team organized by the new government of the German Empire — supported by the first German emperor, Kaiser Wilhelm I.[3] There were also five other German expeditions positioned around the world for the transit, including one on the remote Kerguelen Islands in the middle of the Indian Ocean.

The intrepid German team arrived at the Auckland Islands in October 1874 and remained there until March 1875. It wasn't a comfortable location for a five-month stay, especially for a 19th-century, pioneering scientific expedition that was preparing for just a few, non-guaranteed hours of astronomical triumph, and it reveals just how dedicated and determined they were to achieve their measurements.

The German expedition at Terror Cove. Hugo Seeliger and Hermann Krone are leaning against the tree trunk.

Self-portrait (the first selfie?) of Hermann Krone, Dresden, 1858.

Wilhelm Schur, 28, was an astronomer from Strasbourg and the leader of the expedition. With him was Dr Hugo Seeliger of the Royal Observatory in Bonn, who was 25 at the time and would later be considered the greatest European astronomer of his generation (he would eventually receive a knighthood — turning him into Hugo *von* Seeliger — for his work). There was also a mechanic, a cook, a Swedish carpenter, and two naval officers who helped the astronomers to set up their equipment and take measurements. Significantly, there were two photographers on the expedition as well: Guido Wolfram and Hermann Krone, whose 19-year-old son Johannes accompanied him as an assistant (a local creek was named in his honour, after he fell into it).[4]

Hermann Krone, then 47, became the most well-known German photographer of the 19th century. He was an early adopter of photography, having started out working for his father's lithography business in the 1840s. During his career Krone published photography books, lectured at Dresden University, and set up a museum of photography.

Towards the end of his life, he also took a slight career detour by publishing four large volumes of poetry between 1899 and 1902 (*Dichtungen von Hermann Krone*), including an *Odyssey*-style epic poem, written in German and in varying metres, about his journey to the Auckland Islands.[5] He even invented a new photographic process during the expedition called 'the Auckland dry process'.[6]

Setting up camp in a lonely land

The expedition team arrived at the Auckland Islands, via Melbourne, in October 1874 with more than 100 crates of equipment and supplies. The men cleared some scrub and erected a three-bedroom prefabricated house at Terror Cove, which is just north of the Hardwicke site in Port Ross. They also set up a photographic darkroom, two domed towers, and a magnetic observatory. There was a rain gauge and an automated tide gauge on the beach to measure tide levels, and various brickwork columns for positioning their equipment. The soil was so boggy that they had to dig down several metres to find solid ground.

The sheep they had brought with them for food quickly escaped from their flimsy pen made of twigs, and disappeared forever into the rātā forest. The men also planted a garden, although it's unlikely that much grew in it. However, there was a more successful weatherboard chicken coop, and the hens and geese get an honourable mention in Krone's verse. The resulting egg-whites were also valuable for making photographic plates (the whites helped to bind the chemicals).[7]

What sort of 19th-century technical equipment did they lug across the world to the subantarctic islands? Telescopes and heliometers (split-lens telescopes to calculate the distance between two stars) were used, as well as chronometers to accurately record the local time and longitude. They carried altazimuths to measure the altitude of stars, and anemometers to measure wind direction and speed. A Foucault's pendulum was also set up to show the rotation of the earth.

Most significantly, and for the first time in history, a photoheliograph (a camera attached to an adapted telescope) was used to take close-up photographs of the transit. This was extremely hi-tech for the 1870s, and it also changed the nature of scientific research because the pictures could be analyzed long after the event had finished.

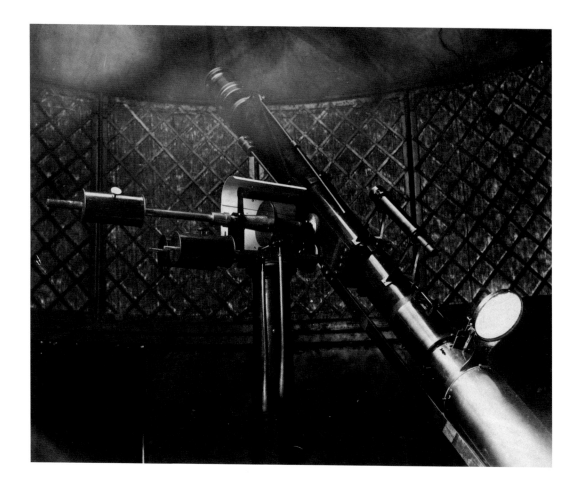

Battling the elements

ABOVE The ground-breaking photoheliograph, 1874.

OPPOSITE Dr Hugo Seeliger (astronomer), Hermann Leyser (mechanic), and Captain-Lieutenant W.J. Becks (Imperial German Navy) looking a bit weary at Terror Cove, 1874.

The men lived at Terror Cove for five gruelling months, struggling to set up their photographic and astronomical equipment and suffering from what Seeliger's expedition report later described as 'extreme hardship' in 'the most wretched [conditions] imaginable'.[8] In other words, they experienced a subantarctic summer, enduring fierce gales and rain, with occasional bouts of hail, snow or sleet.

However, Krone's account in his *Robinsonade* poem about the Auckland Islands (translated into prose) paints a more upbeat and descriptive picture, despite the tough work.

'Threatening rain and dark, massive clouds came rolling out … and a stiff breeze curled the blue waters of the harbour into a heavier sea … We had landed through the foamy surf, and cheerfully started out on our work! … Each day, in the morning, we were rowed in the boat

over to the island [Auckland Island]. There we busily toiled and built. As the twilight fell we were wet through on the outside and on the inside by the sweat from our work, and were bitten terribly by thousands of tiny hungry sandflies. We then returned home hungry to our daily meal on board, only to cheerfully begin our day's work anew after a refreshing slumber as the new morning dawned, with our hands cut to pieces, and in clothing that had remained wet.[9]

Exploration and discovery

Relaxing on the pebbled beach wasn't high on the agenda, then. But during their five-month stay Krone and Wolfram did occasionally take their cameras out to explore and photograph the rātā forest and the cemetery. They also visited and camped in the *General Grant* castaway huts on Enderby Island, which had been abandoned seven years earlier, and sometimes took their rifles out to hunt the pigs and goats on Auckland Island.

Soon after arrival, they discovered to their surprise that they had neighbours. At Erebus Cove they came across a two-masted ship, and slightly inland was a brand-new, two-window weatherboard house. They soon learned that its occupants were a New Zealand shepherd named Fred Nelson and his 'resolute housewife' (see Chapter 8).[10]

In late December, an American ship sailed from New Zealand to check on them and the expedition team were all invited on board to join the crew for Christmas dinner. The Germans were later described by the captain as 'fat and hearty, with no signs of having been in a starving condition on a desolate island'. After the meal Hermann Krone gave a whistling rendition of 'Robin Adair', an old Irish folk tune, which entranced all on board.[11]

Wolfram and Krone's photos are the first known pictures taken of the Auckland Islands, and today they serve as rare and valuable snapshots of some of the islands' ephemeral human history. Krone's reports and verses also provide valuable details, as he recorded the names and dates written on the graves at the cemetery, and also messages inscribed on pieces of wood by castaways and the crews of visiting ships (see Chapter 7).[12]

During their stay the German expedition team also named several local landmarks, which are all mentioned in their expedition accounts. The names weren't formally recognized for another 140 years, until Krone's Creek, Seeliger's Creek and Venus Valley were finally made official by the New Zealand Geographic Board in 2009.[13]

Venus makes an appearance

On the morning of 9 December, transit day, the sky was ominously filled with clouds and the Germans despaired of even seeing the transit, let alone calculating any measurements from it. However, at midday a gentle wind sprang up, and just

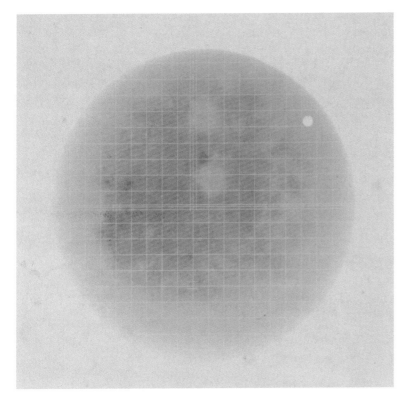

A sight to remember: Venus passing in front of the sun, 1874.

after 1pm the clouds miraculously parted in the right area for the men to record their measurements and take photos as Venus slowly travelled between the Earth and the sun, looking like a dark beauty spot on the sun's bright face.

By 6.26pm, five hours after it began, the show was over. Krone described the post-transit aftermath in his verse:

Zwei Minuten danach	Two minutes later
War alles trübe	Everything was gloomy once more
Und in kurzer Zeit	And shortly thereafter
Begann es zu regnen –	It began to rain —
Und es stürmte und regnete	And it howled and rained
Neun Tage hindurch.	For nine days following.
Mit beispiellosem Glück	With exceptional luck
War unsere Beobachtung	Our observation
Vom Himmel begünstigt …[14]	Had been blessed by the heavens …

They had indeed been very fortunate, and Krone had managed to take 115 pictures of the transit with his photo-heliograph. The bitter hardship of the previous five months, they all agreed, had been worth it. They eventually returned to a very warm welcome in Melbourne and enjoyed all the luxuries of being back in civilization.

Crunching the numbers

So, did the new technology work? Did they achieve their precise measurements after five months of preparing and hoping? Unfortunately, no; the measurements recorded around the globe that day were inconsistent with one another and ultimately no better than the ones recorded in the 1700s, so their expedition couldn't be considered an unqualified success.

However, the photos taken are still of historical value and were remarkable for their technical achievement. In 1882, when the next transit occurred, there were further attempts to capture the measurements, just not by anyone standing on a subantarctic island.

Sadly, all of the original photographic plates from the German expedition were destroyed during an air raid on Potsdam in World War II.[15] In fact, the turmoil of major political events across the 20th century (including two World Wars and the Cold War) would mean that Krone's German reports, poems and photos were left to gather dust in Dresden until a revival of his work in 1998, after the reunification of Germany.[16]

But prints of Krone's and Wolfram's historic photographs have endured. They are scattered around the world and serve as a record of the very first photographs taken of the Auckland Islands. Krone's written account is also a major work of little-known, 19th-century history, and the German expedition teams published 4000 pages of information about their various trips.[17] It just took non-German speakers a while longer to hear of it.

Today, the crumbling remains of the expedition's moss-covered brickwork columns can still be found at Terror Cove, as well as a few old booze bottles and a plinth engraved in English by Johannes Krone: 'German Expedition 1874'.[18]

And the Earth's distance from the sun? The precise measurement (called AU — Astronomical Unit) was finally calculated in the 1960s, thanks to the modern marvel of radar. Without it, space travel and the use of satellites and shuttles would be impossible.[19] In 2012, the International Astronomical Union voted to change the definition of the term 'AU' to a single number, one that's calculated from the speed of light: 149,597,870 (149.6 million) kilometres, or 91 million miles.[20]

The French expedition on Campbell Island

There was a similar expedition of French astronomers to Campbell Island in 1874, but it was somewhat less successful. The clouds cleared only at the beginning of the transit for a couple of minutes, and then for another 20 seconds in the middle of the event; in other words, not long enough to gain any useful measurements. One of the technicians, Paul Duris, died of typhoid during their stay, a disease he'd contracted en route, and was buried on the island.[21]

However, the French expedition left their mark in several other ways. During their

three-and-a-half month stay, Henri Filhol, the expedition doctor who was also a scientist, collected many useful scientific specimens and later published an account of the natural history of the island. The accompanying naval officers also charted a basic map of Campbell Island which was used by subantarctic expeditioners for several decades.

A view of the observatory established on Campbell Island by the French expedition.

But the biggest long-term impact came from the names the team gave to parts of the island group during their stay, including the outlying Jacquemart Island, named for the ship's captain, and Dent Island (the island is shaped like a tooth, or *dent* in French), as well as Venus Bay and Mount Dumas on Campbell Island itself.

The French names are all still in use today, but — as far as we know — there is no surviving epic poem about them.

Courrejolles Peninsula, Campbell Island
(named after the French photographer of the
1874 transit of Venus expedition). The cliffs
are ancient lava flows shaped by rough seas.

7. WRECK-WATCH
Provisions depots and castaway rescue missions (1865–1927)

WITH A SIGNIFICANT NUMBER OF SHIPWRECKS in the late 19th century, and with the world gripped by the personal accounts of the *Grafton, Invercauld* and *General Grant* shipwreck survivors, castaway depots were established in the late 1860s on most of New Zealand's subantarctic islands.

The depots were filled with an assortment of supplies to sustain castaways until their eventual rescue, which could take months or even years. After some confusion regarding the depots' locations, wooden 'fingerposts' were also erected from the late 1880s to direct castaways to the various depots, using the international sign of finger-pointing.

It was a matter of debate at the time as to which country, or countries, should take responsibility for subantarctic castaways. Many shipwrecks — at least, the ones with survivors — occurred on the Auckland Islands, which had only recently become part of New Zealand territory. The ships themselves often departed from Australia, but had been built in America. Many of the passengers or crew were European, and castaways were often rescued by New Zealand-owned sealing ships or government steamers.

With all the countries directly and indirectly involved, there was an initial reluctance to cover costs and try to solve the problem. But political opinion gradually shifted as the shipwrecks kept happening, and awareness of the subantarctic islands' harsh climate grew. A central government was also formed in New Zealand in 1876, after several decades of provincial governments operating on shoestring budgets.[1] Meanwhile, public opinion was in favour of helping the castaways, as shown by the local fundraising efforts in New Zealand and Australia.[2]

The first castaway rescue expedition was the HMSC *Victoria*, sent by the New South Wales, Victoria and Queensland state governments to the Auckland Islands in 1865. On the ship was *Grafton* survivor Thomas Musgrave, who hadn't forgotten the rising smoke he thought he'd seen while stranded and appealed to the Australian governments to search the islands (the three surviving *Invercauld* castaways were rescued five months before the *Victoria* arrived).[3]

ABOVE The 'Victoria Tree' as it was photographed in 1874.

LEFT These days the tree is in a decayed state and surrounded by regenerated rātā forest.

The crew carved a message for castaways on what is now known as the 'Victoria Tree', which is still in Erebus Cove on Auckland Island. The message read: 'HMSC VICTORIA, Norman [the captain's surname], in search of shipwrecked people, Oct 13th 1865.' A message in a bottle was also left at the site.[4]

Vegetables were optimistically planted in the same area, and ten goats and 12 rabbits were released on Enderby Island.[5] However, as the *General Grant* castaways discovered with dismay in 1866, the vegetables had failed to thrive, as had the goats. The introduced rabbits had multiplied but were difficult to catch, and directions were not provided on how to reach New Zealand's mainland. *General Grant* survivor James Teer later appealed to the New Zealand government for provision depots to be established with clothes, blankets, shelter and boats.[6]

Most of the initial depots were set up in 1868 and rudimentary supplies (such as knives and matches) were placed in caches (metal drums) on The Snares, Auckland Island (at two locations), Enderby Island, Campbell Island and Antipodes Island. The *Grafton* survivors' Epigwaitt hut and the *General Grant* survivors' Enderby Island huts were repaired and repurposed for use as castaway depots.

After a sporadic start in the 1860s, the depots were visited and maintained on a six-monthly basis from 1876 by the New Zealand government, using steamers that were also charged with enforcing sealing bans. Animals such as sheep and goats were sporadically released during these voyages to feed potential castaways.[7]

Pastoral farming leases were also offered on some of New Zealand's subantarctic islands in the 1870s (see Chapter 8) and one of the lease conditions was the maintenance of the depot(s) on the island leased. However, the leases were usually short-lived and the depots were generally neglected or 'borrowed' from.[8]

From 1886 the depots' contents were standardized, with improved shelter and supplies.[9] Each depot usually contained tinned biscuits and meat, fishing gear, knives, a small boat, cooking items, a sewing kit, rifles, fat for cooking, matches, a medical kit, blankets, woollen clothing, boots, tea, sugar and smoking pipes.[10]

It may not sound like much today, but it was tempting booty in the late-19th century. Depots were known to be raided by passing sailors or hungry farmers, despite a stern written warning left at the depot entrance.[11] The survivors of the *Derry Castle* became victims of looted depots after their ship was wrecked on the northern reef of Enderby Island in 1887, resulting in the deaths of 15 men. When the eight remaining castaways stumbled across the local depot, only a bottle of salt was left. (But the story has a happy ending: they built a boat, found the Erebus Cove depot on Auckland Island, and were rescued four months later.[12])

The *Dundonald* castaways: so near, yet so far

Discovering a depot must have been cause for relief, if not celebration, but not every island had one. In March 1907, the *Dundonald* castaways were made painfully aware of

Thousands of white-capped albatross nest on the slopes of Disappointment Island.

this fact when they were stranded for seven months on Disappointment Island, which is 8 kilometres (5 miles) off the western coast of Auckland Island and surrounded by wild, hostile seas. Their four-masted ship had been en route to London from Sydney with a cargo of 30,000 bags of wheat when it was wrecked in a bad storm (and because of a faulty compass) against the island's sharp rocks.

Just 16 of the 28 crew managed to clamber from the sinking ship by securing a rope to the rocks and shimmying across the rope above the thrashing sea. One of the survivors later described the gloom of facing their first day stranded on the island, scantily clad and with no food or fire: 'A group of shivering, bleeding castaways standing on the edge of those black cliffs … I cannot describe the cold.'[13]

Assuming they were on Auckland Island, the men started looking for the provisions depot. But they soon realized to their horror that the island they needed was out of reach, across the wild water, and barricaded behind a wall of jagged cliffs. Instead, the men initially survived by eating raw mollymawks and sheltering in tussock huts on Disappointment Island, which is just 10 x 4 kilometres (6 x 2½ miles) and devoid of trees.

Someone providentially found some matches in their pocket, so the men could at least begin roasting the mollymawks and keep warm, but after four months the wet, exposed conditions were almost unbearable and food was running low. They resolved to build a coracle, or small boat, out of flimsy scrub branches and a piece of sailcloth. Their 'oars' were little forked sticks.

Three of the men risked their lives crossing the foam-whipped sea, which had claimed the *Invercauld* and *General Grant* ships 40 years earlier, to reach Auckland Island. However, they couldn't find the depot, so after a week they dejectedly returned to Disappointment Island. During their second try, two months later, the coracle fell apart almost as soon as they departed. During their third attempt the coracle was wrecked at the foot of the cliffs on Auckland Island, but they escaped from the water and scaled the cliffs.[14]

After four days of desperate searching across the island, they triumphantly located the Erebus Cove depot, which had a boat. They quickly returned to collect the others, who didn't recognize them in their depot-retrieved clothes and with fresh haircuts. A few months later, the 15 survivors were rescued by the *Hinemoa* during its annual castaway check. (Jabez Peters, the ship's mate, had died from his wounds and exposure after a couple of weeks on Disappointment Island, and was buried there in a hand-dug grave. After their rescue, the shipwrecked *Dundonald* crew made sure he had a proper burial at Hardwicke Cemetery.)

The ship also carried 26 men from the Philosophical Institute of Canterbury Expedition, who were visiting Auckland and Campbell islands to perform ground-breaking research on the islands' rocks, plants and animals; they photographed the castaways' abandoned tussock huts on Disappointment Island.[15] 'A Surprise Party' was how one newspaper described the unexpected congregation of castaways,

ABOVE The tussock and scrub huts.

LEFT Members of the *Hinemoa* rescue crew stand alongside an unused coracle made by the *Dundonald* survivors.

IN
MEMORY
OF
R.I.P
WRECKED
ON

JABEZ
PETERS

LATE
MATE
BARQUE
DUNDONALD

DISAPPOINTMENT
ISLAND

WHERE
HE DIED
FROM
EXPOSURE
DIED
25 MARCH
1907

The grave marker at Hardwicke Cemetery for Dundonald castaway Jabez Peters.

crew and scientists. The newspaper also divided the names of *Dundonald* survivors and victims into a list entitled, in somewhat poor taste, 'The Quick and the Dead'.[16]

After the *Dundonald* castaways' rescue in 1907, a boatshed was quickly built on Disappointment Island, but the boat it contained was never used.[17]

Spirit of the Dawn: a near-sighted castaway experience

Occasionally castaways were marooned on an island with a depot, but they didn't know it. For example, the 11 survivors of the *Spirit of the Dawn* found themselves stranded for 88 miserable days with no supplies in the winter of 1893. The ship was wrecked in a heavy fog on Antipodes Island while en route to South America from England with a cargo of rice (five drowned, including the captain).[18]

In pitch darkness, the 11 men had somehow made it off the sinking ship and into a small boat, and once dawn broke they reached Antipodes Island. However, in an error of judgement, they failed to secure the boat and it was soon washed off the beach and never seen again. They made a half-hearted attempt to look around the island, but were quickly thwarted by the thick tussock, the rocky terrain and their own weakened state.

With no boat to explore the coastline and no matches to light a fire, they resorted to drinking from penguin eggs (averaging 40 per day in peak season), as well as eating raw birds, limpets and the local plants, and huddling close together in makeshift huts made of sod, tussocks and grass, which they had fashioned beneath an overhanging bluff.

Eventually their flag (made out of some bunting, a red singlet and a broken bit of mast) was sighted and they were rescued after three months by the New Zealand rescue ship *Hinemoa*, whose crew and passengers were shocked by what they encountered. As one witness later described:

'Eleven men, some of whom had very little clothing, were found standing on the rocks — some with pieces of raw penguin flesh in their hands, which they had been eating.'[19]

The *Hinemoa* officers immediately asked the castaways why they hadn't utilized the island's depot, which was located just 4 kilometres (2½ miles) from their camp site and stocked with clothing, bunks, blankets, matches, a hunting rifle, coffee, tobacco and many other provisions. The men were forced to admit that they hadn't ventured more than a kilometre or two from their camp during the 88 days of their exile. Had they explored a bit more of the 12-square-kilometre (5-square-mile) island, they would also have come upon the goats, sheep and cows that had previously been released to sustain any castaways.

This revelation must have been embarrassing for the *Spirit of the Dawn* crew, and the New Zealand press made their opinion on the matter quite clear: 'One almost feels inclined to say their sufferings served them right,' commented the *Southland Daily News*.[20]

Twenty years later, the *Hinemoa*'s second officer declared that he was still incredulous over the men's failure to find the depot:

'It seemed incredible that there should have been so little enterprise … They must have been thoroughly ashamed of themselves. I told them straight that even a pack of women would have shown more curiosity about the island.'[21]

'The curse of the widow and fatherless light …'

Henry Armstrong was a Southland Provincial Government representative from New Zealand who accompanied the voyage south, in the brig *Amherst* in 1868, to establish the first castaway depots. On his return he wrote a detailed report to his superiors, filled with rich descriptions of the various islands he visited.[22]

The *Amherst*'s first stop was The Snares, where they left a marker, a message for castaways, matches, cord and fishhooks.[23] They also lit large fires to attract the attention of anyone who happened to be stranded there, but there was no response.

During their visit Armstrong found the local wildlife extremely irritating, and reacted in a manner that would alarm conservationists today.

'Our progress was painfully slow, the entire surface being literally honeycombed with mutton-bird holes, into which the foot sank deeply at every step, the inmates thereof betokening their dissatisfaction at our presence by giving vent to a half-choked querulous cry. The penguins — ludicrous birds — in hundreds, drawn up in rank and file, stood to oppose us on our march, and it required not a little vigorous kicking to force our way through them.'

But there was some payback from the local birds.

'Mutton-birds darkening the sky in their flight, banging down on the ground in thousands in a most absurd and reckless manner, inflicting severe burets [scratches?] on the heads of several of us.'

Next it was on to the Auckland Islands, where the crew established a depot inside the remains of one of the *General Grant* castaway huts on Enderby Island. On the box deposited inside, Armstrong scribbled a stern note directed at any potential raiders: *'The curse of the widow and fatherless light upon the man who breaks open this box, whilst he has a ship at his back.'* (This threat obviously had little impact, as the castaway depots were regularly raided by passing ships.)

The next day Armstrong and some of the *Amherst* crew took a quick, off-route detour in two small boats. They rowed north of Port Ross and around to the western side of Auckland Island, to try to find the 1866 wreck of the *General Grant* (and, presumably, the missing gold). It is the first-known attempt to find the site of the wreck, and Armstrong wrote in his report that he found some wooden wreck remains and also markings where a ship's mast might have struck the rocks. It must have been disappointing to be one of the first to explore the potential site and not locate any gold. However, he was awestruck by the majestic beauty of the steep cliffs and fierce seas that had caused the doom of several ships.

> 'What can I say of this coast but that I have seen nothing to surpass, or even equal, the grandeur, the savage majesty of its grim storm-beaten sea walls; standing up bold and defiant, sullenly challenging old Ocean to a trial of strength.'

Armstrong continued south into Carnley Harbour, and came across some beach-strewn pieces of the *Grafton* ship. The crew repaired the castaways' old Epigwaitt hut, which was still only a few years old at that stage, and turned it into another castaway depot. The next day they built a third depot at the old Hardwicke site at Port Ross.

After spending a few days at the Auckland Islands, Armstrong reflected that they would be an acceptable place to find oneself shipwrecked:

> 'I am of the opinion that a man may be away on a very much worse shore than the Aucklands. The pigs have overrun the whole Middle [Auckland] Island (a finer breed of wild ones I have never seen), having these, the seals, numerous sea-birds … rabbits on Rose and Enderby Islands, mussels and limpets on every rock, excellent water and firewood … he must be a helpless fellow indeed who cannot soon provide himself with the necessaries of life.'

Today, Armstrong's comments seem a little glib in light of the *Grafton*'s, *Invercauld*'s and *General Grant*'s plights. It would have been easy to make such statements when visiting for a few days in the summer, during deceptively calm weather, on a well-provisioned ship, and with an imminent return home!

Crucially, Armstrong discovered during the voyage that a map of the Auckland Islands produced in 1851 erroneously placed them '35 miles [56 kilometres] to the south of their true position. This glaring error in the latitude will of itself account for the wrecks which have taken place on these Islands.' He urged that this mistake be rectified right away, but inaccurate or out-of-date maps and charts (including a commonly used one that omitted the Auckland Islands entirely from the clipper route) continued to be circulated and depended on for several more decades.

It took another five days for the *Amherst* to reach the shelter of Campbell Island due to strong winds, and then they spent a further four days confined to the ship due to foul weather. Armstrong wryly noted that Perseverance Harbour was 'well-named, although perseverance alone won't take a ship up it'. They released some goats and pigs on the island (which don't appear to have lasted long), set up another depot, then spent two days roaming across the island in search of any castaways.

Part of the reason for their visit to Campbell Island was the possibility of finding the four *General Grant* castaways who had sailed off from the Auckland Islands in search

The *Amherst* spar, placed in Erebus Cove on Auckland Island in 1868 as a signal for shipwrecked sailors. At its base was a small shed containing a case of provisions, a spade and a box of books.

of New Zealand a year earlier, in a small boat and without a map or compass. There was a tiny chance that they might have accidentally sailed south and ended up at Campbell Island, but there was no sign of them.

Next it was on to the Antipodes, which they were lucky to find seeing as their map put the islands 80 kilometres (50 miles) to the east and 16 kilometres (10 miles) to the north of where they actually were. They disembarked and

searched the main island for castaways, but saw nothing but 'the tussock waving in the wind ... and a few parroquets [parakeets] flitting about'.

The *Amherst*'s final stop was the Bounty Islands. By then, the fierce winds of the Southern Ocean had become more than a little tiresome. 'A few strokes of the pen ... cannot convey ... any impression of the sense of weariness and disquietude from which we suffered during that time of constant strife with the elements.' Armstrong found the Bounties particularly rugged. 'Neither man nor beast could exist on the Bounty's, and had I known their nature, I would not have deemed it necessary to visit them,' he wrote grumpily. A depot was eventually established there in 1886, but within a year it had completely disappeared, having been either struck by lightning, blown offshore by gales, or swept away by a heavy sea. A replacement depot was built in 1891, and in 1989 a few planks and a rusty kettle were still there.[24]

The maintenance of New Zealand's subantarctic castaway depots dwindled after 1914 (when the Panama Canal opened), and stopped altogether in 1927 once wireless technology

The rare and endemic Antipodes Island parakeet was originally named 'Uniform Parrakeet' in 1831 by the English poet and illustrator Edward Lear, who later became famous for *The Owl and the Pussycat*. Lear was a keen ornithologist and at the age of 19 created an illustrated book about rare birds, full of lithographs. One of the birds in Lear's book was a parakeet that he saw at London Zoo, but no one could remember where it had come from. Half a century later, Captain Fairchild (who rescued the *Spirit of the Dawn* castaways) saw the same parakeet on Antipodes Island and solved the mystery.

An aerial shot of Ruatara Island, one of the Bounty Islands. The island is named after a Māori rangatira (chief) who camped there for nine months with 13 other men on a sealing expedition in 1808.

improved, steamers replaced sail ships, and the precarious clipper route became less common.[25]

The depot built on Antipodes Island was refurbished in the 1970s and is still in use today as a research hut. A small depot built in 1880 on Enderby Island (known as the 'Stella Hut') is also maintained as a heritage site, but it no longer contains any matches — or tobacco.[26]

The Richardson sisters' subantarctic holiday

Adventure tourism isn't just a 21st-century pastime, and curiosity about the world's little-known subantarctic islands has led more than one person to venture south since they were discovered. Still, the idea of three young sisters sailing there on a lark in the middle of the shipwreck era seems impressively bold, even by today's more liberated standards.

Ethel Richardson and her sisters Fannie and Lillie were the daughters of the New Zealand Minister of Lands, and aged in their late teens and early twenties when they opted for a spur-of-the-moment overseas adventure to visit New Zealand's subantarctic islands on the steamship *Hinemoa,* which was heading south in October 1890 on its annual visit to replenish the islands' castaway depots.

Ethel Richardson kept a diary during their six-week voyage, which was published along with the sisters' sketches and paintings by a descendant more than 120 years later.[27] Despite the freezing climate and their delicate attire (long dresses, knickerbockers, button-up boots, etc.), they very much enjoyed the journey, rowing boats over choppy seas, dodging grumpy sea lions, collecting rare plants and shipwreck memorabilia, and chasing parakeets on the Antipodes.

At their Wellington home the sisters initially tossed a coin as a yes-or-no decider, but ignored its 'no' verdict and went anyway. The three young women were unchaperoned on the ship, but their father trusted the captain and they had travelled with him on the *Hinemoa* before, although not so far south.

After sailing around the southern coast of the South Island to check on the lighthouses, their first subantarctic stop was at The Snares, where they were initially quite shocked by the aggressive 'welcome' from the local fur seals. They also introduced some new animals: 'We landed two kiwis, two possums and two goats … and saw all the penguins by the dozen.'[28]

The *Hinemoa*'s next destination was the Auckland Islands, where the young women explored Enderby Island in the driving rain and then huddled together in Sandy Bay, waiting for the crew to finish their work. 'We went up and looked at the "Derry Castle" huts [castaway huts made by the shipwreck survivors three years previously] … Lillie got some bits to keep … We saw 3 wingless Snipe … I caught one in the long grass, such a dear little brown wretch.'[29]

Further south, they encountered some typically wild weather on Campbell Island, with the view from the top looking much as it does today:

> 'We went up the rough hills to the snow … We could see most of the island, and the sea nearly all round, for miles, and we saw heaps of young Albertrosses [sic] up on top sitting in their nests all among the snow, they were so lovely and clean and soft looking. There were such funny plants up there …'[30]

But the boisterous spring climate proved challenging, and their Victorian-era women's garments were hardly a match for the subantarctic conditions. 'We were soaking up past our knees from the wet tussocky stuff and snow … Lillie was wild with me and she *did swear* because I trod on her dress.'[31]

They played with the local parakeets on Antipodes Island and then carried on to the Bounties, where they were deafened by the noise of thousands of seabirds flocking around the granite rocks. The three sisters returned home with plant specimens and penguin eggs, and were sad the trip was over: '… a jolly good one its [sic] been too in spite of the bad weather'.[32]

One sister, Lillie, eventually married the ship's carpenter, so obviously a subantarctic romance had blossomed. Ethel, the diary's author, became a draughtswoman for Lands and Survey and sold some of her oil and watercolour paintings. Fannie was also an artist and provided plant and animal illustrations for the Forest and Bird Society.

Southern royal albatrosses and megaherbs, Campbell Island.

Their subantarctic voyage had been the trip of a lifetime, and, as for many who have followed in their footsteps, it had an impact on the rest of their lives.

But the islands weren't just a destination for castaways and depot maintenance voyages in the late-19th century. During the same era, they attracted another group entirely: sheep farmers.

8. PASTORAL LEASES
The optimistic farmers and the
isolated sheep (1874–1931)

WILD, UNPREDICTABLE CLIMATE? TICK. Difficult terrain? Tick. Completely removed from civilization? Tick, tick, tick.

Despite this — and the evidence of the failed Hardwicke settlement a few decades earlier — there was more than one farming attempt on New Zealand's subantarctic islands in the late 1800s and early 1900s.

The Auckland, Snares, Bounty, Antipodes and Campbell islands were all absorbed into New Zealand territory in 1863, and the government was keen to extend its agricultural hold on the recently acquired islands, many of which offered a lot of open space for sheep and cattle runs. Pastoral farming was becoming an important part of the colonial country's economy.

Sheep had already been dropped off on some of the subantarctic islands during various government expeditions, as a food source for castaways, and they (the sheep) seemed to fare well enough. As part of the deal, the government also wanted the leaseholders to look after the castaways depots and help anyone who happened to get shipwrecked.[1] From a farmer's perspective, the cheap, generous pastoral leases (some runs were offered for just a few pounds per year, for up to 21 years) were simply too tempting to turn down.

Four leases were offered at auction to begin with: two on Auckland Island, one on Enderby and Rose islands, and one on Adams Island. In the 1890s, showing that no island would be left behind, there were even pastoral leases offered for the Bounty and Antipodes islands — a clear sign that the government had very little knowledge of these distant islands. But no one took up the Bounty Islands lease offer (farming options would have been limited on the bare granite rocks), and the lease taken on the Antipodes Islands was never used.[2]

PASTORAL RUNS

AUCKLAND, ADAMS, AND CAMPBELL ISLANDS.

167,200 Acres.

TO BE OFFERED FOR LEASE BY PUBLIC AUCTION.

NOTICE is hereby given that the under-mentioned PASTORAL RUNS will be offered for Lease, by Public Auction, at the District Land and Survey Office, INVERCARGILL, on WEDNESDAY, the 21st NOVEMBER, 1894, at Noon.

Run 501, being northern part of the Auckland Islands: High and broken; term, 21 years from 1st March, 1895; upset annual rental, £2. Area, 38,600 acres.

Run 502, being southern portion of the Auckland Islands: High, broken country; term, 21 years from 1st March, 1895; upset annual rental, £5. Area, 75,600 acres.

Run 510, being Adams Island: High, broken country: term, 21 years from 1st March, 1895; upset annual rental, £2. Area, 25,000 acres.

Run 511, being the Campbell Island: High, broken country; term, 21 years from 1st March, 1895; upset annual rental, £2. Area, 28,000 acres.

CONDITIONS OF SALE.

Six months' rent in advance and license fee (£1 1s.) to be paid on the fall of the hammer.

G. W. WILLIAMS,

The advertisement for pastoral run leases on New Zealand's subantarctic islands in 1894.

The Monckton farm

In 1873 Dr Francis Monckton, an Invercargill surgeon, became the first New Zealander to attempt subantarctic sheep farming when he leased all of the Auckland Islands from the government.

Dr Monckton had worked as a surgeon during the Crimean War and was reported to be a capable, if rather eccentric, doctor. According to one historian: 'It is said that on one occasion he amputated a man's leg with a carving knife and an axe, and that he would extract people's teeth in the street without any hesitation.'[3] (Presumably they had invited him to do so first.) He had first visited the subantarctic islands in 1865, while he was working as a medical officer on a government ship on the lookout for castaways. In a collision

An engraved print of the lonely Monckton farm, circa 1876, including the Nelsons' washing on the line.

of narratives, one of Dr Monckton's tasks was exhuming and inspecting the body of an unidentified man on Auckland Island (later confirmed to be *Invercauld* castaway James 'John' Mahoney; see Chapter 5). Apparently the weather was awful during his visit, but that obviously didn't deter him from wanting to return and settle there.[4]

Dr Monckton was granted a pastoral lease for a whopping 21 years. Part of the deal included checking and resupplying the castaway depots on the Auckland Islands, as well as taking a boat to circle the coastlines in search of shipwreck victims and helping any that he encountered. He didn't make it to the islands on his first attempt in May 1874 because the seas were too rough. But a few months later in September he dropped off 30 sheep, some timber and a married couple, Mr and Mrs Frederick Nelson, who were to manage the farm. They would live in Erebus Cove, the same area as the abandoned Hardwicke site at Port Ross, in a tiny farmhouse.

The Nelsons quickly sowed grass and oats and planted a garden. They also became acquainted with their temporary

neighbours, the German Transit of Venus expedition crew (see Chapter 6), who admired them and took comfort from their proximity, as German photographer Hermann Krone later wrote:

The Monckton farm, as photographed by a member of the German Transit of Venus expedition.

> 'Both of them hardworking and good, as we later found, they remained loyal neighbours to us, and we to them, the whole time for [our] five months on the lonely islands.'[5]

Dr Monckton had initially planned to quit medicine and join the Nelsons on the farm, but the weather thwarted his repeated attempts to sail there with additional sheep and cattle. At one stage he was forced to release his cargo of cattle on Stewart Island after he took shelter there during a bad storm en route to the Auckland Islands. He couldn't herd them all back onto the ship again, so he abandoned them.

From the beginning, the farm itself was a disaster. The 30 sheep soon ran wild on the island, crops failed to grow, and the

Nelsons went hungry and were eventually forced to raid the nearby castaway depots for supplies. They were taken off the island by a ship in 1877 (the *Gazelle*, on a voyage to seek out the lost gold from the *General Grant*) and the lease was cancelled in 1879.[6]

The abandoned farmhouse was quickly turned into a provisions depot (the one finally reached by the *Dundonald* castaways in 1907), and the ruins were dismantled in the 1940s by the World War II coastwatchers and used to build a scientific laboratory (see Chapter 9). Today, a few scattered chimney bricks in the bush are the only reminder of Dr Monckton's failed dream.

The Fleming farm

Time marched on, and the unquenchable pastoral optimism continued. Twenty years later, more leases were offered for sheep and cattle farming at the northern and southern ends of Auckland Island, as well as Adams Island, Enderby and Rose islands, and Campbell Island further south.

By the early 20th century, there was even a family living down there. A farmer named George Fleming had secured all the Auckland Islands leases in 1900, and he took along his wife and three children as well as a few farmhands. He set up a sheep farm at Carnley Harbour, near the *Grafton* wreck and Epigwaitt site, and he also built a hut on Adams Island.[7]

During the early years of his lease Fleming released about 2000 sheep on Auckland Island.[8] However, mustering proved a challenge because Fleming's dogs got distracted by the local seals and chased them instead of the sheep.[9] The thick scrub also quickly became an issue, and most of the coast-stranded sheep died off within a few years from starvation.[10]

Fleming's lease was eventually cancelled in 1910, but the farm had failed long before that. In 1906, the New Zealand press reported that the roof of the abandoned farmhouse had been ripped off by strong winds, and ships passing through at around the same time saw no more than a dozen sheep in the area.[11]

The ill-fated farming era (2.0) of the Auckland Islands was drawing to a close. Scientists were beginning to realize the importance of the subantarctic islands' unique environments, and Fleming received letters asking him to consider forfeiting his lease. He refused. In his reply, Fleming wrote that he couldn't see any financial gain from reserving land just to look at it, and he certainly wouldn't sanction the use of land for 'picnics' when it could be used for cultivation.[12] Despite Fleming's objections, his lease was cut short and in 1910 Adams Island was declared a Flora and Fauna Reserve. Once all the farming leases (which were barely used, anyway) had expired, reserve status was extended to all the Auckland Islands in 1934. It wasn't quite the end of human habitation on the Auckland Islands, but future residents would derive much more enjoyment from them than most of their predecessors had.

The Tucker Cove sheep farm

Meanwhile, 250 kilometres (150 miles) further south on Campbell Island, there was also some sheep farming underway.

The Tucker Cove sheep farm, with its homestead and wool shed, was located by the shore of Perseverance Harbour. The surrounding scrub had been cleared for pasture and the farm was surrounded by sheep-friendly, tussock-covered hills. This sheep farm lasted for 36 years, from 1895–1931, with the lease changing hands several times. By the early 1920s, there were up to 8000 sheep on the island.[13]

Tucker Cove was named after Captain William Tucker, a former New Zealand mayor who took over the lease in 1900 from J. Gordon, a farmer who had built the farmhouse and woolshed in 1895 and introduced 350 sheep to Campbell Island. In a strategic move, Tucker employed four musterers from the Scottish Shetlands in 1904; his reasoning was that they were already used to cold, windy weather. He expanded the farmhouse to six rooms, and added 6.5 kilometres

Shetland sheep farmers on Campbell Island, 1905. Captain Tucker is standing at the back, with a white hat and beard. Note the musical instruments on the right: fiddle, bagpipes and accordion.

Abandoned whaling try pots (used to render down blubber for oil) at North East Harbour on Campbell Island.

(4 miles) of wire fencing to the sheep yards. He also introduced another 2000 sheep, a few dozen cattle and a couple of horses.[14]

But Tucker hadn't considered the isolation of Campbell Island. Supply ships visited very rarely, so even the hardy Shetlanders didn't linger for long. One of the musterers, Andrew Nicolson, had brought along his two daughters from Scotland to act as cook and housekeeper on Campbell Island. They opted to stay in New Zealand instead, but they did venture south to visit him in 1907.[15]

In 1909, the indomitable Captain Tucker changed tack and hired men who could tend to the sheep in the spring/summer/ autumn seasons and then hunt southern right whales in the winter, when they came into the bays to calve. The first whaling station was set up at North West Bay, and then in 1911 another station was built at North East Harbour. One of the North East whaling party took his wife along in 1911, a woman named Mrs Cook (first name unknown), who is the first woman recorded to have lived on Campbell Island (excluding 'The Lady of the Heather', and also an unidentified woman who may have been marooned on the island with a sealing gang between 1835 and 1839).[16]

The whalers/farmers enjoyed middling success for a few years, but then World War I interrupted Tucker's plans when all of his 11 whalers enlisted. In 1916, Tucker passed the lease to a couple of businessmen from Dunedin named Mathewson and Murray, who set up the Campbell Island Company and hired a number of young New Zealand men as musterers over the next ten years.

The diary of a lonely shepherd

An employee named Alfred Austin kept a diary during his time at Tucker Cove, which was eventually published as *A Musterer's Sojourn (1919–1921)*.[17] Austin kept his journal faithfully, writing every day about the weather, the local wildlife and his farming work.

Maintaining a daily routine must have been good for his mental health in such a remote location. In our plugged-in, 21st-century world, it's difficult to imagine the isolation he must have felt at times. There was no radio, no newspapers, and no phone or any other form of communication with the outside world. Tucker Cove was the only farm on the island, so the small team of four to eight musterers was completely cut off, apart from very occasional ships passing through.

Life for the sheep farmers would have been very challenging at times, especially working outdoors in all weather. Campbell Island is buffeted by strong westerly winds, it rains almost every day, its peaks are often shrouded in mist, and it's not unusual for the island to receive a light snowfall. The mean annual temperature is 6° Celsius (43° Fahrenheit).

To illustrate the island's weather patterns, here is a typical diary entry from Austin in May, 1920:

'Here we are with that same old tale, yes, rain & more rain. To date we have had this month "one" fine day. Vile weather. Dense fog all day, heavy rain towards evening … 29.54 [–1.4 Celsius].'[18]

Fortunately his sense of humour helped him to handle the bleakness of the weather. Once he joked wryly that he was 'thinking of roofing in the island' to deal with the constant rain.[19]

There was, however, plenty to see and do on Campbell Island, which helped to ward off the dreaded 'island sickness' that often cast a dark shadow over those living in small groups cut off from civilization for long periods.[20] Thousands of sheep needed to be shorn, buildings had to be painted and repaired, and firewood (the local dracophyllum scrub) had to be chopped for fuel and for warmth. The farmhouse also had to be anchored down during winter to stop it from blowing away in a gale, as happened to one of their precious boats during a storm. There was also laundry and housekeeping, and giving each other haircuts. Whatever needed doing, they did it; after all, nobody else was going to.

The local wildlife also distracted and entertained them. Seal and bird hunting was a common pastime. They took photos of the shearing and the animals, and developed the pictures themselves. Penguins were sometimes kept as pets. From time to time they were treated to spectacular shows from the Southern Lights aurora, and Austin also enjoyed watching the southern royal albatrosses with their giant wings gliding over the harbour. During the winters, southern right whales would visit the northern bays.

When forced indoors by the weather, there was music to enjoy. Austin had brought his cornet with him, and would play along to records on the farm's gramophone. One of the musterers was a former heavyweight boxing champion and he gave the other men boxing lessons in the woolshed.

The shepherds were mostly young and fit, but started becoming unwell near the end of their stay, which may have been the early signs of scurvy as they had run low on supplies. They were forced to raid the local castaway depot, which was still intermittently checked and restocked in the early 20th century. It didn't help matters when the ship that was supposed to collect them in March 1921 failed to show up. Austin's mild exasperation in those first days and weeks turned to angry disbelief as the months crawled by with no sign of a reprieve.

April 1921: 'Anxiously waiting for that boat.'

November 1921: 'No boat yet? … Food reduced almost to flour, sugar & mutton!!!!'

Austin must have felt immense relief when he finally saw their ticket home arrive in Perseverance Harbour on 28 November 1921 — eight months overdue. His Campbell Island residency had lasted for more than two years, but not by choice. The final diary entry is understandably a little terse: '… the stunt is over & the clock is wound up. Let us forget about it.'[21]

By the end of the 1920s wool prices had dropped sharply, and it was becoming more and more difficult to entice farmers to live on Campbell Island. However, one last person had a go: George Warren took the lease in 1926 and held onto it for five years. He arrived with a small team of men and another 5000 sheep, but struggled against the enormous number of Norway rats (introduced via passing sealing ships in the early 1800s) that had overrun the farm.

In a bit of novel ingenuity, Warren also took along a couple of homing pigeons in the hope of improving communications with the New Zealand mainland. However, one refused to leave the island and then drowned in the sheep-dip tank; the other bravely flew off towards the open sea and was never seen again.[22]

Once again, the isolated conditions couldn't be overcome. From 1929–31 a shepherd named Alex Spence and three other men were left on Campbell Island

Campbell Island sheep, photographed in the 1970s. Today the island is sheep-free.

with no one bothering to check on them. When concerned relatives urged the government to send down a relief ship, the men were found surviving on tea and mutton, and using sheep tallow for candles. They were surprisingly upbeat considering the circumstances, but were very disappointed to learn of the economic depression which had left their bales of wool almost worthless.[23]

The Tucker Cove sheep farm was finally abandoned in 1931, and the 4000 remaining sheep were left behind to either die off or run wild over the uninhabited island. Warren and Mathewson, who still technically owned the sheep, were given six months to remove them in 1938, but failed to act so the sheep became government property.

Applications still came in from people wanting to shear the sheep and sell the wool, but by the mid-1930s Campbell Island had been declared a reserve for flora and fauna, and

The Shacklock Orion wood-coal range from the Tucker Cove farm homestead.

after 20 more years of political dithering the decision was put in writing in 1954.[24] The sheep turned feral and were mostly left to themselves in the following decades, before gaining prominence once more in the 1970s (see Chapter 12).

Today, the only remaining sign of the Tucker Cove homestead on Campbell Island is a rusted Shacklock Orion wood-coal stove sitting by the harbour. The Tucker Cove farm site is one of the NZ Department of Conservation's managed historic sites and is only accessible with a visitor's permit.[25]

9. 'CAPE EXPEDITION'
The enemy raiders and the wartime coastwatchers (1939–45)

IN AUGUST 1939, the captain of a large German cargo steamer called the *Erlangen* found himself to be very much in the wrong place, at the wrong time.

Captain Alfred Grams had just received a telegram from Germany, informing him that war was imminent and that he needed to return immediately. The problem was that both Grams and the *Erlangen* were in New Zealand, almost as far away from Germany as it's possible to be. What's more, the *Erlangen* was low on fuel. Captain Grams told New Zealand port authorities that he was going to sail to New South Wales in Australia. But on 26 August 1939, just a few days before World War II broke out, the *Erlangen* left New Zealand under cover of darkness and vanished.

Well, not literally. But the ship didn't arrive in New South Wales, and it only had enough coal for five days at sea. Where had the *Erlangen* gone?

Captain Grams had quietly decided to black-out the ship and head south to the uninhabited Auckland Islands. The main island is partially covered in rātā forest, and the captain knew that wood would be an acceptable alternative to coal. The secluded location also gave him an opportunity to 'disappear' for several weeks while he decided on his next move.

He certainly didn't talk to anyone else about his plans. It was already an extremely awkward time to be in charge of a German ship in the middle of the Pacific, let alone to be running low on fuel. The political situation was tense; many eyes were watching the movements of his ship, and it didn't go unnoticed when he failed to turn up in Australia. (A New Zealand ship, the HMS *Leander*, did visit the Auckland Islands to see if the *Erlangen* was there, but heavy rain and strong winds prevented the *Leander* from entering Carnley Harbour, where the *Erlangen* was anchored.[1])

A couple of months later, the *Erlangen* turned up in war-neutral Chile. The ship had only just made it to South America thanks to the stolen rātā wood, which had eventually burned out and was then supplemented with most of the ship's wooden fittings. Finally, the crew was reduced to using sails fashioned out of tarpaulin to make the final stretch of the journey.[2]

The story of the *Erlangen's* subantarctic detour soon emerged, and was later confirmed when Auckland Island was found to be missing a significant amount of its southern rātā forest. (The captain also confessed to the thievery after the war and even produced a blurry photo of two crewmen hacking down stunted trees.[3]) The *Erlangen's* 12 officers and 50 Chinese crew had spent five weeks struggling to fell several hectares' worth of tough-barked rātā trees, a discreet distance back from the coast at North Arm in Carnley Harbour, so that their handiwork wouldn't be visible to any passing ships. But once anyone strolled inland, it was obvious — and a few discarded German tools at the site provided further evidence.[4]

The *Erlangen's* arrival in Chile wasn't the end of the ship's dramatic journey, and the captain's attempt to return to Germany (and the ship's eventual scuttling by its own crew when they were intercepted by the British in the Atlantic Ocean) was later immortalized in the 1955 John Wayne/Lana Turner film *The Sea Chase*.

Sailing south on a top-secret mission

Did it really matter that a few remote trees were cut down? Was anyone going to miss them?

Perhaps not, but it was the act of subterfuge that made the New Zealand government nervous; the remote and uninhabited subantarctic islands left the rest of the country vulnerable to the approach of enemy ships. In 1940, things were made much worse when two New Zealand passenger ships en route to England were intercepted by German raiders. The prisoners from one ship, the *Turakina,* reported being taken to a colder climate and an isolated, tussock-covered island that sounded suspiciously like Campbell Island. German ships were also sighted in the Indian Ocean, heading south. It all added up to strong evidence that enemy ships were using the harbours of Auckland and Campbell islands as rendezvous points.[5]

This was enough for the New Zealand War Cabinet to take action, and three groups of men were hastily shipped south in March 1941 to guard the islands' harbours. Two groups were stationed at the northern and southern ends of Auckland Island, and the third group was sent to Campbell Island.

The initiative was given the codename 'Cape Expedition' as a ruse, and the first expeditioners weren't told where they were going in order to keep things as top-secret as possible. They were to keep a lookout for German (and, later, Japanese) aircraft and ships, and immediately report any sightings back to the mainland via a coded radio message.

The men initially wore civilian clothing, and were instructed to call themselves fishermen if they were discovered. However, that changed in 1942 after 17 New

Zealand civilians and coastwatchers on the Gilbert Islands (in the Pacific Ocean, between Papua New Guinea and Hawaii) were executed by Japanese soldiers.[6] The subantarctic coastwatchers from then on were issued uniforms and enlisted in the army.

Each expedition group initially consisted of four men who were rotated annually (although some decided to stay for longer) until the war ended in 1945. They were provided with three years' worth of food and clothing in case it took a while to send down another supply ship. Tiny, windowless 'emergency' huts stocked with supplies and emergency radios were concealed deep in the bush in case they were discovered, and there was also a motorized boat called the *Ranui* with a crew of four to serve as a link between the three stations and provide a means of escape if necessary.

Much of the coastwatchers' written history originates from the northernmost station, known as 'No. 1', and located at Ranui Cove in Port Ross. The group lived in a comfortable, prefabricated four-room house with double plywood walls,

The sawn stumps of trees hacked down by the *Erlangen* crew in 1939 to fuel their ship and flee to South America. Note the abandoned axe head.

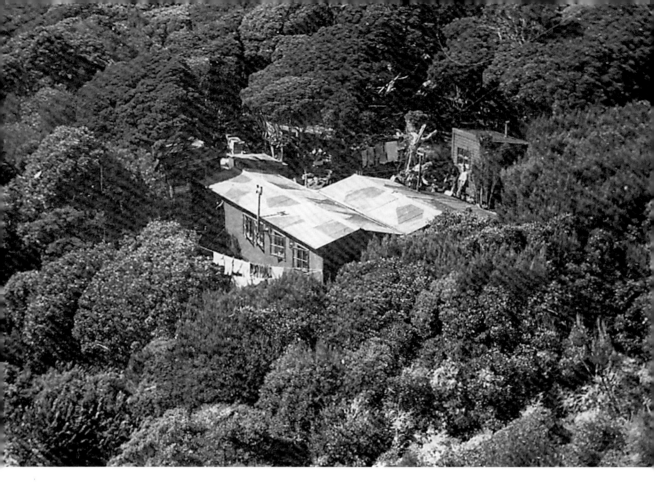

double glazing, stoves for heating (fuelled by coal and rātā wood), and generator-charged batteries for electricity and radio. The house was hidden from view from the water, but near to the coast. There were also storage huts, a science laboratory, a tool shed, and a hut for mapping/surveying work. One of the small buildings, known as 'Falla's laboratory' for Robert Falla, a naturalist and leader of the 1943 party (later Sir Robert), was repurposed from old timber at the 19th-century Monckton farm/castaway depot site nearby.[7]

A short hike up the hill from the camp was a 3 metre x 3 metre (9 foot 8 inch square) lookout for coastwatching duties, where the men would take shifts scanning the horizon, searching for signs of enemy approach. If something was sighted, they were supposed to send a Morse-coded report to the mainland, destroy the radio, alert the others, and then proceed to their emergency hut until a navy ship arrived. They were not armed in the early years, aside from hunting rifles which were only to be used for killing the local goats, sheep, pigs or cattle for meat.[8]

The men must have felt very vulnerable at times, especially in those early, high-alert years. As 1944 coastwatcher Graham Turbott later wrote:

'We could not help imagining the implications of a possible enemy visit — the emergency huts' limitations as long-term shelters if the main stations were destroyed, and the unlikelihood of early relief.'[9]

To begin with, the objective was primarily to keep an eye out for the enemy, with coastwatching duties performed in rostered shifts from dawn to dusk. In winter, that was from 8.30am to 4pm, but in summer the sun rose at 2.30am and didn't set until after 10pm. As Graham Turbott put it: 'Isolation and long spells of monotonous routine were clearly of the essence of coastwatching.'[10]

No doubt their coded radio reports were intercepted, as no enemy ships were sighted. From 1944, coastwatching duties were reduced to three quick checks a day.[11]

Exploring a different world

Crucially, most of the men had been hand-picked for the 'Cape Expedition' because of their strong interest in science. In addition to their coastwatching duties they were encouraged to undertake meteorological observations and surveying work, as well as study the native plants and wildlife. The specimens they collected and documented, as well as their reports on the wildlife they observed, were hugely beneficial and their field studies eventually went on to be published as scientific papers.

Many of the coastwatchers later became world-renowned scientists in their respective fields, including ornithologist Sir Robert Falla; geologist, palaeontologist and ornithologist Sir Charles Fleming; and ornithologist and zoologist Graham Turbott (who published his 'Cape Expedition' memories almost 60 years later, in *Year Away*).

An expedition that could have gone horribly wrong instead became a success, thanks to some foresight and careful planning. The men were chosen because they were able to handle the isolation and dramatic environment, and they worked with the conditions instead of against them (although they still became frustrated by them at times). They had work to occupy them and were given plenty of provisions to make their stay as comfortable as possible.

The daily routine was well structured, and each man took a turn at cooking and housekeeping. They ate well: bread and scones were freshly baked (although repeated attempts to make a jam roly-poly were unsuccessful), meat came from the sheep on nearby Ocean Island to offset the tedium of tinned bully-beef, and they even had fresh eggs for their breakfasts along with porridge and bacon. The well-stocked pantry included tinned soups, vegetables and puddings, along with the added luxuries of rum, tobacco and chocolate. Daily doses of vitamins and tonics were also provided to counteract the lack of fresh produce and sunshine, although not everyone was vigilant in taking them.[12]

ABOVE Auckland Island coastwatchers: (clockwise from top left) Bart Challis, John Douglas, George Anderson, Charles Fleming, Allan Eden.

RIGHT A tongue-in-cheek dinner menu from 'Sarah's Bosom Cafe' (Sarah's Bosom was the former name for Port Ross) in 1942. The planned dessert includes 'fresh Auckland Island oranges' — surely a fantasy.

```
..MENU..
..SARAHS BOSOM CAFE 12/5/42..
..ENTREE..
..TINNED SARDINES OR SARDINES OUT
OF A TIN..
..SOUP..
.. TOO MUCH OTHER RUBBISH..
..MEAT..
..BEST OCEAN ISLAND ROAST LAMB..
..VEGETABLES..
..MASHED SPUDS..
..BOILED SPUDS..
..BAKED PUMPKIN CARROTPARSNIPS AND
ONIONS..
.BOILED PEAS CABBAGE..
..GRAVY A LA MODE..
..SWEETS..
..FRUIT SALAD AND CREAM..
..JELLY AND CREAM..
..FRUIT..
..FRESH AUCKLAND ISLAND ORANGES
APPLES PINEAPPLES PEACHES PAIRS..
..DATES.. ..PRUNES.. ..FIGS..
..POSE FOR PHOTOGRAPH..
```

Daily chores were divided up and became part of the station routine.

The men would while away the long evenings by catching up on scientific work, developing their photos in the blacked-out bathroom, playing cribbage tournaments, and working their way through a selection of books (the epic tome *War and Peace* was read more than once). At one stage they printed a coastwatchers' magazine called *Subantarctic Observer*, with written and artistic contributions from all three stations. They also gave each other lessons in cooking, public speaking and dancing.

All these activities were important to keep the men busy and engaged, as topics of conversation reportedly ran low after spending months on end together, listening to the wind roaring outside and the cold rain hitting the windows.[13] Radio contact with loved ones was not allowed between 1941–43 (apart from urgent cases, such as bereavement). After 1943 this was relaxed and the men could send and receive two personal messages per year, as well as receive mail when the relief ship passed through.

The rotation of coastwatchers was supposed to be annual, but many opted to return to the islands because they enjoyed the scientific and surveying work that came with such a unique posting. It was also the beginning of subantarctic

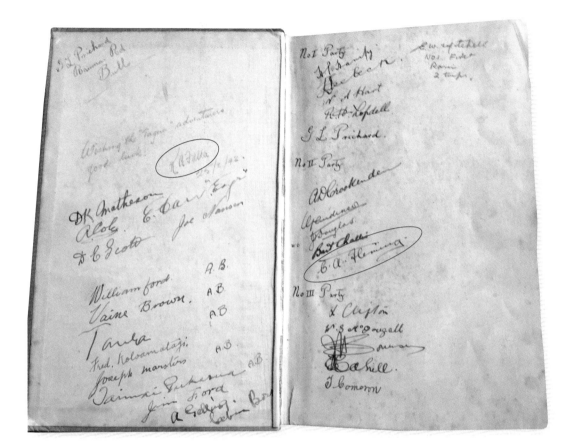

meteorological observations, which would prove to be so useful that a weather station on Campbell Island was permanently established and then maintained for another 50 years after the war ended (it's still there, but has been fully automated since the mid-1990s; see Chapter 11).

Mapping wild, remote islands

Campbell Island and the Auckland Islands had been inaccurately mapped for almost 150 years by the early 1940s (starting with Bristow's sketch in the early 1800s), and the government decided the coastwatching years provided a good opportunity to correct the errors. They needed a surveyor for the job and at the end of 1943 hired Flying Officer Allan Eden, a New Zealander whose life was about to change when they shoulder-tapped him for a position on the Auckland Islands.

In his 1955 memoir, *Islands of Despair*, which recounts his surveying and coastwatching experiences along with

The signatures of the No. 1, No. 2 and No. 3 (Campbell Island) 1942 parties. Note the signatures of Robert Falla and Charles Fleming, who both went on to receive knighthoods for their contributions to science.

entertaining summaries of the islands' history, Eden admits that he'd barely known of the islands' existence before he was sent there. He agreed right away to go as a coastwatcher and as the head of the surveying party, but, as he wrote later, 'I felt a bit sceptical about the added inducement of possible treasure to be salvaged from the wreck of the *General Grant*.'[14]

Eden appears to have thoroughly enjoyed his time on the Auckland Islands, even though he and his men inevitably got caught in wild weather, occasionally tumbled into smelly seal wallows, battled against the expletive-inducing blowflies (and rats, further south on Campbell Island), and had to endure the nocturnal bellowing of sea cows (mother seals) calling to their pups outside their tents during surveying field trips.

The coastwatchers also experienced many close encounters with territorial sea lions, as Eden describes:

> 'It was quite dark ... I had not proceeded far when there was a loud woof, and an angry sea-lion lunged viciously at me from the gloom of the forest floor ... I beat a hasty retreat ... [but] soon discovered that there was more than one sea-lion camped in the forest, and I had many more anxious moments before I reached the open beach. When I returned to camp my tale was received with some amusement ... but it was by no means uncommon for a new man at the islands to pocket his pride and scale a handy tree when surprised by a sea-lion.'[15]

They also regularly encountered the wild goats, pigs, cattle, rabbits and sheep that had been introduced by previous visitors and residents. The pigs were particularly appreciated: 'quite a few of them finished up in our cooking-pots'.

During Eden's posting, the coastwatchers at Ranui Cove stumbled across the remains of the Hardwicke settlement and some of the old castaway depots, visited the local cemetery, and also placed a wooden memorial on Enderby Island for the 15 victims of the 1887 *Derry Castle* shipwreck.[16] At the time there was still some recognizable debris from the ship scattered around the reef, although one man realized to his horror that the white object he was casually kicking around the beach as a football was a human skull.[17]

Challenging hikes

The surveying party had to trek right across Auckland Island to calculate their topographical map measurements, which was no easy feat. The island's steep terrain (peaks rise to 600 metres or 2000 feet), precipitous western cliffs, thick tussock and peaty soil all slowed their progress, and it would take several hours to walk even a few kilometres. The weather could also take dramatic turns for the worse, and thick fog often shrouded the tops of the mountains. But if the fog wasn't there, it was because gale-force winds had blown it away.

Hardwicke Cemetery as it looked in the early 1940s.

Initially Eden had hoped to experience several consecutive fine days in order to make some progress with the surveying, but his naive optimism was met with raised eyebrows by the more seasoned expedition members. The surveying party set up field camps around Auckland Island, but Eden was dismayed to find that the weather constantly hampered their progress and caused them considerable discomfort while they waited for the cloud cover and heavy rain to clear: 'It was very disturbing to realize how little work we were getting done.'[18]

Despite the delays and frustrations, their surveying of the Auckland Islands and Campbell Island was eventually successful. In fact, the Campbell Island topographical map they created was used for another 40 years.[19] One of the surveyors was Leslie Clifton, who had led the Campbell Island party in 1942 and joined Eden's surveying team at the end of 1943. Clifton was killed in an aircraft accident in 1951 (on Mount Ruapehu in New Zealand), and there is a memorial stone for him at Beeman Cove on Campbell Island, marking the spot where his ashes were laid by men working at the meteorological station.

ABOVE Geoff Prichard at the western cliffs of Auckland Island, looking south. Photographed by Bart Challis.

RIGHT Surveying Auckland Island: Allan Eden with theodolite, Les Clifton with book, 1944.

A Gibson's albatross nests amongst the tussock on Adams Island, overlooking Carnley Harbour.

ABOVE & OPPOSITE
'No. 1' station,
photographed in 2007.

Unlike the flimsy habitats of their whaling, sealing, farming and castaway predecessors, the coastwatchers' double-glazed bases were cosy and warm. As Eden recalled:

> 'It was a treat to be able to look out the window at the rain and hear the wind roaring in the trees, all the time knowing that one had dry clothes and warm, dry feet. One could have a hot bath as often as one cared to boil the copper to fill the bath.'[20]

However, the field camps were a different story: 'We got wet through every day, so there was no point in putting on dry clothes.' There were several perks that came with living on a seldom-visited archipelago, such as getting to name invertebrates and landmarks — including a lake on Adams Island that became Lake Turbott after the coastwatcher who found it. Hiking across the islands also gave the men a chance to absorb the islands' natural wonders, while enjoying panoramic views of the harbours and the vast ocean beyond.

But the 'Cape Expedition' was only ever a wartime initiative. The coastwatchers successfully guarded New Zealand's southern islands from the enemy during World War II, then their duties began to wind down: the Tagua Bay station at Carnley Harbour was shut down in 1944, and the Ranui Cove station closed in June 1945. The Campbell Island base remained open as a Meteorological and Ionosphere Station so that New Zealand could continue to receive advance notice of weather approaching from the south-west.

It was the end of human habitation on the Auckland Islands, and since 1945 they have only been visited by scientific researchers and tourists. Today the Auckland Island coastwatching stations are little more than historical relics, with a few mould-covered books leaning on dusty shelves, rusted tins abandoned in the former kitchen, and windows and floors long since infiltrated by the gnarled branches of the local rātā forest.[21]

However, in tribute to the coastwatchers' valuable wartime and scientific contributions, the New Zealand Department of Conservation continues to maintain the two lookout huts on Auckland Island: one at Ranui Cove, overlooking Port Ross, and the other at Tagua Bay, overlooking Carnley Harbour. Both of the weatherboard huts are still painted in their camouflage colours.

10. MACQUARIE ISLAND
The penguin oilers, the crusading scientist, and the expeditioners (1890–today)

IN 1822 AN AUSTRALIAN SHIP'S CAPTAIN named James Douglass informed the *Sydney Gazette*, somewhat angrily: '[Macquarie Island is] the most wretched place of involuntary and slavish exilium … nothing could warrant any civilized creature living on such a spot.'[1]

In contrast, almost 100 years later, the eminent Australian scientist and Antarctic explorer Sir Douglas Mawson described the same island as 'one of the wonder spots of the world' and launched an international campaign to create a protected scientific reserve there.

Macquarie Island's wild beauty must be in the eye of the beholder. It is a large, narrow island, blasted by subantarsctic westerlies and pummelled by heavy surf, in one of the roughest parts of the Southern Ocean between Australia and Antarctica. Its closest neighbour is (uninhabited) Auckland Island, which is more than 600 kilometres (370 miles) to the east. In fact, the climate is so harsh that in the early 1800s Australia decided against making Macquarie a penal colony, fearing that it was too rugged for even their most despised convicts.[2]

An ecological wonder

Macquarie Island is a dependency of the state of Tasmania, which is 1500 kilometres (930 miles) away in a north-west direction. (Yes, visiting non-Aussies do need to carry their passports, but the stamp is a collector's dream.)

The island is a narrow stretch of land (34 kilometres long x 5 kilometres, or 22 x 3 miles, at its widest point) with peaks rising to 430 metres (1400 feet), a jagged coastline shaped by wind and water, and shingle beaches on the eastern side that become very crowded during the summer — but not with tourists.

In peak season (from October onwards), the thrashing surf delivers to shore

hundreds of thousands of royal penguins, who exit the sea and squeeze onto the beaches, jostling for a few inches of space and joining the rockhopper, gentoo and king penguins on the island. Meanwhile, colonies of enormous, blubbery elephant seals also line the shores, rising only for bellowing battles where they stake their territory and gnash holes in their challengers. The noise is cacophonic; the smell is potent.

Rockhopper penguin.

Above all the chaos, a few wandering and light-mantled sooty albatrosses soar through the rain and snow, then perch on their coastal nests looking out to the wild sea.

There are no trees on the island, but there is plenty of greenery. The introduced rabbits, cats and rodents were all eradicated by 2014 and there is an abundance of the megaherb nicknamed 'Macquarie Island cabbage' (*Stilbocarpa polaris*), which provided sealers with much-needed vitamin C, as well as the 'silver-leaf daisy' (*Pleurophyllum hookeri*). Tussock grasses can grow tall in some areas, but are generally controlled by the fierce wind. Small lakes are sprinkled

across the island's undulating plateau, and giant kelp swarms around the coastlines.

Macquarie Island is unique when it comes to geology. It is the only part of the world above sea level to be made entirely from the earth's mantle, a combination of rock and oceanic crust that was squeezed out of the water 600,000 years ago by two tectonic plates, in the manner of a tube of toothpaste.[3] Mainly for this reason, but also because of its unique flora and fauna, it was made a protected UNESCO World Heritage site in 1998.

In such a remote part of the world there are also bound to be myths and mysteries. A nearby 'phantom' island was sighted to the south of Macquarie Island by several 19th-century ships, and was named Emerald Island (after the first ship to 'see' it in 1821). The island came and went, according to various sightings and non-sightings over the years. It has also appeared on several world maps, including in 1987 on an American Express-published desk calendar.[4]

Macquarie Island is undoubtedly real, however, although it has a collection of strange tales like nowhere else in the world.

Joseph Hatch and the penguin digesters

Captain Douglass' disdain for Macquarie Island also extended to the sealers he encountered there during his visit to the island in 1822. 'The men employed in the gangs … appear to be the very refuse of the human species.'[5]

The poorly regarded sealers arrived en masse at Macquarie in the early 1800s during the sealing boom, but the island was also targeted long after that. A London-born chemist, entrepreneur and politician named Joseph Hatch leased Macquarie Island for 30 years, from 1889–1920, harvesting elephant seals (the oil was used for lighting and soap) and

MACQUARIE ISLAND

OPPOSITE TOP
King penguins.

OPPOSITE BOTTOM
Roaring elephant seal.

then penguins for their oil. Royal penguins are much lighter than southern elephant seals; the penguins weigh just 5 kilograms (11 pounds), versus up to 4000 kilograms (8800 pounds) for the elephant seals, so switching species made the work much less taxing for the oilers.

Hatch was a short and vivacious man who had bucketloads of self-confidence and could always pull a crowd. He was a former New Zealand mayor in Invercargill, but had lost his MP seat when it was discovered that he'd been running a shady side business poaching seals from the Auckland Islands. One of his sealing ships, the *Awarua*, had come across the eight survivors of the *Derry Castle* shipwreck on the Auckland Islands in 1887, resulting in media attention in New Zealand and Australia that exposed his illegal enterprise.[6]

It was time to look elsewhere for harvesting opportunities, and Macquarie held appeal because it was Australian territory. From December 1887 Hatch hired a succession of oiling gangs, who set up processing plants for elephant seals, then for king and royal penguins, with the latest in hi-tech oiling equipment: Norwegian-designed, steam-pressure 'digesters'. They were effectively giant bubbling cauldrons that could extract the oil without the animals having to be skinned first.

Around this time there was some confusion over which country or state was in charge of Macquarie Island. New Zealand was about to take possession in 1889 (and include Macquarie on its list of subantarctic islands to visit during its semi-annual castaway checks) when a piece of old legislation revealed that the island was a dependency of Tasmania.[7]

New Zealand's Southland Provincial Government (Hatch lived in Invercargill, part of the Southland region) became concerned about Hatch's mass harvesting of elephant seals and penguins, and asked Tasmania if New Zealand could please absorb Macquarie Island into its own territory. Tasmania's Premier was open to the idea but the proposal went to the House of Assembly, which firmly rejected it. 'Sorry for the seals and sea birds but cannot be helped,' the Premier of Tasmania wrote apologetically in a telegram to the Premier of New Zealand in 1890.[8]

'Turning wild creatures into commodities'

Here's how it worked: unsuspecting penguins were herded into a pen as they waddled up the beach to their rookery, clubbed over the head, bled out, and then taken to the 'Hall of Smells' and shoved into the digesters for steaming. After 12 hours, the resulting oil was scooped off the surface, cooled, and collected into casks for shipment back to New Zealand, where it was refined. Penguin oil was useful at the time in the making of ropes and twine. Each penguin yielded about half a litre (close to a pint) of oil, worth sixpence.[9]

It was an efficient business, at least to begin with. When the king penguins started thinning out, the oilers turned to the smaller and more abundant royal population at

A young elephant seal in a king penguin colony, Macquarie Island. Hatch swapped seals for penguins while running his oil-extracting business.

Nugget Point, at the northern end of the island. Hatch's gang were putting in 12-hour shifts in peak season (during the summer), and working around the clock to maximize their gains. Today it sounds like something out of a Stephen King horror novel, but at its peak there were ten digesters on three sites at Macquarie and up to 3000 penguins were being tossed into them each day. During Hatch's 30-year lease, more than three million penguins are estimated to have been killed.[10]

In a sign of the times, a New Zealand newspaper editorial from 1890 defended Hatch's enterprise.

'It is a native industry and encouragement should be extended to him ... he is creating wealth by turning a variety of wild creatures into commodities serviceable to humanity.'[11]

The business made a decent profit during its heyday, although on their return to New Zealand many of the oilers discovered that their cut of earnings had been whittled right down by the deduction of uncosted provisions, many of which had been inedible or lost at sea en route to the island. In some cases, they returned owing Hatch money.[12] Penguin blood contaminated many of the first oil casks, which had to be discarded. Hatch was also charged steep duties, as he was importing oil into New Zealand from an Australian territory and penguin oil was classified as 'foreign'.[13]

It was an uncomfortable, dangerous profession for the oilers, who lived in freezing and squalid conditions, sharing their quarters with enormous rats, chipping ice off their wet clothing, and topping up their limited diets with elephant-seal tongue 'sandwiches'. Supply ships were often delayed by bad weather, resulting in even more frustration and hardship.

New Zealand government steamers headed south at least twice to retrieve stranded oiling gangs whose families were worried about them. Oilers were also known to occasionally topple into the digesters, resulting in terrible burns.

The rescue ship that sank without a trace

Just getting there was (and still can be) hazardous; Macquarie Island has no wharf, harbour or other sheltered spot to drop anchor, and sudden, violent storms are common. Men sometimes had to fight for their lives while loading or unloading heavy goods, including casks of oil, in the pounding surf.

In 1891, 19 passengers and crew died during a storm off the coast of Macquarie. Eight members of Hatch's oiling gang had only just left the island and were heading back to New Zealand in a small government steamer called the *Kakanui,* which had sailed down to relieve them after they'd endured ten months existing on less than six months' worth of provisions. The men's ragged clothes and shoes had almost worn through. They were desperate to leave and crowded onto the *Kakanui,* but shortly after departure a fierce gale developed and the ship was never seen again.

The resulting New Zealand court of inquiry into the deaths of the 19 men revealed the primitive conditions on the island, but cleared Hatch of any wrongdoing. After all, it wasn't his ship, he had advised the *Kakanui* not to sail, and in a letter delivered to Macquarie Island by the *Kakanui* he had urged the oilers to stay put until he arrived in his own ship (ironically named the *Gratitude*).[14]

The Mellishes of Macquarie

After the *Kakanui* disappeared, there were only two people left on the island: the station manager, Henry Mellish, and his wife, Annie. As the *Kakanui* sailed off into heavy swells and strong winds, Annie fired a farewell salute with her gun. The Mellishes had decided to stay put and wait for Hatch, as per his advice, and they also wanted to guard the oil that had already been collected. It was a decision that saved their lives.

Henry worked on Macquarie Island for 20 years: a remarkable length of time to live on such a wild and remote island in the late-19th century. His wife Annie also spent a few years on the island working as a cook. She is remembered for her shooting prowess while topping up the pantry, and also her knack of pulling together a meal from very

A card made by Joseph Hatch showing a montage of people and ships related to the 1891 sinking of the *Kakanui*. Hatch is at the top right with a bowtie. Henry and Annie Mellish are in the middle..

DESCRIPTIVE SKETCH.

IN the beginning of last year the Schooner "Awarua" belonging to Mr J. Hatch of Invercargill took down eight men together with Mr and Mrs Mellish to be landed at Macquarie Island. Latitude 54 S Longitude 158 E to prosecute the sea elephant and penguin oil trade. Provisions were there and left sufficient to last from nine to twelve months, irrespective of the local supplies of food, comprising native wood-hens, rabbits, mutton birds, penguin and albatross eggs, as well as a large portion of the former bird, with the tongue of the sea elephant, both good eating.

In December 1890 a scare was raised by ill-advised people in Dunedin that stores were only left at the outside for six months, and consequently that the nine men and one female on the Island must be absolutely starving. Acting on this fallacious information the Government hurriedly despatched the S.S. "Kakanui" to the supposed relief of the party, their steamer "Hinemoa" being engaged on other work.

Mr Hatch, as also public opinion at Invercargill, asserted that the "Kakanui" was unsuitable for the work, that there was no occasion for their interference at all as subsequent events have proved beyond doubt, the "Hinemoa" arriving with the information that food still remained; portion of which the Gratitude brought back.

The "Kakanui" left Invercargill jetty on Christmas day and reached the Macquarie Island on January 2nd 1891 *via* Stewart's Island. Left there the following day having taken on board eight men who decided to leave at the urgent request of the Government agent on board, notwithstanding the fact that the supplies were not exhausted and that the headsman, Mellish, did all in his power to dissuade them from doing so. Since the "Kakanui" left nothing has been heard of her, the conclusion being that she has foundered at sea with 19 souls on board, *viz* :— her own crew, and Hatch's men save Mr and Mrs Mellish, who decided to wait the arrival of the ketch "Gratitude" the ordinary relief vessel, which was advised by letter per Captain Best of the "Kakanui," urging the whole party to remain.

The "Kakanui" was built by Messrs R. S. Sparrow & Co. of Dunedin, register 57 tons, commanded by Capt. W. Best, valued at £2500, insured for £1800, and owned by the D. & I. S. S. Coy., Ltd., Mr Keith Ramsay, agent.

Mr Hatch's ketch "Gratitude" 122 tons, built for Mr W. Buckingham of Sydney, and purchased by Mr Hatch in August last for this special trade, (the schooner "Awarua" well known in connection with the saving of the survivors of the "Derry Castle" at Auckland Islands in 1887, having proved too small) was despatched on January 17th, 1891, with stores, casks, and plant for prosecution of the venture. After an absence of two months landing part cargo, taking on board 127 casks Oil, as also Mr and Mrs Mellish, returned on March 18th. She was under the charge of Capt. J. Bramston. During the absence of both vessels the "Hinemoa" was despatched on three special relief trips, was unsuccessful on all occasions in meeting with any traces of the missing ship. A large number of sensational articles, telegrams and letters have appeared in the public press all over the Australian colonies in many of which Mr Hatch, an old representative for Invercargill in the N.Z. Legislature was very roughly handled, but subsequent events have proved his knowledge of the position to be correct.

The photographs have all been executed by Mr Karl Gerstenkorn, photographer, of Invercargill and published for the proprietors.

KEY TO PHOTOGRAPH.

1, S.S. "Kakanui" with Captain W. Best. 2, Mr Hatch's ketch "Gratitude." 3, Mrs Mellish 4, Mr Mellish, who remained on the island, the only survivors of the party. 5, Captain J. Bramston ; 6, Mr J. Hatch, owner ; 7, Mr Thomas, Mate ; 8, H. Donelly, 9, A. Griffiths, 10, J. Winter, 15, C. Olin, crew of the ketch "Gratitude." 16, C. Hunt, Engineer for erecting plant. 17, C. Pratt, 18, J. Dallas, ('leadsman), 19, T. Te Au, 20, T. Wyniott, Native whaleboat crew (of Colac,) for rafting oil and stores to and from island. 11, Mr D. Nickless, 12, T. Bannister, 13, H. A. Wenborn, 14, J. J. Guest, Tourists by the "Gratitude."

Copyright reserved.

little.[15] The oiling gang had quickly run out of flour, tea, coffee and sugar. The casks containing biscuits were later found to be wet and full of mould, and most of the salted meat was inedible. But Annie Mellish was not defeated: instead, she would serve up rabbits (introduced to the island in the 1860s), penguin eggs, elephant-seal tongue, and 'Macquarie Island cabbage' soup, as well as 'pea coffee' made from smashing up burnt split peas with a hammer and mixing them with water. Meanwhile, the plethora of penguin meat was also appreciated, according to Henry Mellish: 'There were plenty of … penguins to be got, and certain portions were capital eating.'[16]

Once they were collected by the *Gratitude* and arrived back in New Zealand for the court of inquiry into the *Kakanui* sinking, both of the Mellishes testified in defence of Hatch. Meanwhile, Hatch organized a public address to raise money for the *Kakanui* Relief Fund and hotly defended his business against what he called the 'ridiculous nonsense of protecting the penguins.'[17]

Mawson's crusade

But from the early 1900s, public opinion began to shift. There was international unease over the ongoing slaughter of birds and mammals, with some big names calling for Hatch to shut down his operations and campaigning for his lease to be revoked. Hatch's counter-argument was that the ongoing slaughter of royal penguins didn't reduce the overall population.[18]

Sir Douglas Mawson first visited Macquarie in 1911, along with Australian journalist and photographer Frank Hurley; both had travelled with Ernest Shackleton on his Antarctic voyages. At the site now known as Wireless Hill, Mawson and his crew set up the first radio relay station from Hobart to Antarctica, and it was the first connection between Australia and the Ice Continent. Hatch's oiling crew helped them with their work, which involved transferring equipment up the hill using a flying fox. Mawson also set up a scientific station to study the plants and wildlife on the island, as well as the weather.

In 1916, Mawson formally appealed to the Australian government to make the island a scientific reserve. They turned him down, but there was an ongoing campaign by British MPs, scientists, international media and the general public (including the British science fiction writer H.G. Wells, who was sufficiently moved to pen a moralizing tale called *An Undying Fire* with an appeal to spare the penguins).

The photographs and stories brought back by Antarctic explorers had raised people's awareness of the southern wildlife, and people were beginning to feel affection and concern for the remote birds and mammals. In particular, journalist Frank Hurley's passionate description in the *Sydney Morning Herald* of unwitting Macquarie Island penguins on a death march triggered a public outcry. In what may have been the first international conservation movement, people from around the world banded together to demand the animals' preservation and protection.[19]

The old penguin digesters.

During a public-speaking circuit with projected slideshows of island scenery, Hatch (who as an ex-politician had the gift of the gab) launched a spirited attack against his accusers and repeatedly defended his enterprise, but he eventually gave up the lease in 1919. For one thing, the business (the literally named Southern Isles Exploitation Company) wasn't going as well as it had been: his ships kept getting broken up in storms, it was becoming expensive to fund supply vessels, and public opinion was mostly against him by that point. Hatch died in Tasmania in 1928, at the ripe old age of 91, leaving six children. His grave in a Hobart cemetery is nameless, without ornament or sentiment.[20]

It was the end of an era, and Macquarie Island was declared a wildlife sanctuary in 1933. Today Hatch's rusted old penguin digesters sit idle in the sand, surrounded by thriving birdlife.

Macquarie Island research station

By the 1940s, the exploitation of Macquarie Island's wildlife was well and truly over. In 1948 Macquarie Island opened a full-time research station, which was managed by the Australian National Antarctic Research Expeditions (ANARE) and staffed with ten to 15 residents at a time. One of the station's early residents was Horst Münstermann, who lived and worked on Macquarie Island in the 1957–58 expedition year. More than half a century later, he still vividly remembers the experience.[21]

Münstermann had arrived in Australia from Germany in 1955, at the age of 21. He was working at Sydney's Mascot Airport in 1957 as an assistant when the man in charge of meteorology turned to him and asked: 'How would you like to attend weather school in Melbourne for three months, and then maybe work in Antarctica?'

'Where is Antarctica?' replied Münstermann, who had only recently arrived in the southern hemisphere.

A few months later, he sailed to remote Macquarie Island for a 13-month posting as a meteorologist. Giant waves crashed over the Danish icebreaker ship *Thala Dan*, with a great deal of pitching and rolling in the wild ocean.

On arrival, the expedition team was 'greeted' on the beach by a long-haired, bearded meteorologist in his birthday suit. 'He was trying to scare us off … I thought to myself, "I'm going home!"' But Münstermann was immediately put to work in a mad dash to unload two years' worth of supplies off the ship while the weather permitted. Everything had to be packed into 'army duck' boats (amphibious vehicles) and transported through the pounding surf to the beach.

Weather and wilderness

There were 16 men on the expedition, including three meteorologists, an aurora physicist, radio officers, a geophysicist, a medical officer, a carpenter, a cook and an officer in charge. Münstermann was quick to pick things up on the job: 'I just learned as I went along, day by day.'

It was the International Geophysical Year, a time of global interest in the Earth's upper atmosphere. There was a lot of weather to monitor and just three men to do the job, so round-the-clock work wasn't unusual for Münstermann in the first

ABOVE The *Thala Dan*

LEFT
An aerial shot of the
research station, 1958.

A more typical welcome on the beach, 1958.

six months. 'I often started a shift at six o'clock in the morning and went right through until lunchtime the next day, in order to have a proper break.'

Hydrogen weather balloons were raised up to 100,000 feet each day to measure the wind speed and direction, with reports radioed back to Melbourne via Morse code. 'Sometimes the wind was so fierce, all you could do was run and hope you wouldn't go up with [the balloon].'

During his time off, Münstermann would explore the island. 'It was a wet place. There are about 320 days of rain and precipitation a year, but the animal life was incredible.' He roamed across the island, visiting the royal penguin rookery with its 800,000 penguins, playing with southern elephant seals, and photographing black-browed albatrosses, blue-eyed shags and rockhopper penguins.

While the station itself was relatively comfortable, the outlying huts in those days were very basic — in fact, some were more 'box' than 'hut'. At Bauer Bay, a popular nesting spot for wandering albatrosses, Münstermann remembers staying overnight with a biologist in a converted weather balloon box that was slightly larger than a coffin. 'It was 7 feet long, 4 feet

high, 4 feet wide [2 x 1 x 1 metres]. When we got into it we were hysterical because we thought we were going to die, we thought we were locked in.' But new discoveries made such temporary discomforts worthwhile. 'You couldn't help but cuddle the albatross chicks. I was the first to take photos of parents coming back to feed their chick, no one had photographed it before.'

Horst Münstermann raising a weather balloon attached to a radiosonde on a calm day, 1958.

Staring death in the face

Scattered around the island are sombre reminders that Macquarie can be a hostile and dangerous place for humans. Nugget Point was the final resting place for a couple of the early 20th-century penguin harvesters, and there are unmarked graves of men who drowned or died of illness, hunger or exposure. At North Head is the grave of John Windsor, a senior meteorologist who died of appendicitis in 1951. Another grave is for Charles Scoble, who drowned in a frozen lake in 1948 while skiing.

Münstermann had his own close shave in similar circumstances when he too fell into a frozen lake, with a 30-kilogram (66-pound) rucksack strapped to his back. It was the middle of winter and he was all alone. Somehow he

Horst Münstermann's quarters, with 'glamour girls' on the wall and bird eggs on the desk, 1958.

managed to haul himself out of the freezing water, breaking through the ice with his elbows in order to reach the bank. Then he had to walk for another two-and-a-half hours, soaking wet and shivering, to reach the nearest hut at Green Gorge.

Today, he shrugs off such feats of endurance: 'When you're young, you can do anything!' Risks and new experiences were all part of the freedom allowed in those days, he adds. 'You were allowed to do anything. You just picked up your camera and walked. You didn't tell anyone where you were going. It was none of their business!'

A man's world

Münstermann also spent a year working at Mawson Station in Antarctica in 1960. Later, when he returned to Germany for a series of public lectures on his expeditions, people were very curious about his men-only stints at Macquarie and Mawson.

'People often asked me, how did you feel about not having any women down there? I had pictures of pretty girls hanging on the walls, but after a while I just ignored them. They're not in your life, so you don't miss them. But

when I came back [to Australia], even from a kilometre away all women looked pretty — even old women! When I got off the boat, this beautiful girl walked past. Someone was introducing their parents to me, and they stuck out their hands [for me to shake], but I just watched the woman!'

Returning to mainland Australia after a year of isolation wasn't easy: 'I hated being back. Traffic, regulations, law and order … all the things you have to abide by when you live in a society. I had problems adjusting to that.'

Münstermann, who is now in his eighties and retired on Australia's Gold Coast, recently made a YouTube video to share his photos and memories of Macquarie Island with a wider audience.[22] During his time on Macquarie he also found three wooden pulleys from 1911 on Wireless Hill, probably left behind by Mawson's expedition team. Münstermann donated the pulleys to Mawson's Huts Replica Museum in Hobart, Tasmania.

Macquarie Island station today

Macquarie Island station is now managed by the Australian Antarctic Division (AAD). In 2016 it was announced that the station would be closed down, but an outcry from scientists and politicians kept it open, and a cash injection from the Australian federal government is funding an upgrade to some of the buildings.[23]

The station usually has 20 to 30 team members (fewer during the winter due to the potential effects of short, sunless days) and women have visited the island as part of expedition teams since the summer of 1959–60. In 1976, the first woman — Dr Zoe Gardner — overwintered on the island.[24]

Macquarie Island's nature reserve is the responsibility of Tasmania Parks and Wildlife Service, which hires a couple of rangers each year to monitor the plants and wildlife, maintain tracks and infrastructure, and also manage tourist visits in the summer. Ongoing research is conducted seasonally about the wildlife and the island's geology, and there is now a collection of 50 years' worth of weather data which provides insights for research on global warming and climate change.[25]

There are 30 buildings at the station, including a modern 'mess' hut displaying historical photos from previous expeditions. Although the weather on the island can still be very challenging, living conditions are much better than those the sealing and oiling gangs endured. It's also a lot easier to communicate with the outside world: the station has internet access, with its own Facebook page and a weekly online newsletter, as well as a live webcam.[26]

However, some things don't change: the elephant seals still snore outside the accommodation huts, the penguins chatter noisily on the beach and in their rookeries, and the gales are as ferocious as ever. 'I feel like I am blindfolded inside a pinball machine sometimes,' one of the residents commented in a station newsletter.[27]

Beak hour: King penguins greeting tourists on Macquarie Island.

11. CAMPBELL ISLAND METEOROLOGICAL STATION
The weather-watchers and the wildlife (1945–95)

WEATHER OBSERVATIONS FROM CAMPBELL ISLAND began in 1941 during the World War II coastwatching era. After the war ended, the island's weather station remained in operation and was eventually staffed with between nine and 11 people at a time before it became fully automated in 1995.

In other words, for 54 years small groups of people, usually rotated annually, sailed 660 kilometres south (400 miles) from mainland New Zealand to live on a remote island and report around the clock on the weather. Participating was a challenge and an adventure, and for many it was a life-changing experience. Several expeditioners returned to live and work at the station more than once.

Reporting from remote outposts

At the time, weather data was manually radioed to New Zealand from several outlying locations: Campbell Island, Raoul Island in the Kermadecs, Chatham Island, Scott Base in Antarctica, and Pitcairn Island. (Australia's Macquarie Island still maintains a staffed weather station, with reports sent to Tasmania.)

On Campbell, synoptic (summary) weather observations were carried out every three hours by met technicians on rotating shifts to measure the ground temperature, air pressure, cloud forms, wind speed and direction. Observations were carried out at 0000, 0300, 0600, 0900, 1200, 1500, 1800 and 2100, all year round and in all weather conditions. An Upper Air Sounding (UAS) was also carried out each day at midday, and also at midnight during the summer. A 2-metre (6½-foot) tall, hydrogen-filled, latex balloon with a radiosonde attached was released into the stratosphere, reaching heights of up to 30,480 metres (100,000 feet). The radiosonde then transmitted continuous data

ABOVE Campbell Island Meteorological Station, 1969.

LEFT Senior Meteorological Observer Dave Paull performing an Upper Air Sounding with balloon and radiosonde, Campbell Island, 1970.

on the temperature, humidity, atmospheric pressure, wind speed and direction.

The met officers had to make their own hydrogen for the balloon out of caustic soda and aluminium shavings (and sometimes magnesium filings), a volatile combo nicknamed 'the bomb'. This process took an hour, and then raising the balloon took another two hours. Eventually the balloon would burst. The data provided by the radiosonde was analyzed by the on-duty met technician and sent north to New Zealand via high-frequency radio telephone.

It was vitally important information, as much of New Zealand's weather approaches from the south so the weather reports provided the mainland with advance notice. But it wasn't just of interest to New Zealand; the weather station was part of a global network. The information they gathered assisted aircraft that were heading to Antarctica in the summer months, including for the USA's 'Operation Deep Freeze' missions which fly from New Zealand to McMurdo Sound.

In the 1940s there were just four or five men stationed on Campbell Island, but over the years this increased to nine workers on an annual rotation: one OIC (Officer In Charge), a mechanic to keep all the equipment running, a radio tech, an ionosphere observer, two met technicians, one DSIR (Department of Scientific and Industrial Research) employee doing geophysics work, a cook, and a senior met observer. Two more met technicians would be added in the summertime to handle the extra shifts.

In 1957, met operations shifted from the old coastwatching huts at Tucker Cove across Perseverance Harbour to where the buildings now stand at Beeman Point.

Mark 'Swampy' Crompton

Meteorologist Mark Crompton lived on Campbell Island for seven years, on and off, between 1969 and 1991 — the longest-recorded human residency in the island's history. He spent much of his free time exploring all the nooks and crannies of the island, which is easier to traverse than Auckland Island (and, unlike Macquarie, devoid of frozen lakes).

Now semi-retired and living on New Zealand's remote West Coast, Crompton remembers coming across an article about Campbell Island in 1962 when he was a schoolboy, and he knew immediately that he wanted to go there. He later discovered that the Ministry of Transport offered postings to Campbell Island for trained meteorological observers, and that was his ticket south.

In 1969, the year Neil Armstrong took the first step on the Moon and the Beatles performed their last show, Crompton took the path (or ocean) less travelled and sailed to Campbell Island. His first glimpse of his new home, just one day shy of his 21st birthday, brought awe and delight: 'It was probably a wild, stormy day with hail bouncing off the ship. But I loved it! I was fascinated.'[1]

Measuring weather patterns wasn't an easy job, especially when the island was experiencing one of its typical weather systems. Wind gusts reach over 96 kilometres

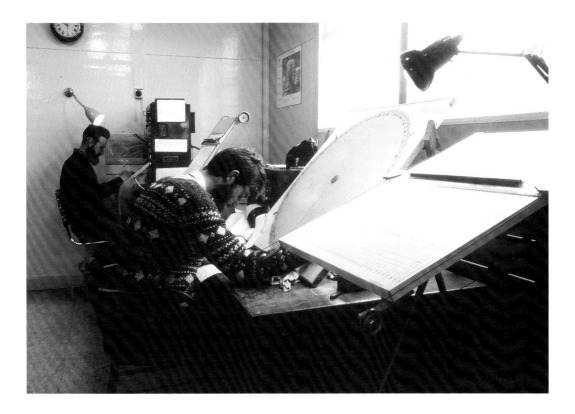

Mark Crompton (front) and Dave Paull in the Campbell Island met office plotting the upper winds, 1970.

(60 miles) per hour at least 100 days per year, a light snowfall can occur in any season, and the sun shines on average for just 650 hours across an entire year (as a point of reference, London gets more than double that), with less than an hour of sun for 215 days a year. It also rains 325 days a year, although not usually for the entire day.[2]

Those are some pretty bleak figures. But the island has a mystical sort of beauty, too, as the met station's Officer in Charge (OIC) James Judd wrote in 1963:

'The weather statistics give a far gloomier picture of the weather than is actually experienced. It is a fact that the fine clear days, if not actually better than those experienced in New Zealand are certainly more appreciated. There is a cleanness about them which one would never experience in a town. This clarity of atmosphere also lends a soft beauty to what is otherwise a rather sombre landscape.'[3]

The strong winds made for some blustery times working outdoors, says Mark Crompton.

A golden moment of sunshine
on Campbell Island.

'The met office was about 100 metres [110 yards] from the hostel, so you can imagine on a June, July or August night at 3am staggering out to the boardwalk to read temperatures in a screaming sou'west gale at minus two [Celsius]. We had a mercury barometer in those days — we used to go out with a torch to read the temperature. Now you can just bring it up online!'

In such a wild climate, there was sometimes a risk of becoming a victim of the weather they were recording. Sometimes the tug of the balloon in strong winds would drag them through the dracophyllum scrub as they raised it, or they'd get knocked on the head by the attached radiosonde as the balloon lifted. Campbell Island is also prone to williwaws: vicious but short-lived squalls that rush down the mountains (as experienced by Captain Hasselberg, to his peril). Crompton was bowled over more than once, but knew enough to not be sitting in a boat while they were prevalent.

'Williwaws can be very violent. They were quite frequent, mostly in a northerly flow. The wind would tumble over Lyle Ridge and spill down into Perseverance Harbour … You can be flattened by them.'

Crompton became well known to the weather crowd for his descriptive and humorous reports, which were eagerly awaited. 'A rare fine day became: "*We will pay for this.*" A wet day became: "*Well, you had better tie everything down, it's going to get much worse.*" And it always did.'[4]

Home comforts

The basic living conditions of the sheep-farming era were in the past. Despite the chilly climate (the mean annual temperature is 6° Celsius, or 43° Fahrenheit), Crompton says the buildings were toasty warm, with hot air piped around by large diesel combustion furnaces. 'We would turn the thermostat up to 24 or 25 degrees [Celsius], it was like Hawaii. We took down 100,000 litres [26,400 gallons] of diesel on the ship [as fuel] each year.' For relaxation there were plenty of books, as well as a pool table, a record player, and then later, a VCR, a film projector, and a gym. Wildlife photography was always a popular pastime, and the station had its own darkroom. Chess and darts matches were played remotely against the Macquarie Island and Scott Base weather stations.[5] As OIC James Judd put it in 1963: 'There is plenty of space and opportunity for the practice of individual hobbies, which range from model making to the playing of bagpipes.'

Living far from civilization and in a cold climate (it was also the 1960s and '70s), there was a tendency towards hirsuteness: 'Electric razors <u>can</u> be used, but rather obviously are not,' Judd wrote pointedly.

What did one eat on Campbell Island in the post-sealing, post-farming era? Initially there were tinned and dried goods in the pantry, with fresh mutton provided by the

Mark Crompton in the Campbell Island staff kitchen, winter 1970.

local sheep. According to Crompton, this became somewhat tedious. 'I got thoroughly sick of Campbell Island sheep! They also tasted quite strange.' (This was due to the sheep eating the local dracophyllum and *Bulbinella rossii*.) But from the early 1980s, when walk-in freezers were installed, food options exponentially increased. 'Food wasn't a big cost — the big cost was the shipping — so the Met Service said to take down whatever food we wanted. We didn't want for anything, we lived like kings! Steak, roast duck, scallops … ' Alcohol was paid for out of their own pockets, but could be purchased duty-free from passing naval ships.

A solitary life

Crompton also spent three years working for the Met Service on Raoul Island in the Kermadecs (1100 kilometres or 680 miles north-east of New Zealand) and had a year on the Chatham Islands too, so he became accustomed to living on remote offshore islands.

Isolation can have many benefits, offering time out from stress-triggering traffic, phones, offices, crowds, shops and news reports. Living on a remote island was also a path to self-sufficiency, becoming an expert out of necessity, growing in confidence, and being part of a small team that depended on one other. There were many advantages that came with working outdoors, such as being surrounded by unique plants and wildlife.

But a posting on Campbell Island didn't suit everyone, and Crompton recalls a few expedition members having to be 'extracted': in other words, collected by ship and whisked back to the New Zealand mainland. With a small group of different personality types living so closely together in a remote environment, a few clashes and meltdowns were probably inevitable. As Crompton recalls:

'The mid-1970s in particular were unsettled, when the OIC was in his mid-50s and a former army sergeant, and much older than the others who were late teens or early 20s. They were all young 'flower power' types, with hair down to their shoulders, looking like they'd just come out of a rock festival in California. It made [the OIC] feel physically sick just looking at them! He got there and started barking orders, but they just told him to take a running jump. Down there, he had no one to back him up.'

The first women at the station

The first woman to visit Campbell Island as part of a field expedition was Brenda May, an entomologist, who spent six weeks there in 1975. But it wasn't until the early 1980s that women were allowed to join the meteorological team at Beeman Cove.[6]

The first two women to live at the station for a 12-month posting were Diane Harris, who worked as a cook (she was also a registered nurse who had worked in Alaska), and Joanne Cowern (now McDougall), who was the senior meteorologist. McDougall was an experienced meteorologist. She'd heard plenty of stories about the southern expeditions, and it was the goal of many met technicians to head south for an adventure. However, when she heard about the station postings on subantarctic Campbell Island and asked to join, she was told by the Met Service that women didn't participate. Many reasons were given, including safety and the cold climate. Undeterred, McDougall put forward her case for going and had to 'tick all the boxes' to convince them that it was a good idea. 'But the time was right. Women scientists had started working at the more remote Antarctic stations and it was happening all over the world.'[7]

She was hired as the senior meteorologist for the 1981–82 expedition. On arrival in Perseverance Harbour, McDougall remembers being amazed by the 'bleak but beautiful' scenery and the close encounters with the local wildlife — although she felt like a unique species herself when the previous year's all-male expedition approached

Joanne McDougall on Campbell Island in 1981.

her with curious fascination, having not set eyes on a woman for 12 months.

McDougall and Harris were the first female residents of Campbell Island since 'Mrs Cook' during the whaling years of the early 20th century, and having two women living at the station involved a few adjustments. For example, it soon became apparent that the annual supply of toilet paper wasn't going to last the distance and an emergency delivery from the mainland had to be ordered.

McDougall's 12-month posting sped by. 'It was all so interesting. It's a bit like being in a flat with people you wouldn't normally live with, but you have your own room, you have fantastic parties, and there were wonderful huts around the island.'

As the met team all worked different shifts, they were allowed to explore the island by themselves during their time off and stay overnight in the various huts.

'Each hut had its own character … in North West Bay you could see the southern

right whales and their calves; down at the beach it would be penguin rush hour, and sea lions and sea elephants with their harems and their pups. The rockhopper colonies were an hour or two away … Southeast Harbour had sea lion pups and giant petrels, Bull Rock had the black-browed and grey-headed mollymawk colonies. On the ridge were the royal albatross and wanderers … It was wonderful for mental health.'

When she wasn't working or exploring the island, McDougall painted portraits of the other expeditioners and developed her photos in the station darkroom. 'It was a major thing and quite competitive; we'd all have cameras, film, photographic paper, and a year's worth of chemicals.'

After leaving Campbell Island at the end of 1982, McDougall set her sights on the Ice Continent, and made history again. In 1986, she became the first woman employed by the New Zealand Met Service to have a posting at Vanda Station, in Antarctica.[8]

McDougall hasn't returned to Campbell Island since her posting there, but her memories of her time on the island have stayed with her. In 2016, she wrote and illustrated a children's book called *A Southern Tale* about the subantarctic wildlife.

'I was really horrified to discover that the [New Zealand] sea lions had become endangered. Our base was surrounded by sea lions; we used to trip over them, they'd give birth outside, and sometimes they even came into our quarters. I must be one of very few people on the planet who can say that they've had a sea lion on their bed!'

Keeping busy during a year away

Team members who lounged around expecting to be looked after didn't last very long, says Mark Crompton, who was the Officer in Charge on several expeditions.

'The best way to cope was to keep busy: people who got out, did things, built a boat, did some botanical work, whatever — if they did something, they were all right … But we got some that sat around the base marking each day off on the calendar. That way, a year can take a long time to go!'

Crompton kept very busy, with multiple roles during his time on Campbell Island. In addition to the regular weather reports, he also did a lot of scientific and conservation work over the years. In 1984, he hiked up Mount Honey (540 metres or 1770 feet high) every week on his day off — even through the bitterly cold winter — to monitor a couple of botanical and micro-climatological stations for botanist Colin Meurk, recording weekly data on air and soil temperatures, wind speed, snow depth, and rainfall.

Crompton also helped with the sheep eradication between 1970 and 1990 (the wild descendants of the Tucker Cove sheep farm; see Chapter 12 for more details about the eradication) and he lent a hand during the 1970s bird-banding project for Wildlife Service, led by ornithologist Dr Chris Robertson, to measure the ocean range of albatrosses: 'I must've banded a thousand albatrosses!' (Albatrosses spend most of their lives at sea and can fly thousands of kilometres; many of the banded birds were later recovered off the southern coasts of Chile and Argentina.)

A philatelist's dream

Like Macquarie Island, Campbell Island had its own post office from the early 1950s — they must surely have been two of the most remote post offices on the planet, and Macquarie's is still running — with a unique Campbell Island postmark.

The island's exotic postmark was eagerly sought by philatelists (mail-related collectors) from around the world, who would send self-addressed envelopes to the island so they could add the postmark to their collections. But incoming mail was infrequent, for obvious reasons, and also erratic. For example, there were supposed to be at least two mail drops a year by Orion aircraft in the 1980s, but sometimes the gusty winds thwarted them. The mail was also dropped off-course at least once, taking several days to locate in the dense tussock.[9]

Crompton was the 'postmaster' for three years as part of his OIC duties, and required special training for the role. But despite being kept busy with his various

The rare Campbell Island 'Poppleton' cachet, a philatelist's dream. George Poppleton was the 1959–60 OIC and designed the first 'Antarctic' version of the cachet. This second version originates from 1963 with the 'Sub-antarctic' correction.

roles and responsibilities, there was still time for fun and recreation. In the 1970s, Crompton and three others ran to the top of every single mountain peak on Campbell Island in one go, an impressive feat that took 36 consecutive hours. Perhaps he had a slight competitive advantage: he wears a size 13 shoe.

Working in the wild

Living in such a remote location was an adventure, but there were risks involved. Expedition members had training to deal with emergencies and the appointed medical officer for each expedition would also spend time in the emergency department of a city hospital, learning how to sew up wounds and deal with trauma-level injuries. Such preparation was vital: from Campbell Island the nearest hospital was almost 700 kilometres (435 miles) away, across the open sea.

Over the decades there was the occasional illness or accident that required emergency evacuation. Medical events between 1945 and 1995 included a stroke, an abscess, a thumb squashed by a door that slammed in the wind, and a case of appendicitis in 1946 that required immediate evacuation by flying boat — the first successful aircraft landing at Campbell Island (or at least, in its harbour). But more often than not, patients were picked up by naval vessels, which took a few days to get there.[10]

Given the remoteness and the severe weather, it's perhaps surprising that there weren't more serious problems over half a century. But Mark Crompton says as OIC he was always mindful of the risks, even when performing seemingly straightforward tasks.

'I always had in the back of my mind that if anything happens, you're [more than] 600 kilometres [375 miles] away from Invercargill by sea. So you have to keep that in mind, whatever you're doing. Accidents in particular can happen in the kitchen. If you're doing field work by steep cliffs …'

The weather can change suddenly, too; thick mists can drop over the mountains like a curtain, making it difficult to get one's bearings. The land is uneven and boggy, with dips and holes hidden in the tussock. And there can be other dangers lurking such as the notoriously territorial sea lions, which weigh up to 400 kilograms (880 pounds) and don't appreciate surprises.

Some viewed the sea lions as free entertainment, but Crompton says he showed respect for the wildlife. 'I was always aware that I was in their territory, not the other way around, and I used to steer clear of them. Others used to rile them up for a chase, but I didn't feel it was right.' But sometimes encounters can be accidental. During a historical and scientific expedition to Campbell Island in 2010, one of the group was walking through some dense tussock in Tucker Cove when he unwittingly trod on a sleeping sea lion, which didn't take kindly to the interruption. It whipped around and bit the man on the knee, causing profuse bleeding. The injury was successfully treated without an infection developing, but wildlife attacks can have severe consequences for those who find themselves in the wrong place at the wrong time.

The shark attack

At 3.30 pm on Friday, 24 April 1992, OIC Mike Fraser, 32, was attacked by a 4-metre (13-foot) white pointer shark while snorkelling with four other people at North West Bay.

An experienced diver, Fraser had separated from the others to swim a bit further out from the coast when he felt something ram into the right side of his body and push him under the water. At first, he assumed it was just a playful seal pup. But when he surfaced, he saw the huge jaws of a shark. He screamed, and the shark pulled him back under the water.

He tried punching and kicking the shark, but saw that his left arm was useless and his right arm was clamped between the shark's jaws, so he used his knees and feet instead. He then felt himself released and knew he must have lost his arm. He lay on his back and kicked away from the pool of blood, knowing he had little time and energy left. He was struggling to breathe, going into shock, and the shore was 30 metres (100 feet) away.

Then he felt a hand under his chin, and was told to stay still.

Department of Conservation ranger Jacinda Amey, 23 (who was visiting the island to perform a yellow-eyed penguin census), had started swimming out to Fraser as soon as the shark retreated. She pulled him back to shore and the team quickly got to work.[11]

Meteorologist Linda Danen and technician Robin Humphrey stemmed the flow of blood from Fraser's severed arm by using the strap of a snorkel mask as a tourniquet, then used a plastic bag and tape as a dressing. Gus McAllister, the station mechanic, sprinted the 9.5-kilometre (6-mile) hike back across the island to Beeman Base to raise the alarm and pick up medical supplies. It took him just 30 minutes to get there, compared with the 90 minutes it had taken the group to reach the bay.

A government research ship, the *Tangaroa*, was three hours away from Campbell Island and responded to the station's radio alert. But evacuation by ship wouldn't work; Fraser had lost a large amount of blood, and time was running out.

Almost 700 kilometres (435 miles) away on the New Zealand mainland, helicopter search and rescue pilot John Funnell got a phone call at 4.30pm to tell him that a man had been attacked by a shark on Campbell Island and needed to be evacuated by chopper. Could he help? Sure, Funnell replied, no problem. Then he hung up and thought: *How the hell am I going to do it?*[12]

He contacted long-distance pilot and navigator Grant Biel and paramedic Pat Wynne, and within a few hours the three of them were in the air, the New Zealand mainland disappearing behind them as they flew south. They carried medical supplies, including four units of blood, and three 200-litre (53-gallon) drums of

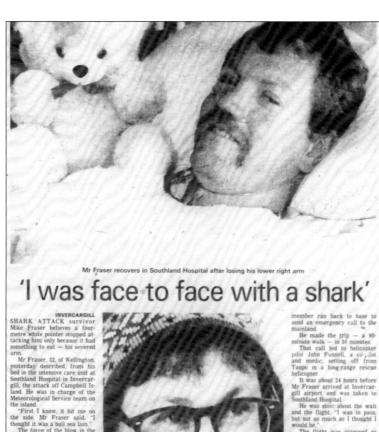

Mr Fraser recovers in Southland Hospital after losing his lower right arm

'I was face to face with a shark'

INVERCARGILL

SHARK ATTACK survivor Mike Fraser believes a four-metre white pointer stopped attacking him only because it had something to eat — his severed arm.

Mr Fraser, 32, of Wellington, yesterday described, from his bed in the intensive care unit at Southland Hospital in Invercargill, the attack off Campbell Island. He was in charge of the Meteorological Service team on the island.

"First I knew, it hit me on the side. Mr Fraser said. "I thought it was a bull sea lion."

The force of the blow in the Friday afternoon attack knocked him backwards under the water.

"I got back to the surface and I was face to face with a shark — its mouth, basically."

Mr Fraser, who had been snorkelling in about five metres of water, thrashed about trying to fend off the white pointer with his arms.

"It was pure instinct. With something that size, you don't know what to do."

The shark started biting into his lower right arm and Mr Fraser discovered his left arm was "floppy and useless" with a broken wrist.

"I started using my knees and feet. I didn't know what to do. I thought my number was up. I could not defend myself."

Suddenly the shark pulled away and swam off.

"I think that's when my arm came off," Mr Fraser said.

"It had a mouthful of my arm and had a feed. The fact my arm came off may have satisfied him a bit."

Mr Fraser lay on his back

Miss Amey . . . pulled Mr Fraser to safety

and started trying to struggle the 30 metres to shore. He had lost a lot of blood and was having trouble breathing when Jacinda Amey reached him.

Miss Amey, 23, a Conservation Department officer from Tuatapere, was one of five people who had gone snorkelling in North-West Bay.

She grabbed Mr Fraser under the chin and started towing him in.

"I talked to her later, and

she said when she saw me break free she knew it was a shark," Mr Fraser said.

If Miss Amey had not come to get him, reaching the shore would have been impossible, he said.

On the beach, another woman on the Met team worked to stop the bleeding and prevent him going into shock.

A mayday call was sent out on a portable radio from the beach while another Met team

member ran back to base to send an emergency call to the mainland.

He made the trip — a 90-minute walk — in 30 minutes.

That call led to helicopter pilot John Funnell, a co-pilot and medic, setting off from Taupo in a long-range rescue helicopter.

It was about 24 hours before Mr Fraser arrived at Invercargill airport and was taken to Southland Hospital.

He was stoic about the wait and the flight. "I was in pain, but not as much as I thought I would be."

The flight was cramped as he was wedged in between extra fuel tanks needed for the long distance.

No previous shark sightings had been reported at Campbell Island, Mr Fraser said.

"You would have more of a chance running into a shark in Wellington harbour than on Campbell."

A diver with 10 years' experience and an instructor's ticket, he has dived with sharks before.

His work with the Met Service for the past 15 years has meant spending time on Raoul Island in the Kermadecs.

"You saw a shark every dive you did there. If you didn't see a shark that was a novelty," he said.

The attack has not discouraged him from diving, but it could be more difficult as he was right-handed.

Surgeons will examine his arm tomorrow, then further plastic surgery work will be done in Christchurch or Upper Hutt. He will probably begin physiotherapy soon — NZPA

The Dominion, 28 April 1992. Pictured are Mike Fraser, in his hospital bed, and Jacinda Amey.

A1 jet fuel which would need to be changed over mid-flight. An aircraft flew above them for part of the journey, radioing data coordinates.

Meanwhile, the Campbell Island team worked continuously over Fraser at North West Bay during the long night, keeping him warm, trying to keep him conscious, and injecting him with pethidine for pain relief.

The following morning the rescue helicopter landed safely

on Campbell Island, thanks to some navigation tips radioed from the *Tangaroa* to guide them past the outlying Dent Island in the early dawn light and thick cloud. First, they flew Fraser over to the met station, where Wynne performed a quick operation on Fraser's badly damaged left hand. Next, they transferred Fraser back into the helicopter and flew to Invercargill, where he was rushed to hospital within 24 hours of the shark attack.

It had been a dangerous rescue mission flying the 1400 kilometre (870 miles) return trip over the open sea, dealing with thick cloud cover at Campbell Island, no land in sight for several hours of the journey, intermittent GPS signals, and heavy fuel drums wedged in next to them for the two long, uncomfortable flights. But they made it, and Fraser survived to tell the tale.

It was a world-first achievement as a single-engine helicopter rescue. At the time, no one had been confident that such a rescue mission was even possible.

A week later, Fraser told newspaper reporters from his hospital bed: 'I thought my number was up … The fact my arm came off may have satisfied [the shark] a bit.'[13]

Fraser lost his lower right arm in the attack, but underwent several operations to regain most of the use of his left arm. He returned to Campbell Island as the OIC for the station's final year of manual operation, in 1994–95. DOC ranger Jacinda Amey and helicopter pilot John Funnell received awards for bravery, but both insisted that it was a team effort.

Mark Crompton was not stationed on Campbell Island during the year of the shark attack, but knows those who were involved. 'That shark would've been circling, just waiting for the victim to die. Jacinda was very brave to go in.'

Historical decline

The met station became fully automated in 1995, and apart from seasonal scientific and tourist visits the island is now uninhabited. These days, weather data from Campbell Island (and also from Enderby Island further north) is automatically transmitted via satellite to Wellington. As a result, the dozen-odd small buildings at Beeman Point sit empty, with shuttered windows, creating a miniature ghost-town effect. The silent huts are guarded by snoozing sea lions. The small railway track, which used to have a trolley wagon to transport cargo up to the hostel from the wharf, is now overgrown with tussock and megaherbs. The wharf crane is frozen, and the little 'street' lights are extinguished.

Crompton spent seven years of his life at Campbell Island, New Zealand's southernmost territory and a place many New Zealanders have probably never heard of — something Crompton is well aware of:

'A lot of people know about Scott Base, Edmund Hillary and the Antarctic history, but the average New Zealander has very low awareness [of the subantarctic

The boardwalk and empty met buildings in 2016. Note the increase in dracophyllum scrub.

OPPOSITE The island is now uninhabited, with the 'Welcome' sign reserved only for visitors.

islands]. *People might know there are some islands south of New Zealand with penguins, whales and seals, where it's cold, wet and windy, but that's about it. The islands have a very low profile.'*

The met station is jointly managed by the Department of Conservation and NZ MetService, but is seldom used. Crompton feels strongly that there should be a subantarctic base there, similar to what Australia has on Macquarie Island.

'The logical place for [a base] is Campbell Island. All the databases of the botanical and biological, invertebrate, entomological, and weather are on Campbell. Why reinvent the wheel? Ideally, if money wasn't a problem, you'd demolish all the old buildings and put in a small, modern facility that could accommodate seven to ten people — but it doesn't look like that will happen in my lifetime.'

Campbell Island today

Crompton returned to the island in 2010 as part of the Campbell Island Bicentennial Expedition, marking 200 years since Captain Hasselburg first sighted its mist-covered mountains from the *Perseverance*.

On arrival, Crompton couldn't believe how much the island had changed since the sheep and rats were eradicated in the 1990s and early 2000s, causing a dramatic regeneration of megaherbs including the Ross lily (*Bulbinella rossii)* and the Campbell Island daisy (*Pleurophyllum speciosum)*. But ultimately, he says, it's not the places you form close relationships with, it's the people. He has stayed in touch with a lot of the former met workers, and they still catch up and reminisce about their adventures on the island.

Crompton still thinks about Campbell Island every day, more than a quarter of a century after his final posting there in 1991.

'We were very lucky, very privileged to have had the opportunity to be there. Sometimes I'd sit having morning tea and look out the window, down the harbour and see southern royal albatrosses and [light-mantled] sooty albatrosses banking on the wind, just metres away. Where else would you see that?'

12. CONSERVATION
The sheep shooters, the teal tackle, and the subantarctic rangers
(1960s–today)

THE WHALERS, SEALERS, EXPLORERS, COLONISTS, CASTAWAYS AND FARMERS have faded into the past. These days, instead of trying to exploit or survive on the subantarctic islands, people are more interested in studying and protecting them. Their status as conservation icons is official: New Zealand's and Australia's subantarctic islands are all UNESCO World Heritage sites, giving them the same level of reverence and guardianship as the pyramids in Egypt and the Grand Canyon in the United States.

Macquarie Island became a state nature reserve in 1972. It was declared predator-free in 2014 after the cats, rodents and rabbits were all eradicated due to a seven-year, AU$25 million project that involved a combination of aerial baiting, ground trapping and detector dogs. Since then, the island's native vegetation has been regenerating with vigour.

By 1934, all of New Zealand's subantarctic islands had become protected nature reserves — although there was a request in 1955 from the Winston Churchill-led British government to 'borrow' the Antipodes Islands for hydrogen-bomb testing (the request was turned down by the New Zealand government).[1]

Since the 1960s, the New Zealand Lands and Survey Department, Wildlife Service (Department of Internal Affairs), DSIR (Department of Scientific and Industrial Research) and the Department of Conservation (from 1987) have all been their guardians, restricting visitor numbers and working to restore the islands to their former glory. It's still a risky job, too: one DOC ranger had to be evacuated from Enderby Island by helicopter in 2017 after her wound from a sea lion bite became infected.[2]

Restoring a fragile ecosystem

Fighting two centuries' worth of introduced pests on wild, inhospitable islands has not been an easy task.

It all started in the early 1800s when the Norway rats were introduced to Campbell Island by sealing and whaling ships. Next, cats were introduced to control the rats, and then from the late 1800s thousands of sheep were imported for farming. The sheep munched on the island's native vegetation, including the endemic megaherbs, while the rats ate native bird eggs and killed off the smaller birds on the main island.

Meanwhile, pigs, sheep, cattle, goats, rabbits, cats and mice were all introduced to the Auckland Islands during the 19th century (horses, dogs and chickens were also introduced, but they didn't last) to feed the sealing and whaling gangs, the settlers and the castaways.

The larger animals chomped on and trampled over the native plants, killed the birds, destroyed their nesting habitats and broke their eggs. The rabbits on Enderby Island also dug burrows that became death-traps for the local sea lion pups, which toppled into the holes and suffocated.

However, from the 1970s a strategic and systematic eradication of introduced pests began to be carried out,

An Auckland Island feral goat, once part of the world's most southerly goat population, photographed in the 1970s. Goats were introduced to the Auckland Islands during the 1800s to feed sailors and castaways, but the remaining population was eradicated from the main island in the early 1990s. They are now extinct.

The silver-grey Enderby Island rabbits (now eradicated from the island) are one of the world's rarest rabbit breeds. Twelve rabbits were introduced by the HMCS *Victoria* of Australia in 1865 as a source of food for future castaways. By the time of eradication, there were estimated to be several thousand on Enderby Island. A few dozen of the species, thought to have originated from the British Silver Grey breed but evolved during 130 years of isolation, were rescued by the NZ Rare Breeds Society and transported to the New Zealand mainland.

involving methods that included shooting, trapping and dropping poison baits.

Enderby Island has been officially predator-free since 2001, after the cattle and rabbits were removed or exterminated in the 1990s. The New Zealand Rare Breeds Society rescued some of the introduced species, which had evolved over time to adapt to the harsh conditions. The Enderby Island cattle, for example (isolated for decades after being abandoned in the early 1900s when pastoral farming failed), developed longer bodies and shorter legs, and also acquired a taste for seaweed.[3]

Campbell Island was declared predator-free in 2006, and its rat-free status was a world first for a large island. The Snares and Bounties managed to sidestep long-term introduced predators, as did Adams Island.

In June 2016, there was a 'Million Dollar Mouse' blitz on the Antipodes Islands to rid them of mice, the only introduced pest on the islands. The campaign involved public fundraising with donations matched by the Morgan Foundation, and with support from the Department of Conservation, Island Conservation, and World Wildlife Fund NZ. There were two bait drops involving 65,000 kilograms (64 tons) of Pestoff cereal bait by two helicopters during the subantarctic winter. In 2018, the project was declared to be a success.[4]

New Zealand's and Australia's subantarctic islands have

ABOVE The megaherb *Anisotome latifolia*, or 'Auckland Islands carrot', growing on Enderby Island. Megaherbs have unusually large leaves and are endemic to the subantarctic region.

LEFT *Pleurophyllum speciosum*, or 'Campbell Island daisy'.

become examples to the world of what can be achieved in terms of predator eradication. However, the battle is not over yet: an estimated 1000 pigs still need to be eradicated from Auckland Island, as well as mice and a small number of feral cats. The impact of these introduced animals is noticeable, with trampled vegetation and fewer birds and nesting areas than on the nearby, predator-free Enderby Island. In early 2017, a project leader was announced and planning is now underway to eradicate the remaining predators. It will be a case of last but certainly not least: Auckland Island is Australasia's largest subantarctic island, 42 kilometres long and 23 kilometres wide (24 x 14 miles), with 50,000 hectares (123,000 acres) of steep, boggy terrain and dense forest scrub. Its southern and western coasts are constantly battered by ferocious waves, whipped up by frequent southwesterly gales.

Protecting the natives

The native plant life on the predator-free subantarctic islands is thriving, but sadly that's not always the case for the wildlife. New Zealand (formerly Hooker's) sea lions and yellow-eyed penguins (hoiho) are still endangered for a variety of reasons, including fisheries bycatch, food limitations, diseases, changing ocean temperatures, and predators. Fisheries also pose a threat to some species of albatross, which spend most of their lives at sea and are slow breeders. Over 85 per cent of the world's albatross species live on the world's subantarctic islands.

The southern right whale population is slowly recovering, according to observations conducted in 2017 around the Auckland Islands, a winter-time breeding zone for the rare mammals. These days, the use of drones makes whale-surveying more straightforward than it used to be and the footage is mesmerizing.[5]

From about the time of the new millennium, marine reserves were created to protect the local sea life from fisheries and a few name changes took place. In 1998, The Snares became Snares Islands/Tini Heke ('tiniheke' in Māori means 'to delude, or deceive'). The Auckland Islands Marine Reserve was established in 2002 for 12 nautical miles (i.e. 22 surrounding kilometres) and renamed Auckland Islands/Motu Maha ('multiple islands' in Māori). In 2014, Campbell Island's marine reserve was created and the main island was renamed Campbell Island/Motu Ihupuku ('island of the fur seal'). The Antipodes Island/Moutere Mahue Marine Reserve was also created in 2014 ('moutere mahue' means 'abandoned islands') and so was the Bounty Islands/Moutere Hauriri Marine Reserve ('hauriri' means 'angry wind').[6]

Historic sites: protect or abandon?

There is so much human history on these remote specks of land that it raises a conservation conundrum: should the islands' historic sites be preserved as memorials and because they're of interest to tourists, or left to decay in favour of the natural environment?

A big part of the conundrum is the time and money required for such restoration work and maintenance. Is it worth putting resources into areas that are seldom visited, to maintain bits of wood that were never made to last?

Currently there's a 'compromise' approach. Access to sites is restricted and many of the New Zealand subantarctic islands' historic sites are maintained by the Department of Conservation (e.g. Hardwicke Cemetery, with its six graves, the Stella Hut on Enderby Island, the depot on Antipodes Island, and a couple of the coastwatcher lookout huts on Auckland Island).[7] However, others (including the coastwatching bases, the *Grafton* wreck, and the Victoria Tree) are now in a badly decayed state. Meanwhile, historic sites such as the abandoned pastoral farms and the Hardwicke settlement are being slowly swallowed up by the peaty earth and the forest. Apart from the *Derry Castle* memorial plaque on Enderby Island, there is no memorial for the many shipwreck victims of the Auckland Islands.

On Macquarie Island, tourist access to protected wildlife areas and historic sites is also tightly restricted, maintained by Tasmania Parks & Wildlife Services, and enforced by the rangers who live on the island.

Fencing and sheep shooting

The gradual eradication of predators from New Zealand's and Australia's subantarctic islands has involved many conservationists and scientists over the years, including Dr Christopher Robertson. Robertson has worked as an ornithologist for more than 40 years, and in 2008 he was awarded the Queen's Service Medal for services to ornithology. He has spent much of his life working on remote, inhospitable islands, often clinging to steep rocks in howling winds and driving rain, to study the habits and habitats of rare birds.

In the early days of his scientific career, Robertson worked with Sir Robert Falla and Sir Charles Fleming (both former World War II subantarctic coastwatchers), as well as the pioneer ornithologist Lance Richdale, who fought for the protection of southern birds including albatrosses and hoiho.

In the 1970s and 1980s, part of Robertson's role at the Wildlife Service was to monitor birds on remote offshore islands and help others to get rid of the introduced animals that were threatening the birds' habitats, including the feral sheep on Campbell Island. For many decades after the Tucker Cove farm was abandoned there was political debate about whether or not to eradicate the sheep, which were running wild and increasing in number after an initial decline when the farm closed. By the late 1960s, there were estimated to be about 3000 sheep on the island.[8]

The sheep eradication was an epic project that lasted for two decades, involving many people and organizations. A couple of very long fences were built to divide the task into three stages. In 1970, a 2.2-kilometre (1.3-mile) fence was built across Campbell Island by NZ Wildlife Service and the Lands and Survey Department. The

ABOVE Light-mantled
sooty albatross.

RIGHT Campbell Island
sheep looking towards
Dent Island, 1970.

1300 sheep on the northern side of the fence were shot with
.22 long rifles, and 800 photographs were taken across the
island to record before-and-after changes to the vegetation.

In 1984, a second fence was built by Lands and Survey
from North West Bay to the South Coast preparatory and

Fencing and sheep shooting party, Campbell Island, January–February 1970. Chris Robertson is standing at the back, with a pipe.

a similar number of sheep were shot on the south-western side of the island. The remaining sheep were culled in the late 1980s, along with the few dozen remaining cattle (leaving a feast for the scavenging skuas). The gradual fencing of the island also provided time to measure the difference made to the vegetation and birdlife when no sheep were present.

While animal lovers might baulk at the idea of systematically culling thousands of sheep, Robertson points out that it was simply what had to be done to restore the islands and protect the native wildlife.

> 'It needed doing, so we did it. You don't necessarily want to do it, but that's part of the job. [The time that the sheep were introduced] was part of an era when people thought they could control things.'[9]

Wildlife teams initially stayed in the old World War II coastwatchers' camp in Tucker Cove Valley, as one hut was still standing (more or less) in the early 1970s. The hut was not heated and the glass windows had all fallen out. Blowflies were irritatingly ubiquitous. Showers were permitted weekly over at the Beeman Cove met station, but there was always the risk of falling into a seal wallow during the long walk back to

the hut. The men put up some plastic sheeting to keep out the wind and the blowflies, but living conditions were far from palatial and they worked outside through hail, rain and gales, building fences and shooting sheep across the 112 square kilometre (43 square mile) island. 'We never got totally dry on Campbell,' recalls Robertson. 'We didn't bother putting on dry socks in the morning because they'd be wet within 20 minutes.' They quickly learned that it was a good idea to have 'a tot of whisky' after a long day of field work.

It wasn't quite '*hasta la vista*' for all of the Campbell Island sheep, though. A dozen were later saved for the Rare Breeds Conservation Society in New Zealand, who valued the sheep for their unique genetic qualities (developed over several decades of isolation), including lack of foot-rot, the ability to self-shed their wool, and their resistance to certain diseases.[10] Today there are still about 30 Campbell Island sheep in existence, but not on Campbell Island; they live on a farm in the South Island. The rare sheep made international headlines in 2017, when five pregnant ewes were slaughtered by unidentified vandals.

'TEAM RAT'

No one, however, had any interest in preserving the tens of thousands of Norway rats running riot across Campbell Island and killing the native birds. In 2001, 120 tonnes of cereal bait containing the toxin Brodifacoum was dropped over the

A southern royal
albatross guards its nest.

entire island during a month in winter by the Department of
Conservation as part of the world's largest rodent eradication
project, involving 19 people (and hundreds more offsite),
many years of planning, and four helicopters flying almost 700
kilometres (435 miles) south of New Zealand into potentially
difficult weather. The project's chief helicopter pilot, Peter
Garden, was later made an Officer of the New Zealand Order
of Merit for services to aviation and conservation.[11]

The bait-drop blitz worked, and in 2006 the island was
officially declared to be predator-free (once the rats were gone,
the cats died out naturally). Pete McClelland, who managed the
rat eradication project for the Department of Conservation,
says it was four times the size of anything attempted previously:
'People said it couldn't be done, but it led the way for other
eradications, like on Macquarie.' (As well as the Falklands,
South Georgia Island and the Galápagos Islands.)[12]

BIRDWATCHING AT THE ENDS OF THE EARTH

Conservation work on subantarctic islands wasn't just about
terminating unwanted species, however. In the 1970s there
was also a large-scale bird-banding project for southern royal
albatrosses to measure the birds' ocean range and feeding
area. Albatrosses travel thousands of kilometres across the
open sea, and some banded juvenile birds were recovered on

the coast of Chile within four days of departing Campbell Island.

These days scientists can attach satellite transmitters and GPS trackers to birds for real-time data, and drones can be used to access and film remote areas. But back in the 1970s and 1980s, it was one bird and one band at a time. Small albatrosses/mollymawks often favour steep clifftop locations for nesting, on isolated islands surrounded by wild, inhospitable seas, so Robertson had some logistically challenging and hair-raising workdays.

Did he sometimes long for civilization during these cold and remote expeditions?

'It was just a different "office" for a time … Most modern expeditions wouldn't live in the sort of conditions that we lived in, but that was part of being there at those times. I was one of the last to do extreme island operations in a tent. Now they need huts and helicopters!'

THE TEAL TACKLE

Such dedicated field work sometimes yielded immense rewards, especially during one particular encounter in 1975. Robertson was exploring Dent Island, a tiny island 2 kilometres (1.2 miles) off Campbell Island, with fellow Wildlife Service officer Rodney Russ when Russ spotted what he initially thought was a rat scuttling through the dense tussock.

Both men then realized to their delight that it was a female Campbell Island flightless teal, a bird that many had believed to be extinct. Only the isolated location of Dent Island, which acted as a natural quarantine zone, had saved a few of the species from the thousands of egg-guzzling, nest-destroying Norway rats that had been residing on Campbell Island since the early 1800s.

Russ leapt into the tussock and emerged triumphantly holding one of the world's rarest ducks. She was safely stored inside a pair of Robertson's nylon overtrousers, which he deftly knotted at the bottom of each leg to secure the bird in a sort of makeshift carrier bag, and the two men returned to Campbell Island to show the others.

A few of the estimated 50 teal on Dent Island were later transported to a wildlife sanctuary in New Zealand for a captive breeding programme. After the rats were eradicated from Campbell Island in the early 2000s, 150 teal were released there over three years and they are slowly increasing in number (there are now estimated to be over 500). Today they can be spotted sedately cruising around the shoreline of Perseverance Harbour.[13]

ONE OF THE WORLD'S MOST REMOTE CAMP SITES

Former Department of Scientific and Industrial Research (DSIR) scientist Rowley Taylor was another 'extreme' expeditioner of the 1970s. Taylor and Robertson worked

Wildlife Service ranger Rodney Russ holding the rediscovered Campbell Island flightless teal, Dent Island, 1975.

together on a number of subantarctic expeditions, and both camped on the rugged Antipodes Islands during the 1978 BAAS (Bounty, Antipodes, Auckland and Snares) Expedition, which was organized by the Wildlife Service and involved 26 scientists. Taylor recalls:

'We had no concerns for health and safety. [At the Antipodes] we didn't have life jackets, we had a clinker [wooden] dinghy and a Zodiac inflatable … Even I was worried about it, we didn't have a spare motor in case something went wrong … but that's just what we did.'[14]

To the untrained eye, the Bounty Islands are little more than a group of wind-blasted rocks. Nevertheless, during the BAAS Expedition Robertson spent two further weeks camping on one of them (Proclamation Island) in a small tent, which he had specially made to ensure it held fast in severe weather.

He was there to study the local birdlife, along with fellow scientists Don Horning and Gerry van Tets. The three men — who jokingly referred to themselves during the expedition as the 'New Zealand governor' (Robertson), the 'American ambassador' (Horning), and the 'Australian ambassador' (van Tets) because of their respective nationalities and their sole

occupation of the archipelago — were the first people to camp on the Bounty Islands in at least 100 years.[15]

During their short residency they named several parts of the islands, including Bradley's Cove, named after the colourful Captain Ian Bradley of HMNZS *Waikato*, the ship that delivered them to their remote outpost. On arrival, Bradley dressed himself over his wetsuit in a Royal Navy lieutenant's uniform circa 1870, and rolled out a scroll to declare the Bounties for Her Majesty in a 'proper' re-enactment of a similar but ship-based proclamation a century earlier. He then proceeded to go diving, almost drowned, and had to be fished out of the water by Horning — hence the cove's name in Bradley's honour.[16]

But even during such a far-flung scientific expedition, administrative matters had to be dealt with. While camping on the Bounties, Robertson cast his Special Vote in the New Zealand 1978 General Election and it was delivered 800 kilometres (500 miles) back to the mainland by the HMNZS *Waikato*, along with the votes of Campbell Island staff. Every vote counts, including subantarctic votes.

OPPOSITE TOP & MIDDLE
Camping on Antipodes Island next to the old castaway depot, which was repaired and upgraded into a research hut during the 1978 BAAS Expedition.

OPPOSITE BOTTOM
Camping on the Bounties, 1978.

ABOVE
Captain Ian Bradley of HMNZS *Waikato* re-enacting the 1870 proclamation.

WORKING IN THE WILDERNESS

There were certain challenges that came with working on remote islands during the 1970s and 1980s: for example, frequently tramping down steep, uneven hills resulted in a painful condition known as 'subantarctic knee'.

It also wasn't unheard of to get caught in the mist that drifts over Campbell Island's hills, relying on human footprints or sheep tracks for navigation. Attempts at clever 'shortcuts' during field trips could also backfire, resulting in startling encounters with barking sea lions, getting caught in sleet and gales, and eventually a wet, cold and tired return to the expedition base at midnight.

Of course, scientific expeditions weren't supposed to be holidays. It was work and it was worth the discomfort, says Robertson; they were part of a new frontier of scientific discovery.

'It was a pioneering age ... such an interesting time! Back in those days, not much of anything was known so there were a lot of discoveries. Even now, I'm still surprised at what an interesting group I was associated with. There weren't many of them [in the Wildlife Service] but they were a team, and they're still a team — they still have reunions.'

As with all expeditions to remote locations, there were disparate personalities and dynamics to manage. But ultimately, Robertson says, it was about everyone banding together as equals: 'When you're in trouble halfway up a cliff, you can't pull rank!'

Tracking whales and tagging seals

Nadine Gibbs (now Bott) 'summered' — and wintered — multiple times on the Auckland Islands and Campbell Island in the late 1990s. As a marine ecologist, she did everything from anaesthetizing to performing autopsies on New Zealand sea lions, tagging pups, counting yellow-eyed penguins (hoiho), and tracking southern right whales. However, her first trip to the subantarctic islands coincided with distressing circumstances.

In 1998, what's known as a 'mass mortality event' killed off approximately 20 per cent of adult New Zealand sea lions (rāpoka in Māori) and 50 per cent of their pups at their primary breeding colonies on the Auckland Islands. All scientists knew was that something stress-related had triggered a bacterial infection that killed off a large number of one of the world's rarest seal species. (The New Zealand sea lion population is now classed as Nationally Critical, and declining.[17])

Bott was 23 and in the middle of her Master's degree at the time, studying marine anatomy, when she was shoulder-tapped by the Department of Conservation and asked if she wanted to be part of their annual sea lion research. She sailed south as a volunteer and was bedridden by seasickness, as the tiny fishing boat chartered for the 36-hour journey rolled over the giant waves of the Southern Ocean. However, on arrival at the research hut on Enderby Island, she was spellbound. 'Until you've been there, you can't comprehend the splendour of the place, the uniqueness, the wildness.'[18]

As the daughter of a wildlife conservationist, Bott had spent much of her childhood outdoors and surrounded by animals. Still, travelling to the subantarctic islands was a giant leap out of her comfort zone and her limits were constantly tested. Just a few days into the expedition she fell and broke her wrist, but didn't want to be evacuated and miss out on the rest of the trip. The doctor of a passing tourist ship plastered up the injury and she carried on.

WHALE WATCHING IN THE WINTER

Bott's marine autopsy experience came in handy during that first expedition and she was soon asked to head back to the Auckland Islands for a winter expedition to study the behaviour of southern right whales, especially mother–calf relationships.

Her job was to help with land-based tracking of the whales, using a theodolite to measure their positions in the harbour

A southern right whale off the coast of Auckland Island.

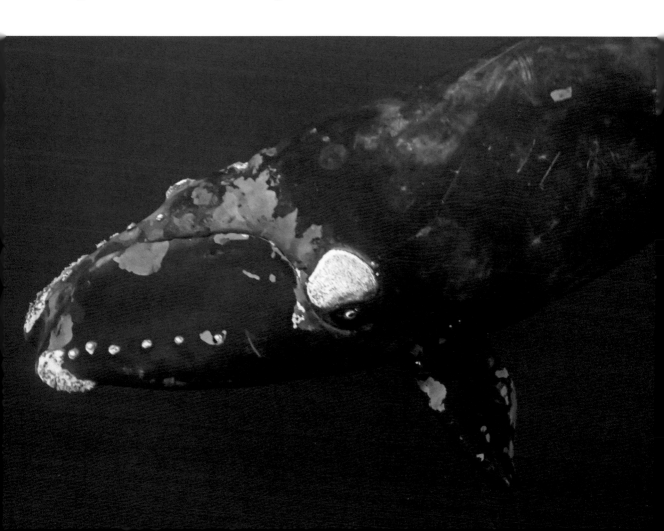

A female New Zealand sea lion ('sea cow') swims through a forest of giant kelp off Enderby Island

and deciding, based on a series of movements, whether they were travelling, socializing or breaching (rising up and breaking the surface of the water).

Each southern right whale has a unique pattern of callosities, or raised white patches, on its head, so photo IDs were used to monitor individual whales. The species can grow to over 15 metres (50 feet) long and were called 'right' whales in the 19th century because they were valued by whalers for their oil, but today they are admired for different reasons. They don't have a dorsal fin, unlike many other whale species, and Bott says they tend to be very interactive. 'The boys used to rub up against the boat, thinking we were female [whales].' However, she also discovered that southern right whales can be temperamental. One day during the expedition, the group found themselves facing a potential *Moby-Dick* situation.

'There was a mother and calf [in Laurie Harbour] and our boat must have been quite far, maybe 100 or even 200 metres (600 feet) away from her. We started up the engine and she started breaching, and came closer and closer, still breaching. We all felt the hairs rising on the back of our necks! We thought, "This has the potential to turn bad … let's get out of here!"'

UP CLOSE WITH SEA LIONS

Bott also spent a summer tagging sea cows (female sea lions) to measure how far the cows were travelling each day to provide for their young, as there was a theory that a lack of food might have contributed to the mass mortality event in 1998. Squid is a popular source of food and sea cows were having to compete with squid fisheries, venturing further out to sea and leaving their pups for longer periods. New Zealand sea lions have clearly defined gender roles. During the breeding season in summer, the females hunt for food and tend to their young while the males guard their turf on the beach, angrily and noisily defending it from other sea lions.

The tagging work was intense, says Bott. First, the team had to locate breeding females. Then they tagged the pup, weighed it and took a DNA sample. They also captured the cow in a net, with one person jumping on her back and pulling up her flippers so that she couldn't move, and another holding her head so that she couldn't turn around and bite the first person. An anaesthetic mask was quickly placed over the cow's face. Once she was sedated, a radio tag was attached to track her movements on and off the beach, as well as a satellite dive transmitter to log her 'dive profile', recording information about where she was going, how often, and the depths she reached.

New Zealand sea cows are one of hardest-working foragers in the seal world, says Bott; they can dive to great depths, but it forces them to operate at the very limit of their abilities. The study showed they were venturing far beyond the 12 nautical miles (22 kilometres) that encompasses the protected marine reserve around the Auckland Islands.

Nadine Bott with sea lion pups, Auckland Islands, 1998.

During their downtime, the expedition team would head to an area they nicknamed the 'puppy pool'. It provided them with some much-needed bonding time with the local wildlife, says Bott. 'It was where the pups played, and we'd just hang out with them. They'd come and climb over us, [and we'd be] interacting in a way that we didn't want anything from them, just being there.'

Despite hardships experienced during some of the expeditions, Bott says people's dedication didn't waver. 'The commitment and the passion was amazing. We never bucked any rules. We were just so happy to be there … we'd do whatever we could [to help].'

Working in such demanding conditions was also an opportunity for her to meet, and be mentored by, some of the bigger names in subantarctic conservation.

'The real leaders stand out and they're inspiring. One of the biggest experiences for me was meeting hard-working, passionate and capable people. It makes you feel like you can deal with anything in life after that.'

The boardwalk on Enderby Island protects the island's fragile megaherbs.

The islands' 21st-century guardians

'Subantarctic' is not a word that appears very often on business cards, but for DOC's senior subantarctic ranger, Jo Hiscock, it's another day at the office (or, sometimes, on a remote offshore island).

The Southland-based subantarctic team consists of three or four rangers who manage visitor permits, oversee quarantine regulations on subantarctic island-bound ships, work with the tourism industry, maintain the islands' infrastructure (such as the Campbell Island Col Lyall boardwalk), coordinate research projects and transport, and also perform some of their own research, such as yellow-eyed penguin surveys.

Hiscock has been senior subantarctic ranger since 2013, and has spent ten years in the subantarctic team. It's also part of Hiscock's job to help people reach New Zealand's subantarctic islands if they want to go there, by putting them in touch with boats that need more passengers — a sort of expedition matchmaking service. However, Hiscock says

that while she has noticed a gradual increase in *awareness* of New Zealand's subantarctic islands (locally and globally), that hasn't resulted in more people actually wanting to hop on a ship and travel there. 'There's a highly variable number of visitors each year, but there's not an upward trend in visitors, and it usually depends on research that's being done.'[19]

Research funding is increasingly hard to come by, however. Hiscock says that although there are more subantarctic research projects running these days (studying the local wildlife populations, the effects of climate change, and the impact of fisheries, for example), they tend to have a lifespan of just a year or so, which is a much shorter duration than they used to be. And because annual variation can be quite high, the data collected won't always be an accurate snapshot. (One exception is a long-term study of wandering albatrosses, undertaken for more than two decades on Antipodes and Adams islands by scientists Kath Walker and Graeme Elliott.)

A yellow-eyed penguin (hoiho), Enderby Island. New Zealand's Yellow-Eyed Penguin Trust works with DOC to monitor and protect the endangered species.

RARE AND VULNERABLE

Hiscock has taken part in several yellow-eyed penguin (hoiho) surveys over the years. Yellow-eyed penguins are one of the world's rarest penguin species and in New Zealand are classed as 'Nationally Endangered' with small populations at the bottom of the South Island, on Rakiura/Stewart Island and adjacent islands, and also a genetically distinct population on Campbell Island and the Auckland Islands. Threats to the subantarctic yellow-eyed penguins include predation at sea by sea lions and fur seals, diseases and fisheries bycatch.[20]

It's tricky to form a clear picture of trends from the remote subantarctic population, says Hiscock, due to 'incomplete' counts in previous decades that were restricted to limited breeding areas. The penguins are also wanderers, taking turns to hunt in the ocean and nesting in well-concealed areas — including in dense forests on the Auckland Islands and tall tussock on Campbell, as well as on exposed cliffs— so locating and counting breeding pairs can be a challenge.

GPS tracking should make it easier to monitor the penguins in future and Hiscock says a large proportion of the penguins on Enderby Island now have transponders (little glass microchips) attached. But the overall population seems to be declining: there are now thought to be just 250 breeding pairs on the New Zealand mainland.[21]

PERMIT ONLY

For human visitors, exploring the subantarctic islands is not the free-for-all experience that it once was. Since the removal of many of the introduced predators, access to most areas is tightly restricted to allow the islands' native plants and animals to recover.

Technically the islands are also no-fly zones, so flights are saved for emergencies or as part of what Hiscock calls 'sensible research', such as aerial surveys. The islands are still remote, but 'not as remote as they used to be' — for example, it takes two-and-a-half hours to reach the Auckland Islands by helicopter from New Zealand's South Island, assuming the weather is favourable. The Snares, Aucklands and Campbell Island are all within helicopter range, and Enderby and Campbell both have fuel depots for re-tanking. In a practical sense, fuel has replaced the coffee, tobacco and woollen clothing of the old provisions depots.

However, it's a different story for the Antipodes and Bounties, which are about 800 kilometres (500 miles) away from New Zealand's South Island. If an emergency happened there, a ship (often a naval ship, as the NZ Navy supports DOC research trips) would have to travel a good portion of that distance to be within helicopter range. But DOC staff working in the subantarctic region are trained to be self-sufficient. They understand that if they break a leg, evacuation could take up to two or three days depending on the weather and the location.

Senior Subantarctic Ranger Jo Hiscock on the 'little marbles', the Bounty Islands.

CHANGING WATERS

Hiscock has spent time on all of New Zealand's subantarctic islands and enjoys their unique characteristics, but she has a soft spot for one of the lesser-known and least-visited groups.

> *'The Bounties are absolutely magic. They're little granite rocks full of seals and albatrosses and prions; each of those rocks is taken up by something. They're teeming with wildlife, little marbles in the ocean, in the middle of nowhere. It's really cool.'*

But there are shifts happening in the subantarctic ecosystem, Hiscock says, and the impact is noticeable on the islands' wildlife. 'It's hard to pinpoint the impact of fisheries, shifting ocean currents, and also climate change — all factors that could be affecting food supplies.' The scientific world is watching these small islands in the middle of the ocean, UNESCO World Heritage sites that are paradoxically fierce and fragile, to see what will happen next. They are considered to be pure and almost completely untouched, but for how long? The islands' rare, endemic plants and wildlife depend on them for survival, and decisions made today could affect their future.

Ultimately, it's a matter of securing the funds for more research, says Hiscock, which will hopefully tell us how to keep protecting these wonderfully unique little dots at the end of the world. 'They're so full of wildlife, full of history, valuable for research and so untouched … they are absolute gems.'

13. TOURISM
The minister, the comic artist, and the descendant (1968–today)

IN 1936, WHEN HE WAS WRITING THE FINAL PAGES of his doctoral thesis on the history of the Auckland Islands (published posthumously in 1948), Fergus McLaren concluded:

> '[A]s far as can be seen, the islands will have no future history. The bleak climate, the unproductive soil, and the isolation of the Auckland Islands under the changed conditions of a modern world, suggest that, in the loneliness of the Sub-Antarctic Ocean, they will be "world forgetting, by the world forgot".'

Well, he was partly right; the isolation of New Zealand's and Australia's subantarctic islands has resulted in relatively few visitors (and no residents, apart from the rotating staff on Macquarie Island) since the closing of the New Zealand coastwatching and meteorological stations in 1945 and 1995 respectively. Despite the marvels of modern technology, there's still really only one way to reach most of the subantarctic islands: by sailing across the wild, open sea.

Unless you happen to be the pilot of a rescue helicopter or conducting aerial research, 99.99 per cent of visitors still travel the old-fashioned way, using the same turbulent over-water method as the sealers, whalers and early explorers did two centuries ago. Because of this, it generally takes longer to travel from New Zealand or Australia to the subantarctic islands than it does to reach London Heathrow by plane.

Who can go there?

Because of their remoteness, but also to protect them, the subantarctic islands are only visited by a small handful of scientists, conservationists and tourists each year.

The islands are UNESCO World Heritage sites, so visitor numbers are strictly capped.

Australia's Macquarie Island is managed by Tasmania Parks & Wildlife Service, and tourists can visit with a permit — but you'll be taking a gamble with the weather. There's always a possibility that you'll arrive only to find that the swells are too rough to permit landing. (Still, you'll see plenty of the unique wildlife from the ship.)

Meanwhile, fewer than 1000 people a year are allowed to visit New Zealand's subantarctic islands, although the exact number fluctuates year on year depending on the number of research projects and Antarctic expeditions. Department of Conservation permits can be issued for a fee, and a DOC representative must be on board the ship.[2]

Only a handful of areas can be visited on Auckland, Enderby and Campbell islands, with varying annual quotas depending on the site. Visits to The Snares and Antipodes Island involve circuits around the coastlines only, if the weather allows for it, with no stepping on land (aside from DOC-approved research programmes). The Bounties are deemed too rough for small boats, but can be viewed from a ship at a safe distance.

There are also strict quarantine and biohazard rules. All pockets and bags must be checked and vacuumed, and shoes must be scrubbed and treated each time a new island is visited. A rogue seed or insect hitching a ride (not to mention a mouse) could cause irreparable harm. But plants and insects aren't the only potential threats, and human visitors are a mixed blessing. Much of the conservation work is government-funded, but tourism is also necessary to fund research, upgrades and site maintenance (and to help people learn about the islands). On the other hand, too many visitors could disturb the wildlife and negatively impact on the islands' fragile ecosystems.

The voyage is also not for the faint-hearted. The climate can be hostile, the terrain is rough (apart from Enderby and Campbell islands' boardwalks), and no one is immune to danger. In 2003, an expedition group of 15 people, including two New Zealand mayors and Conservation Minister Chris Carter, found themselves stranded on Adams Island, the southernmost island of the Aucklands, after the weather took a sudden turn for the worse and their planned chopper pick-up had to be cancelled. Instead, they had to trek for several challenging hours (including wading across an icy, thigh-high river) to reach the shore for evacuation by boat. Several people lacked adequate clothing for the conditions, and were wet and shivering by the time they were rescued in the late evening.[3]

The history of subantarctic tourism

Despite the risks of a hostile climate and open-sea travel (or maybe because of them), subantarctic tourism isn't a recent development. Curious people of all ages, including politicians' families, began visiting the islands in the 1880s as paying passengers on government steamships during their semi-annual trips south to check for castaways and seal poachers. There was a 40-year visitor lag after 1927, when the castaway rescue

A light-mantled sooty albatross soars in the late afternoon sun, Campbell Island.

The locals greeting a tourist ship, Auckland Islands.

missions ceased, and then dedicated tourist ships started heading south from the late 1960s thanks to Lindblad Travel, a New York-based travel agency.

However, it wasn't until the late 1980s that subantarctic tourism became a regular business, partly due to biologist Rodney Russ (the Campbell Island teal discoverer) and his family business Heritage Expeditions, originally called Southern Heritage Tours. The company combines tourism with conservation and education by employing historians, wildlife photographers and scientists as expedition guides. Public awareness of the subantarctic islands was growing in the late-20th century, thanks to TV wildlife documentaries, advertising and conservation organizations.[4] The islands were also a convenient stopover for ships en route to Antarctica.

Getting away from it all

The remoteness of the islands is a drawcard for a hardy few who want to explore the unique plants and wildlife, visit the scenes of human triumph and tragedy, or simply get away from the chaos and pressures of everyday life. On the islands there are no traffic jams, no gloom-and-doom news reports, no eternal scrolling through social media feeds, and no meetings, appointments or deadlines.

Instead, there is a constant need for flexibility and spontaneity. In an era when travel can be carefully planned down to the finest detail through agents and peer-review websites, the subantarctic islands don't allow for any of that. After all, how do you rate an albatross, check into a non-existent hotel, or follow a daily itinerary when the weather can change from bright sunshine to fierce hailstorm in a matter of minutes?

Because of the time spent sailing across the open sea just to reach the islands, the limited time on land also passes very quickly — as the scientist and writer W.H. Guthrie-Smith expressed so passionately in 1936 after a fleeting visit to the Antipodes Islands.

'Alas! that there should not have been days, weeks, months to be spent when there were only hours … Oh! If only on the Antipodes Islands I could have recovered days sad in the loneliness of cities, wasted in futilities, squandered in the daily ineptitudes of life.'[5]

How to get there

There are half a dozen concessionaires and most of them travel for a small window of time during the subantarctic 'summer' (November to February). Heritage Expeditions began as a small family business, and today is still one of very few companies in the world running organized tours to New Zealand's and Australia's subantarctic islands. It's also possible to visit on a privately chartered boat or volunteer for a research trip; a good place to start is to get in touch with DOC's Southland office in New Zealand, or Tasmania Parks & Wildlife Service in Australia.

Who are the people choosing to part with their hard-earned cash to sail over turbulent seas in order to visit remote, wild islands? As it turns out, there's a range of ages, nationalities and motives. Some tourists are birdwatchers or botanists. Others are history buffs or just have a keen sense of adventure. Reclining on a tropical sun lounger with a cocktail in hand simply isn't their preferred holiday option. They want to get away from it all, but also have an adventure and learn something new. They want to be tested and inspired. Their families often think they are mad.

DEREK LIGHTBOURNE, MINISTER AND BOTANY ENTHUSIAST

Derek Lightbourne describes himself as an 'active retiree'. Now in his mid-seventies, he has voyaged to the islands of the Southern Ocean three times in the last ten years. Along with his many years of serving in the church, he always had a strong interest in travel and the outdoors. On retirement, he resolved to 'do the best first'; for him, this meant visiting the remote islands he had read so much about in history books, as well as experiencing the unique plants and wildlife of the islands.

Lightbourne was apprehensive at the beginning of his first expedition, sailing south by himself in 2007 and encountering the rough seas, but says the journey changed him forever.[6]

> *'It was like an imprint in my life, that's how I would describe it. For quite a long time after, I lived the experience. For example, I'd go to the beach and see seagulls but in my mind's eye they looked like albatrosses, or see a yellow flower and it looked like the* Bulbinella.'

During his first expedition Lightbourne also made it to Macquarie Island, for which he needed to produce his New Zealand passport twice (when the ship departed from and returned to New Zealand) for inspection by an Australian Customs official. The highlight, however, was being surrounded by all the penguins.

> *'They were in the hundreds of thousands. Down there [on Macquarie], the colourful king and royal penguins are in abundance. I was sitting on the beach because they say to go no closer than 5 metres [16 feet], but if they come up to you, that's fine. Well, they did, they were very curious. The smell was strong, it came out to meet you as you arrived at shore.'*

Lightbourne's second expedition south, in 2016, had an unexpected focus on the islands' history with Rodney Russ as expedition leader and a Hardwicke descendant (me) on board the ship.

> *'Walking on the islands brought a strong sense of the presence of history. Sitting on the beach at Sandy Bay on Enderby Island, I thought of the Hardwicke settlers farming on the island and their families playing on the beach, and also the desperate castaways [15 years later] walking along the same beach in search of food and awaiting rescue.'*

Having been enriched by his expeditions south, and eager to share his knowledge of a seldom-visited part of the world, Lightbourne regularly gives slideshow lectures to local retirement and garden groups about the islands' history and their unique flora and fauna. His audiences are fascinated, but are also emphatic that they will never go

there: 'People say: "I'd love to visit, but … you wouldn't get me on that ship!"'

Derek Lightbourne with the royal penguins and elephant seals on Macquarie Island.

GISELLE CLARKSON, COMIC ARTIST

Every year, Heritage Expeditions' Enderby Trust offers a handful of scholarships (heavily subsidized trips) for people aged between 18 and 30 wanting to travel to New Zealand's and Australia's remote offshore islands. To be eligible, applicants need to explain in 400 words why they want to visit the islands and what they plan to do with their acquired knowledge after they return from the expedition.

New Zealand illustrator and comic artist Giselle Clarkson was one of the 2016 scholarship winners. In late 2016, at the age of 27, she visited The Snares, the Auckland Islands, Campbell Island, Antipodes Island, the Bounties, Chatham

Island and Macquarie Island — an intrepid and enlightening voyage through the Roaring Forties and Furious Fifties that most people will never experience.

Clarkson's interest in New Zealand's and Australia's offshore islands wasn't new. She'd always been interested in conservation work, enjoyed hiking and had studied photography, so before long these experiences combined to see her start creating conservation-themed comics, sharing stories about New Zealand plants and wildlife. When applications opened for the Enderby Trust Scholarships in 2016, Clarkson submitted her entry as an illustrated essay. In her application, she included her plans for spreading the word about conservation in comic form after she returned. It worked: she was rewarded with a coveted place on the *Spirit of Enderby*'s 19-day 'Birding Down Under' expedition.

For Clarkson, every part of the journey was incredible:

> 'I got just as much out of … travelling on a ship, and the people and the situations you end up in — I got as much out of that as getting right up close to the albatrosses, seeing the rafts of penguins, and seeing Hardwicke and Enderby … The whole experience was life-changing.'[7]

Thanks to social media, her resulting artwork has gained plenty of attention. Since returning from the expedition Clarkson has created non-fiction comics and illustrations about the subantarctic islands for several organizations, including a large, multi-page feature in the *New Zealand School Journal*, a series distributed nationwide to primary and intermediate schools. Clarkson says she particularly enjoys presenting stories about the islands to a younger audience: 'You can be funny and goofy, you can get excited about it. I want kids to care. If the kids are into it, you get their parents swept up in the same thing!'

There was plenty of inspiration for her comics during the trip. At Macquarie Island (even though they couldn't disembark from the ship due to rough weather) she saw king and royal penguins on the beach, orca whales circling the coast, and snow covering the hills in mid-summer. The Snares, Antipodes and Bounty Islands all have landing restrictions, but she explored some of their coastlines in a Zodiac and saw a fascinating array of rare and endemic birds. The 'Birding Down Under' expedition attracts dedicated birdwatchers from all around the world, clutching checklists with hundreds or even thousands of bird species to tick off. Their dogged determination and enthusiasm left an impression on Clarkson.

> 'None of them were going to miss out. Even those that got really seasick, they'd spend the entire day on the [ship's] bridge … If they missed a single bird, if there was some rare bird that came flying past the ship and they missed it, they'd never have forgiven themselves!'

Giselle Clarkson meets the eastern rockhopper penguins (and vice-versa) on Antipodes Island.

For those who specialized in penguin-watching, they needed to see just a couple more species to complete their checklists (there are 17 recognized penguin species in the world).

'We got to the Antipodes, and for some people those were the last two species in the world they had to see, so when they saw the erect-crested penguins and eastern rockhoppers everyone cheered and there were rounds of applause and [cries of] "Whiskeys in the bar!"'

Each year when Enderby Trust Scholarship applications open, Facebook and Twitter fire up with posts, likes and shares from conservation groups and previous recipients. Clarkson isn't surprised.

'People who have been [to the islands] on a scholarship are like, "It's open! Go! What are you doing? Apply, apply!" They write posts about how it changed their lives, put their careers in a completely different direction. Basically, that it was the defining point that made other stuff happen ... It's a big thing. You want to keep shouting about it.'

My story

I grew up with the tale of my stoic ancestors and their challenging time in the ill-fated town of Hardwicke, and for several years I had toyed with the idea of going to the Auckland Islands myself. But day-to-day life distracted me; I lived in a bustling city, and like many other people I was juggling work and young children. Visiting the subantarctic islands seemed like a distant pipe dream, a Shackletonesque ambition best left to others.

Besides, I wasn't sure that going there would be a sensible idea. I'd read so many tragic stories about the islands; what if all the gloom somehow infiltrated my system, or my ship got wrecked on a reef? What would Raynal, the *Grafton* castaway, have written as a review of the islands on TripAdvisor? 'Zero stars; would not visit again.'

Still, I was fascinated by the remote, ecologically unique subantarctic islands. Being a writer by profession I'd decided to write a book about them, but I knew I couldn't describe them convincingly without going there. Besides, I was curious to see my great-great grandmother's unusual birthplace and go somewhere that very few people had visited, yet was actually a part of New Zealand. I wouldn't even need my passport!

I started making vague, 'next year' plans, and someone I spoke with suggested that I contact Heritage Expeditions owner Rodney Russ to ask if he would be leading a trip down to the islands in a year's time. I'd heard a lot about Russ, a conservationist and guide with a lifelong interest the subantarctic islands, and there were rumours of his imminent retirement. I knew it might be my only chance to go with him.

I casually typed a quick email about my family history, my wish to visit the Hardwicke site in a year's time, and my plan to write a book about the islands. Russ is a man of the sea, so I'd hoped to hear back in six months, if ever. Instead, he replied immediately with just one sentence: 'What's your phone number?'

Our short conversation proved to be life-changing: 'You can come along on our "Forgotten Islands" expedition next week if you like, we have a spare berth.'

'Yes please!' I replied, feeling thrilled. However, after hanging up, anxiety consumed me. Did I really want to drop everything and sail south for a week with strangers, having no contact with my family? No, I couldn't do it. I wasn't ready; it was too soon.

I wrote an email turning down the offer, and felt immense relief.

But when I woke up the next day, my relief had turned to regret. It wasn't how I used to live my life, saying no because I was scared. During my pre-children years I had leapt out of planes, jumped off bridges and trekked through the jungles of Borneo. Besides, would I really be any more 'ready' in a year's time? Who was to say the opportunity would even still be there?

In her 1997 book *Wake of the Invercauld*, castaway descendant Madelene Ferguson Allen wrote about her personal reasons for travelling from Canada to the Auckland Islands: 'Life is to be lived, and I was … tired of the routine of life. Here was the chance of a real-life adventure, to go to the ends of the earth with a purpose.'[8] I felt the same way; my life was great, but I couldn't remember the last time I had taken a giant leap outside my comfort zone.

I wrote back to Rodney Russ and asked if I could come after all. Yes, he replied, but please don't keep changing your mind … !

It was mid-December, so while everyone around me was hanging tinsel, wrapping Christmas presents and spending their spare time at the beach, I was hurriedly stuffing thermal and waterproof clothing into a backpack. The packing list was daunting: gumboots, hiking boots, thermals, balaclava, gloves, hats, rain and wind jacket … I had to borrow most of the recommended items, having never visited anywhere as cold, rugged or isolated as the subantarctic islands.

My friends and family were all excited and tremendously supportive, although not everyone understood where I was going. 'Will you stay in a lodge when you get there?' someone asked.

I flew down to Invercargill, a place I had also never been, to our meeting point at a hotel. I had no idea who else was coming, and it turned out to be all sorts of people: retired couples, science students, conservationists, a TV news crew, solo holidaymakers, and a technician coming to check the automated weather stations on Enderby and Campbell islands.

We bussed to Bluff, a tiny town at the southern tip of New Zealand, then clambered aboard the *Spirit of Enderby* (a reassuringly solid-looking, 72-metre or 230-foot icebreaker ship) for our first briefing. Russ introduced the ship's crew and some of the passengers, including me. I felt like a subantarctic-wide celebrity with my Hardwicke family background. My cabin was comfy, my room-mate was lovely, and our first dinner was three-course and restaurant quality. What had I been so worried about? This would be easy!

STORMY SEAS

Still, the butterflies hadn't quite disappeared. 'This is our last chance to abort,' a fellow passenger joked as the ship inched away from the dock. Stormy seas were predicted, and Russ euphemistically warned of an 'uncomfortable' night ahead. A parade of shipwreck images ran through my mind, and I tried to pull myself together. This was an ice-strengthened vessel sailing with GPS navigation in the 21st century, not a flimsy wooden sailboat with a drunken captain clutching a dodgy map. Surely I wouldn't beg the crew to toss me overboard, as my poor great-great-great grandmother had done on her way to Hardwicke?

And yet … once we got going, the rhythmical rocking I had naively anticipated soon felt as though I were gripping hold of a bucking bronco. 'Oh my god!' I exclaimed. 'We'd better climb into our bunks,' said Chris, my sensible and more experienced cabin mate. Meanwhile, small, unsecured items flew up and down the cabin as the ship pitched and rolled in all directions through the darkness.

My seasickness patches were not up to the challenge, and my dinner soon made an unwelcome reappearance. Fortunately, sickness bags were strategically placed around the ship for such moments. The pills I'd packed (and should have taken earlier) were more effective for the nausea, but they left me feeling drowsy and I slept a lot while we were at sea. Lying in bed was the safest, most comfortable place to be, anyway.

'Remember: when you're moving around, have one hand on the ship *at all times*,' Russ repeatedly reminded us over the intercom, and it didn't pay to be blasé. One night in the bathroom I forgot for a moment and went flying into the walk-in shower, grabbing hold of the tap for an impromptu blast of cold water overhead. Navigating from my cabin to the convivial ship's lounge involved grasping handrails when we were at sea, lurching from side to side as if I'd overindulged on the rum.

It was incredibly humbling, being surrounded on all sides by the powerful Southern Ocean with no land in sight. The waves rose several metres high (up to 16 feet) during that first memorable night. But calm seas would have been almost disappointing, and certainly anticlimactic. After all, I hadn't come for a sedate harbour cruise, I was there to experience the so-called 'liquid Himalayas' in all — or at least some — of their formidable glory.

THE 'FORGOTTEN ISLANDS'

The weather was too rough to approach The Snares by Zodiac the next day, but we were close enough to peer through binoculars at the punk-rocker-resembling Snares

crested penguins on land and admire the flocks of sooty shearwaters (also called mutton birds, or tītī), giant petrels, and albatrosses circling overhead.

'You're doing well,' one of the guides said encouragingly, as I leaned palely against the ship. But the cold air on my face felt good and the next day, once we reached the shelter of Enderby Island, I felt much better and managed some breakfast. After quarantine (washing boots, vacuuming pockets) we jumped into Zodiacs and headed to shore, where we were welcomed by 'beachmaster' sea lions lounging at Sandy Bay, waiting impatiently for their female counterparts to arrive so the breeding season could commence.

Male sea lions (bulls) are huge. They weigh about 400 kilograms (880 pounds), offer loud roars for trespassers, and have a long, glossy mane of hair. Unlike fur seals, sea lions stand upright on their flippers and 'flollop' around. We respected their personal space and photographed the yellow-eyed penguins (hoiho) that waddled down the sand dunes to meet us.

Waves pound against the northern reefs of Enderby Island, with megaherbs (*Anisotome latifolia*) in the foreground.

A friendly yellow-eyed penguin (hoiho) on Enderby Island.

Ambling along the narrow boardwalk that leads across the relatively flat island, we were surrounded on both sides by blossoming megaherbs, with stems growing up to 2 metres (more than 6 feet) tall and giant, rippled leaves that soak up the limited subantarctic sunshine. It felt like another era or even another planet, with the solitude and the exotic plants. I'm no birdwatcher, but it was still exciting to encounter rare birds, such as the subantarctic snipe, that only exist on or around the islands.

At the end of the boardwalk we found ourselves on the wind-blasted northern side of Enderby Island. We were given the option to either turn back to the beach or keep going on a five-hour, pathless trek around the island. The group split into two; I wavered. I'd never done a 'proper' hike, let alone gone off-track, but I knew it might be my only chance to roam across a subantarctic island. 'Come on!' encouraged Chris, my cabin mate. That did it; I took a deep breath, turned east, and followed the others along the gusty cliff-edge towards the unknown.

During that wild, challenging trek I saw waterfalls blown

A sea lion at the edge of the rātā forest, Enderby Island.

back upwards and pale blue frothing seas pounding at the black cliffs, the sea surging back and forth as if from a monster's mouth. No wonder there were shipwrecks, I thought; what ship would stand a chance in those waters? The ocean's merciless power is confirmed by the *Derry Castle* memorial plaque on the island for the 15 men who were killed there in 1887.

Red-crowned kākāriki parakeets flew above us, adding a colourful touch. The sun shone brightly overhead (Enderby Island is known as the 'Riviera of the subantarctic' as it receives much more sun than the other islands), and as we pushed through the scrub and over the undulating, peaty land I started peeling off my layers of cold-weather gear, feeling foolish in my thermals. Soon we entered the shade of the goblinesque rātā forest. The ground was a bed of ferns and megaherbs, and the branches were filled with the flute-like melody of bellbirds. The rātā flowers were in bloom, their orange-red blossoms framing the gnarled branches. It all felt like something out of a fairytale.

The twisted branches and megaherbs of the rātā forest.

I realized that I had been wrong in my pessimistic expectations. The islands weren't bleak (especially since I wasn't shipwrecked there); they were beautiful, one of the most beautiful places I'd encountered in my world travels. Enderby Island has been described as 'the jewel in the crown' of the subantarctic islands,[9] although the island's sharp, dramatic beauty can be tricky to capture in photos.

Experiencing the timeless quality of an uninhabited island, free from buildings or development, is also rare. What I was seeing was identical to that of R.E. Malone, who visited Hardwicke in 1852 on the *Fantome* and rowed across the harbour to explore Enderby Island: 'Landing at a cove close to a sandy beach, we walked through thick bush, stunted, twisted, and gnarled trees … '[10]

However, some things clearly *had* changed, based on Malone's casual hit-list of the local species: 'While there our fellows killed 302 toois [tui], 144 wild duck, 12 sea-lions, 6 parrots, 2 snipe, 8 bullocks and cows, and 3 calves …' (There are no cattle on the islands now, and I can say in all honesty that we shot nothing.)

THE ABANDONED TOWN IN THE MIDDLE OF NOWHERE

It was late afternoon by the time we made it back to the ship, armed with hundreds of photos, and I have never appreciated a hot shower more. However, I couldn't relax just yet; we were due to sail south the next day, and I knew that evening would probably be my one chance to visit Hardwicke, which was tantalizingly close, across Port Ross. The wind had picked up, though, and the conditions weren't looking promising. What if I couldn't go? I'd braced myself for the possibility, knowing how unpredictable the weather could be, but still … to venture south and not step ashore at the site where my great-great grandmother Harriet was born would have been so disappointing.

I needn't have worried. During dinner, Russ tapped me on the shoulder. 'Eat quickly and get your gear on. I'll meet you outside.' I bolted down a few bites, hurriedly put all my layers and boots back on, and rushed outside into the overcast evening. Russ and his crew had readied the Zodiac and I climbed into it.

We zoomed across the harbour to Auckland Island's Davis Cove, site of the Hardwicke settlement, which was covered in dense rātā trees. Russ jumped out of the boat and I followed him, snapping photos as he pointed at half-buried bricks, the faint indentations of roads, and bits of broken glass.

I tried to imagine a 14-room Government House, a warehouse and family cottages. Mothers, calling their young children to dinner. Mackworth, frowning in his dark coat and sideburns (I imagine him as Colin Firth's Mr Darcy from *Pride and Prejudice*) while passing a sentence on yet another drunken sailor. All was quiet in the forest, but I could sense the echoes of history.

We continued on to the neighbouring Erebus Cove, hurrying past the few remaining bricks of the failed Monckton farm and up a short boardwalk to reach Hardwicke Cemetery. It felt strange to visit a picket-fenced cemetery in the middle of nowhere, with only six graves, silent in the shelter of the trees. Photos of the cemetery had not prepared me for its smallness, or the loneliness of its location.

I looked down at Isabel Younger's crooked grindstone from 1850, with her grieving father's inscription of her infant initials. There too were the castaway graves of 'John' Mahoney, Jabez Peters and David McLelland, no longer just characters in books but real people who had been laid to rest there so long ago.

But there wasn't time for lingering or reflection. The wind was picking up and we needed to get back to the ship. As we clambered back into the Zodiac, I looked out at the choppy sea with trepidation; the ship looked far away. But I also knew that I was in safe hands. As soon as we left the sheltered cove the waves grew higher, the wind blasted fierce against my face, and we were flying across the grey sea: bump, bump, *splash*. I was immediately soaked, and completely elated.

Then I fell off my seat — but the right way, into the bottom of the Zodiac. That turned out to be a good thing because it sheltered me from the roughest few seconds before we reached the ship. I was hoisted up and there were hugs, cheers and applause. After many years of dreaming about it, I'd made it to my ancestor's

ABOVE The tiny and remote Hardwicke Cemetery on Auckland Island. There is a history of passing ships' crews tending to the little cemetery, starting from the late-19th century. These days it is a Heritage Site and managed by the NZ Department of Conservation.

OPPOSITE TOP Back in the Zodiac after my visit to the Hardwicke site, now overgrown with rātā trees.

OPPOSITE BOTTOM My return to the *Spirit of Enderby* from the Hardwicke site with Rodney Russ. Auckland Island is in the background.

birthplace at one of the most remote parts of the globe. It was a day I'd always remember, and a story I would be able to share with my own children.

Later that evening I sat alone on the ship's bridge and gazed out the large windows at the wind-rippled sea and the cold, driving rain. I looked over to Port Ross and tried to comprehend how a few dozen working-class families from England had lasted there for almost three years (let alone the Maungahuka settlers for 14 years) — especially the women in their Victorian-era dresses, caring for their young children and having babies, while dealing with drunken whaling crews, disillusioned husbands, terrible weather and a constant shortage of food.

In contrast, 164 years later I was enjoying all the comforts of a heated ship, with hot water on tap, wearing warm, weather-resistant clothing, and enjoying three-course meals (when I could keep them down). Yet how the wind howled outside, and how the ship shook, even with two anchors dropped in a sheltered port. Some things hadn't changed.

Conditions were too stormy the next day to venture ashore, so we sailed past Carnley Harbour, site of the *Grafton* wreck and the rātā-thieving *Erlangen*, heading further south to Campbell Island.

Our first morning in Perseverance Harbour dawned overcast and calm. In Zodiacs we searched the coastline for the rare Campbell Island teal and saw three. We visited the 'World's Loneliest Tree', which was looking verdant, if solitary, and photographed the rusted old Tucker Cove farm range sitting in the swampy grass. I took a selfie (from a respectful distance) with a majestic sea lion by the harbour.

We then arrived at the derelict huts of the former met station, carefully sidestepping another dozing sea lion. Traipsing in single file up the narrow, 3-kilometre (1.8-mile) Col Lyall Saddle boardwalk (my thoughts turned gratefully to the people who had placed these thousands of small planks, one after the other), we were surrounded by dracophyllum and flourishing megaherbs that looked as if they'd escaped from *Alice in Wonderland*: the yellow lily, *Bulbinella rossi*, and the Campbell Island daisy with its corrugated leaves, *Pleurophyllum speciosum*. The British botanist Sir Joseph

There is only one tree on Campbell Island: an introduced Sitka spruce native to the west coast of North America. Known as 'the loneliest tree in the world', it was planted at Camp Cove in the early 1900s during a visit by New Zealand Governor Lord Ranfurly. *The Guinness World Records* confirms it to be the world's most remote tree, as its nearest tree-neighbour is 220 kilometres (137 miles) away on the Auckland Islands. Over the decades, visiting scientists or met station residents would cut branches off the solitary spruce in December for a Christmas tree.

Hooker had been similarly filled with awe when he stumbled across these magnificent megaherbs in 1840 with James Clark Ross's expedition.

Up, up into the grey mist we went. Small white dots were scattered across the tussock-covered hills: nesting southern royal albatrosses, gradually taking shape as we approached them. Surprisingly large and white, they seemed completely unfazed by our presence. A few glided overhead, letting the wind carry their giant wings. Meanwhile, the adolescents on the ground were busy 'gamming' or practising their courtship ritual by spreading their wings, facing one another, and dancing from side to side; I tried to make a video of their odd clicking and yowling sounds on my phone, but all that was recorded was the roaring wind at the top of the ridge. Southern royal albatrosses are remarkable birds; they will spend up to 85 per cent of their lives at sea, returning to the island every few years from the age of ten to mate with a life-partner, and nesting within metres of where they themselves were hatched.

I knew little about Campbell Island before my visit, having focused most of my attention on the Auckland Islands because of my family history, but going there was an eye-opening experience. It was so much more than standing on a wind-

The ribbed leaves of *Pleurophyllum speciosum*, known as the Campbell Island daisy. Its large leaves help the native megaherb to absorb the intermittent sunshine.

A selfie with a nesting southern royal albatross.

blasted ridge; it was like entering a prehistoric era where wildlife and nature reigned, and I was hooked. As Russ told the accompanying news crew: 'You can read all the books, you can watch all the documentaries … but until you stand up here amongst the tussock and see the albatross, it's then that you take ownership.'[11]

The strong winds eventually got to me, and we had been told to head back to the ship when we were ready. I decided to venture back down the ridge by myself — following the boardwalk, so there was no chance of wandering off and getting lost (I did *not* want to become another 'Lady of the Heather', roaming across the island in gloomy exile). Within a few minutes, I was surrounded by total silence. I had never known such silence.

Before the expedition, I had assumed that going offline (literally and figuratively) for a week would be a struggle, but I had enjoyed the peace much more than I'd anticipated. The previous month had been filled with the outcome of the US election, the 'Brexit' result in Britain, and — closer to home —

a strong, midnight earthquake in my quake-prone city in New Zealand. Frankly, a short reprieve from all the tension and commentary was welcome. I'd also enjoyed getting to know the other passengers on the ship and having real conversations with people instead of simply 'liking' their Facebook posts.

I took my time heading back to the ship, stopping to photograph the exotic plants, enjoying the solitude, and taking in the views of the hills and Perseverance Harbour, exactly how it must have looked hundreds of years ago, with not a person in sight. At other times in my life I have visited locations that proved to be disappointingly crowded, such as the once-buried historic town of Pompeii in Italy. Not the case on Campbell; there were just 50 of us on the whole island.

At the bottom of the boardwalk, next to the old met station in Beeman Cove, I encountered the same sea lion we'd passed when we started out. However, this time I was very aware that I was alone — and he was awake, and watching me with interest. I looked nervously at him. He stared back at me. Suddenly he rose, and started to approach. My heart

The sound of silence on Col Lyall boardwalk.

hammered, and I struggled to plan a tactical response. Should I wave my arms and shout, or play statues? Should I look down deferentially, or would that imply too much vulnerability? Too much over-thinking, more like. I slowly backed away, and then scurried back up the boardwalk until I found some of the others.

The next day a few of us chose to hop back into the Zodiac for our final few hours at Campbell Island, and as we cruised around Perseverance Harbour, the final resting place of Captain Hasselburg, we were followed by playful young sea lions that dipped in and out of the water like dolphins. The weather was windy and wet, and it was the coldest I had felt during the whole trip. Even my waterproof gear was losing its battle against the elements. Still, I couldn't keep the smile off my face. I knew that I was incredibly fortunate to visit a place so remote, beautiful and dramatic, a seldom-seen World Heritage site filled with unique plants and rare wildlife, and with so much fascinating history. I had been afraid to come, but I'd done it anyway — and I already wanted to return. I had felt the pull of the subantarctic islands, and now I understood it. Visiting them had changed my life.

While in the midst of all these deep and profound thoughts, I was smacked in the face by a williwaw that had barrelled down the mountain and blasted us with its ferocious spray. But it was all right; our little boat didn't flip over. We all laughed in surprise, and returned home in one piece.

Besides, the islands belong to Mother Nature. It seemed only fitting that she should have the last word.

Pleurophyllum crineferum, another member of the daisy family.

Tourists enjoying Campbell
Island's magnificent megaherbs.

ACKNOWLEDGEMENTS

FIRSTLY, I AM INDEBTED TO the 'subantarctic writers' of the 19th and 20th centuries. In particular: Conon Fraser, Ian Kerr, Madelene Ferguson Allen, Allan W. Eden, Henry Armstrong, Keith Eunson, J.S. Cumpston, François Raynal, William Mackworth and Fergus McLaren.

Many people have been generous with their time, knowledge and resources while I was writing this book. In particular, I would like to thank Rodney Russ and the staff at Heritage Expeditions, Gareth St John Thomas and Anouska Jones of Exisle Publishing, Dr Christopher Robertson (ornithologist, mentor and friend), Rev. Derek Lightbourne (fellow passenger and kindred spirit), Mark Crompton, Giselle Clarkson, Joanne McDougall, Horst Münstermann, Kim Westerskov, Jo Hiscock, Rowley Taylor, Pete McClelland, the Prichard family, James and David Bade, Elliot Dawson, Sarah Howell, Ian and Gwyneth Armitage, Rachael Egerton, Gareth Winter at Wairarapa Archives, Michael Goldstein, Oliver Riddell, Jenny Phillips, Gail Gauldie, Chris and Yvonne Hall, John McCrystal, Gus Anning, and Chris Andrews.

Special thanks to my husband, Richard Hall, for his patience in listening to countless anecdotes about remote locations, and for minding our children while I travelled to New Zealand's subantarctic islands.

To my daughters, Ruby and Violet, for being able to identify southern right whales from the ages of seven and three, respectively, and also for understanding and tolerating 'Mummy is writing' and 'Mummy is going away on a ship'.

Thanks to Katherine Hurst, Michal McCracken, Nadine Bott and Eleisha McNeill for their ongoing support and encouragement, especially while I vanished into my studio to type for several consecutive months.

Thanks to Belinda Griffiths, Basia Smolnicki, and Hayley May for letting me rent a 'room of my own' in Shelly Bay with a view of the sea. It was most inspiring on wild, windy Wellington mornings!

Finally, thanks to the friendly staff at the Chocolate Fish Cafe for fuelling me with caffeine on a daily basis (without which this book would definitely not have been possible).

APPENDIX

Subantarctic island groups outside of the Antarctic Convergence (excluding many of the smaller rocks and islets):

- **Antipodes Islands/Moutere Mahue (NZ)**
  — Antipodes Island
  — Bollons Island

- **Auckland Islands/Motu Maha/Maungahuka (NZ)**
  — Adams Island
  — Auckland Island
  — Davis Island
  — Disappointment Island
  — Enderby Island
  — Ewing Island
  — Figure of Eight Island
  — Green Island
  — Ocean Island
  — Rose Island
  — Shoe Island

- **Bounty Islands/Moutere Hauriri (NZ)**
  — Depot Island
  — Lion Island
  — Penguin Island
  — Proclamation Island
  — Ruatara Island
  — Spider Island

- **Campbell Island group (NZ)**
  — Campbell Island/Motu Ihupuku
  — Dent Island
  — Folly Island
  — Jacquemart Island

- **Îles de Crozet (Crozet Islands) (France)**
  — Île aux Cochons (Pig Island)
  — Île de la Possession (Possession Island)
  — Île des Pingouins (Penguin Island)
  — Île de l'Est (East Island)
  — Îlots des Apôtres (Apostle Islets)

- **Diego Ramirez Islands (Chile)**
  — Águila Islet
  — Isla Bartolomé
  — Isla Gonzalo

- **'Emerald Island'**
  (a phantom island near Macquarie sighted multiple times in the 19th century; unclaimed)

- **Falkland Islands (Britain)**

- **Macquarie Island (Australia)**

- **Prince Edward Islands (South Africa)**
  — Marion Island
  — Prince Edward Island

- **Île Amsterdam (France)**
  — Île Saint Paul (Saint Paul Island)

- **The Snares/Snares Islands/Tini Heke (NZ)**

- **Tierra del Fuego (Chile and Argentina)**

Snares crested penguins.

ENDNOTES

INTRODUCTION

1. Cumpston, J.S. *Macquarie Island*. Antarctic Division, Department of External Affairs, Australia, 1968. v.
2. 'List of Antarctic and Subantarctic Islands.' Wikipedia. en.wikipedia.org/wiki/List_of_ Antarctic_and_subantarctic_islands
3. 'Te Reo Māori pronunciation guide.' Victoria University of Wellington.

CHAPTER 1. DISCOVERY: THE SEALING CAPTAIN, THE 'SHIP'S WIFE', AND THE LONELY GHOST (1780–1830)

1. In 1809, the captain changed the spelling of his surname from Hasselburg to Hasselburgh (Cumpston, 1968. 2.). For consistency's sake I've gone with Hasselburg, which is also how Ian Kerr (1976) spells it. Thanks to writer and historian Rhys Richards for confirming that there is no definitive 'right' way.
2. 'Seven stories high: record monster wave in Southern Ocean.' *The New Zealand Herald*, 9 May 2018.
3. 'Romantic Episodes: Southern New Zealand and its Outlying Islands.' *Otago Witness*, 10 November 1898. Retrieved via Papers Past.
4. Cumpston, 1968. 2–3.
5. Carrick admits that 'these are not the exact words used … in [the captain's] letters'. ('Romantic Episodes: Southern New Zealand and its Outlying Islands.' *Otago Witness*, 10 November 1898.)
6. ibid.
7. 'Macquarie Island: A Brief History.' Australian Antarctic Division website (www.antarctica.gov.au).
8. The story of the coordinates con-job is described in more detail in J.S. Cumpston's *Macquarie Island*, Australia Dept. of External Affairs, Antarctic Division, 1968. 11–12.
9. Druett, Joan. *Island of the Lost*. Allen & Unwin, 2007. 17–18.
10. Smith, Ian W.G. 'The New Zealand Sealing Industry History, Archaeology, and Heritage Management.' New Zealand Department of Conservation, 2002. 6.
11. Redwood, Rosaline. *Forgotten Islands of the South Pacific*. Reed, 1950. 62.
12. Phillips, Jock. 'Sealing — The sealers.' *Te Ara — the Encyclopedia of New Zealand*. Published 12 June 2006.
13. McNab, Robert. *Murihiku: A History of the South Island of New Zealand and the Islands Adjacent and Lying to the South, from 1642 to 1835*. Whitcombe and Tombs Limited, 1909. 285–86. (accessed via http://nzetc.victoria.ac.nz/tm/ scholarly/tei-McNMuri.html)
14. ibid. 288.
15. Fraser, Conon. *Beyond the Roaring Forties: New Zealand's Subantarctic Islands*. Government Printing Office, 1986. 85–86.
16. Mackworth, W. and Munce, W. *The Enderby Settlement Diaries*. Dingwall, Gregory, Fraser, Robertson (eds.). Wild Press and Wordsell Press, 1999. Entry dated 25 October 1950.
17. Kerr, Ian. *Campbell Island: A History*. A.H. & A.W. Reed, 1976. 15.
18. ibid.
19. As confirmed by meteorologist Mark Crompton, who lived for seven years on Campbell Island (see Chapter 11).
20. 'Romantic Episodes.' *Otago Witness*, 10 November 1898.
21. Kerr, 1976. 15.
22. The Jacobite uprisings involved several attempts in the late 18th century to restore the Stuarts to the British throne. King James Stuart II (of Britain and Ireland) and VII (of Scotland), Charles Stuart's grandfather, had been overthrown in 1688 because of his Roman Catholicism and his belief in the divinity of kings. The failure of the Jacobite uprisings caused Charles to eventually flee Scotland for France.
23. Eden, Allan W. *Islands of Despair: Being an Account of a Survey Expedition to the Sub- Antarctic Islands of New Zealand*. The Anchor Press, 1955. 25.

24. Kerr, 1976. 160–64.
25. Lawson, Will. *The Lady of the Heather.* Angus and Robertson, 1945.
26. Russ, Rodney and Terauds, Aleks. *Galapagos of the Antarctic: Wild Islands South of New Zealand.* Heritage Expeditions, 2009. 161–64.
27. McNab, 1909. 223–24.
28. 'Outlying Islands: Snares, the Maroons.' *Sydney Gazette*, 5 April 1817.
29. Warne, Kennedy. 'A Wing and a Snare, Part 2: Islands of Birds.' *New Zealand Geographic.* March–April 2003.

CHAPTER 2. EXPLORATION: THE POLAR EXPLORERS, THE CAPTAIN'S WIFE, AND THE BOTANIST WITH A SECRET (1760–1840)

1. McLaren, Fergus. *The Eventful Story of the Auckland Islands.* Reed, 1948. 20.
2. Bristow, quoted in Fraser, 1986. 82.
3. Anderson, Atholl. 'Prehistoric Archeology in the Auckland Islands, New Zealand Subantarctic Region.' Dingwall, Paul R., Jones, Kevin L., Egerton, Rachael (eds.). *In Care of the Southern Ocean: An Archaeological and Historical Survey of the Auckland Islands.* NZ Archaeological Association, 2009.
4. Lloyd Esler, personal communication. The information comes from Esler's 2014 book *Whaling and Sealing in Southern New Zealand.* 'Privateering' involved government-sanctioned takeovers and looting of foreign ships.
5. Druett, Joan. *Hen Frigates: Passion and Peril, Nineteenth-Century Women at Sea.* Simon & Schuster, 1999.
6. Fairhead, James. *The Captain and 'the Cannibal': An Epic Story of Exploration, Kidnapping, and the Broadway Stage.* Yale University Press, 2015. 316.
7. Chipman, Elizabeth. *Women on the Ice.* Melbourne University Press, 1986. 129–30.
8. Morrell, Abby Jane. *Captain's Wife: Narrative of a Voyage in the Schooner Antarctic. 1829, 1830, 1831.* (McInerney, Vincent (ed.)) Seaforth Publishing, 2012. Kindle edition, location 298.
9. Chipman, 1986. 130.
10. *Captain's Wife*, 2012, location 318.
11. ibid., location 124.
12. ibid., location 360.
13. ibid., location 381.
14. ibid., location 398.
15. ibid.
16. ibid.
17. ibid., location 1806.
18. Morrell, Abby, quoted in Chipman, 1986. 130.
19. Morrell, B., quoted in Fraser, 1986. 90–92.
20. Fairhead, 2015. 142.
21. *Captain's Wife*, 2012., location 58.
22. Morrell, Benjamin. *A Narrative of Four Voyages: The South Sea, North and South Pacific Ocean, Chinese Sea, Ethiopic and Southern Atlantic Ocean, Indian and Antarctic Ocean from the Year 1822 to the Year 1831.* Harper & Brothers, 1832. 379–80.
23. *Captain's Wife*, 2012., location 1847.
24. Jones, Kevin L. 'Terror Cove, Port Ross. The German Transit of Venus Expedition 1874 and other Scientific and Discovery Expeditions from 1840 to the Start of World War One.' *In Care of the Southern Ocean.* NZ Archaeological Association, 2009. 96–100.
25. 'Ross (lunar crater).' Wikipedia. Retrieved 1 November 2017.
26. McLaren, 1948. 35.
27. ibid.
28. *In Care of the Southern Ocean*, 2009. 100.
29. D'Urville, quoted in Fraser, 1986. 94.
30. D'Urville, quoted in Allen, Madelene Ferguson. *Wake of the* Invercauld: *Shipwrecked in the Subantarctic: A Great Granddaughter's Pilgrimage.* Exisle Publishing, 1997. 157.
31. Ross, quoted in Fraser, 1986. 99.
32. 'Mutiny on the *Bounty*.' Wikipedia.
33. Russ and Terauds, 2009. 63–65.
34. ibid. 81–85.
35. Schalansky, Judith. *Atlas of Remote Islands: Fifty Islands I Have Never Set Foot On and Never Will.* Penguin Books, 2010. 90.
36. Carrick, 1892. Quoted in Taylor, Rowley. *Straight Through From London: The Antipodes and Bounty Islands, New Zealand.* Heritage Expeditions, 2006. 9.
37. Ridley, Glynis. *The Discovery of Jeanne Baret: A Story of Science, the High Seas, and the First Woman to Circumnavigate the Globe.* Broadway Paperbacks, 2010.
38. ibid. 108.
39. Bougainville's journal, May 1768. Quoted in Ridley, 2010.
40. 'New to nature No 70: Solanum baretiae.' *The Guardian.* 8 April 2012. (Commerson did try to name a plant species after Baret, but it later turned out that someone else had already discovered it so the name was disregarded.)

CHAPTER 3. MAUNGAHUKA: THE WARRIORS AND THE SLAVES (1842–56)

1. The exact date of arrival is unknown, with contradictory records for either late 1842 or late 1843. Shand (1893), King (1989) and Fraser (2014)

all say late 1842. Either way, the Maungahuka colonists were the sole occupants of the Auckland Islands, apart from passing sealing and whaling crews, for at least six years before British settlers arrived in December 1849 (see Chapter 4).

2. Their arrival and subsequent colonization of the Chathams is described in King, Michael. *Moriori: A People Rediscovered*. Viking, 1989. 58–65.

3. Mikaere, Buddy. 'Maungahuka — the nearest Maori settlement to the South Pole.' *Tu Tangata* magazine, nos. 31 and 32, 1986.

4. Denise Davis and Māui Solomon. 'Moriori — Origins of the Moriori people.' *Te Ara — the Encyclopedia of New Zealand*, https://.teara.govt. nz/en/moriori/page-1

5. King, 1989. 62.

6. Denise Davis and Māui Solomon, 'Moriori', *Te Ara — the Encyclopedia of New Zealand*, https:// www.teara.govt.nz/en/moriori

7. King, 1989. 66.

8. ibid. 66.

9. ibid. 71.

10. ibid. 73.

11. ibid. 72.

12. ibid.

13. Fraser, Conon. *The Enderby Settlement: Britain's Whaling Venture on the Subantarctic Auckland Islands 1849–52*. Otago University Press, 2014. 29–30.

14. Shand, A. 'The Occupation of the Chatham Islands by the Maoris in 1835.' *The Journal of the Polynesian Society*, Volume 2, No. 2, June 1893. 78. (accessed via www.jps.auckland.ac.nz)

15. King,1989. 78.

16. ibid. 81.

17. Mikaere, 1986.

18. Loveridge, Donald (Dr). 'The Settlement of the Auckland Islands in the 1840s and 1850s: The Maungahuka Colony, the Enderby Colony and the Crown.' Waitangi research paper, 1995. 21.

19. Falla, Robert. 'A Vanished Township.' Yaldwyn, J.C. (ed.). *Preliminary Results of the Auckland Islands Expedition 1972–73*. Department of Lands & Survey, Wellington. 391.

20. Shand, 1893. 80.

21. Mikaere, 1986.

22. Fraser, 2014. 30.

23. Mackworth, W. and Munce, W. *The Enderby Settlement Diaries*. Dingwall, Fraser, Gregory, Robertson (eds). Wild Press and Wordsell Press, 1999. See entries from 17 March 1852 and 13 July 1852.

24. Mikaere, 1986. The letter and waiata are held in the Sir George Grey Special Collections, Auckland City Libraries, NZ.

25. Fraser, 2014. 206.

26. Shand, 1893. 82.

27. Mikaere, 1986.

28. King, 1989. 84.

29. McMillan, Karen. 'Rohana Tapu.' *Forget-them-not our past: Women of the Chatham Islands: Mahine, Wāhine, Frau*. Glentaniki, 1993. 9–13.

30. King, 1989. 64.

31. ibid. 70

32. ibid. 80.

33. Malone, R. *Three Years' Cruise in the Australasian Colonies*. London, 1854. 64.

34. King, 1989. 80.

35. ibid. 88.

36. ibid.

37. ibid. 70.

CHAPTER 4. HARDWICKE: THE SMALL TOWN AT THE END OF THE WORLD (1849–52)

1. Assistant Commissioner William Mackworth's letter to his mother in England, published in Fraser, Conon. *The Enderby Settlement: Britain's Whaling Venture on the Subantarctic Auckland Islands 1849–52*. Otago University Press, 2014. 22.

2. Mackworth, W. and Munce, W. *The Enderby Settlement Diaries*. Dingwall, Fraser, Gregory, Robertson (eds). Wild Press and Wordsell Press, 1999. Entry from 2 January 1850.

3. There are contradictory reports and opinions on whether the settlement was named Hardwicke at the official ceremony on 1 January 1850, or whether it was going to be the name of an established town that never eventuated. Mackworth's diary refers to the settlement variously as 'Port Ross', 'the settlement', and 'the Colony'. But Malone (1854) refers to it as Hardwicke. Fraser (2014) mentions the contradictions and thus calls it 'the Enderby settlement'. My opinion is that Hardwicke has been the commonly used name when referring to the settlement since at least 1854, including in Carrick (1892), McLaren (1948), and Eden (1955), so I have used it here.

4. Fraser, 2014. 46–47.

5. ibid. 34.

6. ibid. 25.

7. Trollope, Joanna. *Britannia's Daughters: Women of the British Empire*. Random House, 1983. 25.

8. McLaren, 1948. 49.

9. 'The Auckland Islands, and the First Settlement Upon them.' *Colonist*, Volume IX, Issue 844, 1 December 1865, page 2. Retrieved via Papers Past.

10. Loveridge, 1995. 36–42.

11. Mackworth. *ESD*. 11 January 1850.

12. Munce. *ESD*. 20 November 1850.
13. Mackworth. *ESD*. 6 January 1850.
14. Fraser, 2014. 29.
15. Mackworth. *ESD*. 10 January 1850.
16. ibid. 19–22 March 1850.
17. A nickname coined by Bishop Selwyn of New Zealand. The Bishop tried to visit the Auckland Islands, but was thwarted by bad weather.
18. *Southern Cross*, 29 March 1850. Retrieved via Papers Past.
19. King, 1989. 82.
20. *ESD*. XI
21. Mackworth. *ESD*. 1 January 1850.
22. ibid. 25 May 1851.
23. McLaren, 1948. Appendix III.
24. Fraser, 2014. 21, 73–74, 102.
25. ibid. 90–91.
26. *Wairarapa Times–Age*, 23 April 1938.
27. Manson, Cecilia and Cecil. 'Granny Cripps, a Famous Hostess of the Nineties.' Wairarapa Worthies No. 3, *Dominion*, 3 April 1954.
28. Macgregor, Miriam. *Petticoat Pioneers: North Island Women of the Colonial Era, Book One*. Reed, 1973. 52–55.
29. ibid.
30. Isaac Cripps' 1849 contract with the Southern Whale Fishery Company. Alexander Turnbull Library. Ref: MS-Papers-0347.
31. *Wairarapa Times–Age*, 23 April 1938.
32. Munce, *ESD*. 31 December 1851.
33. Fraser, 2014. 81.
34. Munce, *ESD*. 11 December 1851.
35. Harriet Cripps' signed baptism certificate, March 1852. Alexander Turnbull Library. Ref: MS-Papers-0347.
36. Macgregor, 1973. Harriet, their Hardwicke-born daughter, died in New Zealand aged 43, in 1894. She left seven children.
37. Fraser, C. 'Life in the Colony.' *ESD*. 199.
38. Dingwall, P. 'Farming and Gardening.' *ESD*. 234.
39. ibid.
40. Malone, R. *Three Years' Cruise in the Australiasian Colonies*. London, 1854. 66. (accessed via www.enzb.auckland.ac.nz)
41. Price, Des. 'Auckland Islands Settlement Doomed to Fail.' *NZ Genealogist*, September/October 1999.
42. Malone, 1854. 65.
43. Fraser, 2014. 62.
44. Mackworth. *ESD*. 4 February 1850.
45. ibid. 7 February 1851.
46. McLaren, 1948. 56.
47. Mackworth. *ESD*. 12 May 1851.
48. ibid. 12 February 1850.
49. ibid. 17–19 October 1850.
50. Munce. *ESD*. 19 October 1850.
51. ibid. 21 and 28 November 1851.
52. Mackworth. *ESD*. 18 March 1852.
53. Fraser, 2014. 118, 122, 167. Also in McLaren, 1948, who euphemistically describes the visits as 'some trouble'. 53. And King, 1989, who calls it 'Minor problems such as … European men chasing Maori women'. 83.
54. Journalist Robert Carrick, quoting Hardwicke's civil engineer Thomas Younger in later years. *Auckland Islands*. Ref: qMS-0397, Alexander Turnbull Library.
55. Fraser, Conon. 'Life on Campbell Island.' *A Musterer's Sojourn on Campbell Island: the Diary of Alfred Austin, 1919–1921*. Dingwall, Paul and Gregory, Geoff (eds.). Department of Conservation, 2004. 105.
56. Mackworth. *ESD*. 14 and 27 October 1850.
57. ibid. 5 May 1852.
58. ibid. 11 July 1852.
59. Fraser, 2014. 90 and 99.
60. Munce. *ESD*. 4 December 1850.
61. Fraser, 2014. 95–96.
62. Macdonald, Charlotte and Porter, Frances (eds.). *My Hand Will Write What My Heart Dictates: The Unsettled Lives of Women in Nineteenth-Century New Zealand As Revealed to Sisters, Family and Friends*. Auckland University Press with Bridget Williams Books, 1996. 254, 259, 270, 497–98.
63. Macdonald, Charlotte; Penfold, Merimeri; Williams, Bridget (eds.). *The Book of New Zealand Women: Ko Kui Ma Te Kaupapa*. Bridget Williams Books, 1991. 257–60.
64. Mackworth. *ESD*. 17 March 1850.
65. Dingwall, P. 'Whaling and Shipping.' *ESD*. 219.
66. Fraser, 2014. 31–43.
67. Mackworth and Munce. *ESD*. 31 August 1851.
68. In the 1860s, after a mysterious 'I.Y.' gravestone was discovered on Auckland Island, an article ran in a New Zealand newspaper and Thomas Younger was tracked down and interviewed about both his daughter's death and the grindstone. 'The Auckland Islands, and the First Settlement Upon Them.' *Colonist*, volume IX, issue 844, 1 December 1865. Retrieved via Papers Past.
69. King, 1989. 87.
70. Enderby, Charles. 'Abstract of Reports from the Commissioner of the Southern Whale Fishery Company to the Directors', 1850. Quoted in Dingwall, P. 'Farming and Gardening', *ESD*. 233.
71. Fraser, 2014. 183–195.
72. The Auckland Islands were absorbed into New Zealand's territory in 1863. In 1898, a letter arrived in New Zealand from a distant relative of Charles Enderby in England, claiming ownership of the islands. Her claim was not upheld. (Scadden, 1988.)

73. *Otago Witness*, 21 August 1852. Retrieved via Papers Past.
74. Fraser, 2014. 209–213.
75. Scadden, 1988.
76. Mackworth. *ESD*. 4 August 1852.
77. Krone, Hermann, translated and quoted in Bade, James. 'Hermann Krone's Record of the German Scientific Expedition to the Auckland Islands to Observe the Transit of Venus, 1874–1875.' From James Braund (ed.). *Ferdinand Hochstetter and the Contribution of German-Speaking Scientists to New Zealand Natural History in the Nineteenth Century*. Germanica Pacifica Vol. 10. Peter Lang Publishing, 2012. 96.
78. Fotheringham, B. 'The Southern Whale Fishery Company.' M. Phil. thesis, Scott Polar Research Institute, Cambridge University, 1995. 8.

CHAPTER 5. SHIPWRECKS: THE *GRAFTON*, THE *INVERCAULD*, AND THE *GENERAL GRANT* (1864–67)

1. Carrick, Robert. *New Zealand's Lone Lands: Being Brief Notes of a Visit to the Outlying Islands of the Colony*. George Didsbury, Government Printer, 1892. 31.
2. Armstrong, Henry. 'Cruise of the Brig Amherst: Official Report.' *Southland Gazette*, Volume 6, No. 9. 11 April 1868.
3. Pope, Lindsay. 'Wild Splendour.' *NZ Geographic*. October–December 1990.
4. Raynal, François. *Wrecked on a Reef; or, Twenty Months Among the Auckland Isles*. T. Nelson and Sons, 1884. 82.
5. ibid.
6. ibid. 109.
7. ibid. 165.
8. Musgrave, Thomas. *Castaway on the Auckland Isles: A Narrative of the Wreck of the 'Grafton' and of the escape of the crew after twenty months suffering*. Lockwood & Co, 1866. 33.
9. ibid. 84.
10. Raynal, 1884. 194.
11. ibid. 287.
12. Mortelier, Christiane. *Wrecked on a Reef or Twenty Months among the Auckland Isles – A facsimile of the text and illustrations of the 1880 edition published by Thomas Nelson & Sons, London, Edinburgh, and New York, with additional commentaries by Christiane Mortelier*. Steele Roberts, 2003. 242.
13. Fraser, 1986. 113.
14. Allen, Madelene Ferguson, quoting Robert Holding from his previously unpublished account written in 1919. *Wake of the* Invercauld: *Shipwrecked in the Sub-Antarctic: A Great Granddaughter's Pilgrimage*. Exisle Publishing, 1997. 85. Allen was adopted, and while researching her birth family she discovered that her great-grandfather was Robert Holding, an *Invercauld* survivor.
15. Allen, 1997. 90.
16. Allen, quoting Holding, 1997. 82.
17. Allen, 1997. Holding gives an account of one man pushing another, named Fritz. out of their makeshift tent for being a 'nuisance'. The next morning, Fritz was found face-down and dead. A few days later, the body had clearly been tampered with. 'Harvey had been eating some of Fritz,' wrote Holding. 152.
18. Allen, 1997. Holding's account. 150.
19. Initially Mahoney's identity remained a mystery, and his body was exhumed at least twice for inspection. These days Mahoney's plot is undisturbed and his gravestone serves as the only memorial to the *Invercauld* shipwreck.
20. Fraser, 1986. 112.
21. Allen, 1997. 156.
22. 'Narrative by William Sanguilly.' Published on www.wreckofthegeneralgrant.com (maintained by a descendant of the Jewell family).
23. ibid. All the survivors spoke well of the captain in their accounts of the shipwreck.
24. Eunson, Keith. *The Wreck of the* General Grant. Reed, 1974. 51.
25. Mary Ann's dramatic exit from the ship is described in Eunson (1974) and also in a letter from Joseph Jewell to his parents, written in 1868 and published on www.wreckofthegeneralgrant.com.
26. ibid.
27. Ormsby, Mary Louise. 'Teer, James', first published in the Dictionary of New Zealand Biography, vol. 2, 1993. *Te Ara – the Encyclopedia of New Zealand*, https://teara.govt.nz/en/biographies/2t35/teer-james
28. Eunson, 1974. 60.
29. 'Narrative of William Sanguilly.' www.wreckofthegeneralgrant.com. It's not clear if this was a serious discussion or simply a nervous joke amongst the group.
30. 'Wreck of the General Grant: Narrative of the Wreck, and Sufferings of the Survivors on the Auckland Islands.' *New Zealand Herald*, 28 January 1878. Retrieved via Papers Past. This is James Teer's account.
31. Letter from Joseph Jewell to his parents, 1868. Published on www.wreckofthegeneralgrant.com.
32. ibid.
33. Eunson, 1974. 73–74.
34. McLelland, aged 61, was buried at Hardwicke Cemetery.
35. *Southland Times*, 27 January 1868. Retrieved via Papers Past.

36. Eunson, 1976. 119.
37. Joseph Jewell in a letter to his parents, 1868. www.wreckofthegeneralgrant.com.
38. 'The Survivors — a New Life.' www.wreckofthegeneralgrant.com
39. For more about the numerous gold-salvaging attempts, read The General Grant's Gold by Madelene Ferguson Allen and Ken Scadden. Exisle Publishing, 2003.
40. 'A Strange Narrative.' *Otago Daily Times*, 19 December 1889.
41. 'Crozet Islands.' Wikipedia.
42. 'A Strange Narrative.' *Otago Daily Times*, 19 December 1889.
43. ibid.
44. *Pall Mall Gazette*, 9 May 1888. Quoted in 'Tamaris, Messages from the Sea.' www.messagesfromthesea.com/tag/tamaris/
45. 'A Strange Narrative.' *Otago Daily Times*, 19 December 1889.

CHAPTER 6. THE TRANSIT OF VENUS: THE ASTRONOMERS, THE PHOTOGRAPHERS, AND THE EPIC POEM (1874–75)

1. Dawson, Elliot W. and Duerbeck, Hilmar W. 'The German Transit of Venus Expedition at the Auckland Islands 1874–1875.' The Hutton Foundation New Zealand, Special Papers No. 3, 2008. Accessed via www.academia.edu.
2. Orchiston, W. 'The 1874 transit of Venus: New Zealand's first foray into international astronomy.' *Journal of the Royal Society of New Zealand*, 42:2, 145–52, DOI: 10.1080/03036758.2012.676053. 2012.
3. Dawson and Duerbeck. 2008. 4.
4. Bade, James. 'Hermann Krone's Record of the German Scientific Expedition to the Auckland Islands to Observe the Transit of Venus, 1874–1875.' From James Braund (ed.). *Ferdinand Hochstetter and the Contribution of German-Speaking Scientists to New Zealand Natural History in the Nineteenth Century*. Germanica Pacifica series, volume 10. Peter Lang Publishing, 2012. 95. The book includes rare English translations (by the University of Auckland) of Krone's writing.
5. One of Krone's epic poems is called *Die Robinsonade auf den Auckland-Inseln* (loosely translated as 'Castaway Narrative on the Auckland Islands') from the second volume of his *Dichtungen* series: *Vater und Sohn auf der Welt-Reise, 1874, 1875* ('Father and Son on a World Trip').
6. Jones, Kevin. 'Terror Cove, Port Ross: The German Transit of Venus Expedition 1874 and other Scientific and Discovery Expeditions from 1840 to the Start of World War One.' *In Care of the Southern Ocean*, 2009. 89.
7. Dawson and Duerbeck, 2008. 14 and 21.
8. Seeliger, quoted in Fraser, 1986. 145.
9. Krone, *Robinsonade*. Quoted in Bade, 2012. 93. A rare copy of Krone's *Robinsonade* in German can be found at the Alexander Turnbull Library, Wellington, NZ.
10. Bade, 2012. 104. Nineteenth-century writers never bothered to include the resolute Mrs Nelson's first name in their accounts of the short-lived farm.
11. Dawson and Duerbeck, 2008. 17.
12. Bade, 2012. 99–104.
13. Due to an application by David Bade, who wrote his University Honours in Geography dissertation about the Auckland Islands.
14. Dawson and Duerbeck, 2008. 14. Thanks to Marta Machura for checking my translation.
15. ibid. 16.
16. Bade, 2012. 90.
17. Dawson and Duerbeck, 2008. 4.
18. Photographic comparisons of the Terror Cove sites in 1874 and 2007 can be found in Armitage, Ian. 'The 1874 Transit of Venus Expedition at the Auckland Islands, Then and Now.' The Hutton Foundation New Zealand Special Papers No. 5, 2011.
19. Dawson and Duerbeck, 2008. 4.
20. 'How Far is the Earth From the Sun?' 17 September 2012. Published on www.space.com.
21. Fraser, 1986. 144–145.

CHAPTER 7. WRECK-WATCH: THE PROVISIONS DEPOTS AND CASTAWAY RESCUE MISSIONS (1865–1927)

1. Egerton, Burgess, Petchey, Dingwall. 'The Auckland Islands Shipwreck Era.' *In Care of the Southern Ocean*, 2009. 152.
2. ibid. 152–53.
3. ibid. 155.
4. ibid. 155–56.
5. 'The Enderby Island Rabbit – a Remarkable Story.' NZ Rare Breeds Society. www.rarebreeds.co.nz/endrabbitswhitman.html
6. Eunson, 1976. 113.
7. *In Care of the Southern Ocean*, 2009. 154.
8. ibid.
9. ibid.
10. Eden, 1955. 118.
11. Taylor, 2006. 170.
12. *In Care of the Southern Ocean*, 2009. 139. Eden, 1955. 39–42.
13. *Dundonald* survivor Charles Eyre, quoted in Fraser, 1986. 119.

14. Survivor Charles Eyre's account. *Feilding Star.* volume II, issue 435. 2 December 1907. Retrieved via Papers Past.
15. Fraser, 1986. 148–50.
16. *Feilding Star.* volume II, issue 435. 2 Dec 1907. Retrieved via Papers Past.
17. Eden, 1955. 149.
18. The men's shipwreck and eventual rescue is described in detail in Taylor, 2006. 139–54.
19. *Otago Witness,* 7 December 1893. Retrieved via Papers Past.
20. *Southland Daily News,* 1893. Quoted in Taylor, 2006. 152.
21. *Otago Daily Times,* 1913. Quoted in ibid.
22. Armstrong, Henry. 'Cruise of the Brig *Amherst*: Official Report.' *Southland Gazette,* Volume 6, No. 9. 11 April 1868.
23. Fraser, 1986. 116.
24. Taylor, 2006. 129–136.
25. *In Care of the Southern Ocean,* 2009. 154.
26. 'Stella Hut.' NZ Department of Conservation. www.doc.govt.nz/parks-and-recreation/places-to-go/southland/places/subantarctic-islands/auckland-islands/heritage-sites/stella-hut
27. Cass, Cynthia. *We Three Go South: The 1890 Diary of Ethel Richardson's Trip to the Sub-Antarctic.* Phantom House Books, 2015.
28. ibid. 85.
29. ibid. 88.
30. ibid. 100–101.
31. ibid. 102.
32. ibid. 136.

CHAPTER 8. PASTORAL LEASES: THE OPTIMISTIC FARMERS AND THE ISOLATED SHEEP (1874–1931)

1. Dingwall, P. 'Pastoral Farming at the Auckland Islands.' *In Care of the Southern Ocean,* 2009. 107.
2. Taylor, 2006. 183–86.
3. Eden, 1955. 81.
4. *In Care of the Southern Ocean,* 2009. 107.
5. Hermann Krone, quoted in Bade, James, 2012. 104.
6. Fraser, 1986. 124.
7. *In Care of the Southern Ocean,* 2009. 113.
8. McLaren, 1948. 93.
9. Eden, 1955. 83.
10. *In Care of the Southern Ocean,* 2009. 115.
11. ibid.
12. Eden, 1955. 84.
13. Kerr, 1976. 90.
14. ibid. 76–81.
15. ibid. 82.
16. Chipman, 1986. 37–38.
17. Dingwall, P. and Gregory. G. (eds.) *A Musterer's Sojourn on Campbell Island: the Diary of Alfred Austin, 1919–1921.* Department of Conservation, 2004.
18. ibid. Entry from 14 May 1921.
19. ibid. 12 July 1921.
20. Fraser, Conon. 'Life on Campbell Island.' ibid. 105.
21. ibid. 28 November 1921.
22. Eden, 1955. 22–23.
23. Fraser, 1986. 129.
24. Kerr, 1976. 115.
25. 'Actively Managed Historic Places: Southland Conservancy.' Department of Conservation. www.doc.govt.nz/Documents/conservation/historic/national-register-amhp/southland-historic-sites.pdf

CHAPTER 9. 'CAPE EXPEDITION': THE ENEMY RAIDERS AND THE WARTIME COASTWATCHERS (1939–45)

1. Bagley, Jones, Dingwall and Edkins. 'The *Erlangen* Incident and the Cape Expedition of World War II.' *In Care of the Southern Ocean,* 2009. 193.
2. Fraser, 1986. 155–56.
3. *In Care of the Southern Ocean,* 2009. 193.
4. ibid. 193–94.
5. Eden, 1955. 1–2. Turbott, 2012.1.
6. 'New Zealand coastwatchers executed by the Japanese.' NZHistory. Ministry for Culture and Heritage, updated 11 July 2017: nzhistory.govt.nz/page/nz-coastwatchers-executed-japanese
7. *In Care of the Southern Ocean,* 2009. 204.
8. Fraser, 1986. 156.
9. Turbott, 2002. 37–38.
10. ibid. 2.
11. ibid. 10.
12. Turbott, 2002. 18. Eden, 1955. 155.
13. 'Coastwatchers: Long, lonely stint waiting for the enemy.' *Otago Daily Times,* 15 August 1992. The article summarizes some of the oral history recorded from interviews conducted with former coastwatchers in the 1990s (the interviews can be accessed at Invercargill Library in NZ) and paints a somewhat bleaker picture than other published accounts. The two most comprehensive accounts published by coastwatchers (Eden, 1955 and Turbott, 2002) were written by men who lived at the Ranui Cove station in 1944 doing meteorological, scientific, and surveying work. Others' experiences, including from 1941–43 when dawn-to-dusk coastwatching was in full operation, may well have differed.
14. Eden, 1955. 4.
15. ibid. 11–12.
16. The memorial from the 1940s has since been replaced twice, most recently by a granite plaque

in 1996 by Rodney Russ of Heritage Expeditions. It is the only shipwreck memorial plaque on the Auckland Islands.

17. Eden, 1955. 43.

18. ibid. 61.

19. Fraser, 1986. 162. However, Eden wasn't impressed by Campbell Island, describing it as 'too small and too dreary'. (Eden, 1955. 28.)

20. Eden, 1955. 70.

21. 'Coastwatchers: Long, lonely stint waiting for the enemy.' *Otago Daily Times*, 15 August 1992.

CHAPTER 10. MACQUARIE ISLAND: THE PENGUIN OILERS, THE CRUSADING SCIENTIST, AND THE EXPEDITIONERS (1890–TODAY)

1. Cumpston, 1968. 60. Captain Douglass's opinion was backed up more than a century later by World War II coastwatcher and surveyor Allan Eden, who wrote: 'Macquarie Island is desolate and miserable to an extent that cannot readily be conceived.' (Eden, 1955. 177.)

2. 'Macquarie Island: A Brief History.' Australian Antarctic Division. www.antarctica.gov.au/about-antarctica/history/stations/macquarie-island

3. 'Geoheritage'. Tasmania Parks and Wildlife Service. www.parks.tas.gov.au/index.aspx?base=620

4. 'Emerald Island (phantom)'. https://en.wikipedia.org/wiki/Emerald_Island_(phantom).

5. Cumpston, 1968. 60.

6. Cumpston, 1968. 133. Hatch had initially denied that his ship was involved in illegal sealing, but this was evidence that he couldn't refute.

7. Chapple, Geoff. 'Harvest of Souls.' *NZ Geographic*. July–August 2005.

8. Cumpston, 1968. 149.

9. Fraser, 1986. 139.

10. Chapple, Geoff. 'Harvest of Souls.' *NZ Geographic*. July–August 2005.

11. *Southland Times*, 21 May 1890. Retrieved via Papers Past.

12. Fraser, 1986. 139.

13. *West Coast Times*, 2 June 1890. Retrieved via Papers Past.

14. Cumpston, 1968. 157, 160.

15. Chipman, 1986. 42.

16. 'The *Kakanui*.' *Evening Star*, 6 February 1891. Retrieved via Papers Past.

17. Cumpston, 1968. 163.

18. Subsequent scientific research showed that he may have been right. (Fraser, 1986. 139.)

19. Chapple, Geoff. 'Harvest of Souls.' *NZ Geographic*. July–August 2005.

20. ibid.

21. Horst Münstermann, personal communication.

22. 'Macquarie Island 1958.' YouTube. www.youtube.com/watch?v=NoSGe-E_d7U

23. 'Decision to close AAD research station on Macquarie Island reversed.' *The Mercury*, 16 September 2016.

24. Chipman, 1986. 44, 46.

25. 'Macquarie Island.' Tasmania Parks and Wildlife Service, 2001 (handbook).

26. www.facebook.com/MacquarieIslandStationSubAntarctic; www.antarctica.gov.au/webcams/macquarie-island

27. 'This week at Macquarie — 12 May 2017.' Australian Antarctic Division (www.antarctica.gov.au).

CHAPTER 11. CAMPBELL ISLAND METEOROLOGICAL STATION: THE WEATHER-WATCHERS AND THE WILDLIFE (1945–95)

1. Mark Crompton, personal communication.

2. 'Campbell Island.' https://en.wikipedia.org/wiki/Campbell_Island,_New_Zealand.

3. Judd's description of life on Campbell Island can be found in Jurisich, Mark. 'A Postal History of Campbell Island/Motu Ihupuku (NZ).' August 2017 (Monograph. 4th edition).

4. 'Mark Crompton, Weather Guru.' The Coasters Club (www.thecoastersclub.co.nz).

5. MacKenzie, Raewyn. 'Life on Campbell Island.' *NZ Geographic*. January–March 1989.

6. Chipman, 1986. 39, 185.

7. Joanne McDougall, personal communication.

8. 'Women in Weather.' iWonder Weather: NZ's Weather History. MetService. www.iwonderweather.co.nz/women-in-weather

9. Fraser, 1986. 166.

10. Kerr, 1976. 137–39.

11. Global Shark Attack File, 24 April 1992. Shark Research Institute. www.sharkattackfile.net/spreadsheets/pdf_directory/1992.04.24-Fraser.pdf

12. Funnell, John. *Rescue Pilot: The Daring Adventures of a New Zealand Search and Rescue Pilot.* Penguin Random House NZ, 2016. 170.

13. 'I was face to face with a shark.' *The Dominion*, 28 April 1992.

CHAPTER 12. CONSERVATION: THE SHEEP SHOOTERS, THE TEAL TACKLE, AND THE SUBANTARCTIC RANGERS (1960S–TODAY)

1. Arnold, L. and Pyne, K. *Britain and the H-Bomb.* Palgrave Macmillan, 2001. 96.

2. 'Researcher evacuated from remote island off New Zealand coast after cut from sea lion tooth.' 13 January 2017. Stuff.co.nz.

3. *Otago Daily Times*, 10 July 1998. One of the

last surviving Enderby Island cattle, 'Lady', also became the first large mammal to be cloned in the 1990s. (NZ Rare Breeds Society, www.rarebreeds.co.nz/enderby.html)

4. Visit milliondollarmouse.org.nz for more details on the eradication of mice from the Antipodes Islands.

5. 'Drones capture unique habitat of whales in the Auckland Islands.' Newshub, 23 August 2017.

6. Māori translations courtesy of DOC, Learning Media NZ, and Stewart Island Museum.

7. 'Actively Managed Historic Places: Southland Conservancy.' Department of Conservation.

8. Kerr, 1976. 126–27.

9. Chris Robertson, personal communication.

10. 'The Feral Sheep of Campbell Island.' (NZ Rare Breeds Society, www.rarebreeds.co.nz/campbella.html)

11. 'Eradication helicopter pilot Peter Garden recognized for international work.' 31 December 2016. Stuff.co.nz.

12. Pete McClelland, personal communication. Also 'Campbell Island rat eradication.' Department of Conservation. www.doc.govt.nz/our-work/campbell-island-rat-eradication

13. There is a similar story involving the elusive Campbell Island snipe, thought to be extinct for 150 years. It was rediscovered in 1997 on the outlying Jacquemart Island, which is the southernmost island in New Zealand territory, and has since successfully reintroduced itself (it can fly, unlike the teal) on Campbell Island.

14. Rowley Taylor, personal communication.

15. Taylor, 2006. 260.

16. Chris Robertson, personal communication.

17. 'New Zealand sea lion/rāpoka/whakahao.' NZ Department of Conservation. www.doc.govt.nz/sealion

18. Nadine Bott, personal communication.

19. Jo Hiscock, personal communication.

20. 'Yellow-eyed penguin/hoiho.' NZ Department of Conservation. www.doc.govt.nz/nature/native-animals/birds/birds-a-z/penguins/yellow-eyed-penguin-hoiho

21. 'Hoiho population falls to record low.' Radio New Zealand, 25 November 2017.

CHAPTER 13. TOURISM: THE MINISTER, THE COMIC ARTIST, AND THE DESCENDANT (1968–TODAY)

1. McLaren, 1948. 103.

2. 'Visiting the subantarctic islands.' NZ Department of Conservation. www.doc.govt.nz/parks-and-recreation/places-to-go/southland/places/subantarctic-islands/visiting-the-subantarctic-islands

3. 'VIPs endure icy tramp before island rescue.' The New Zealand Herald, 29 January 2003.

4. Stewart, Emma J., Espiner, Stephen, Liggett, Daniela, and Taylor, Zac. 'The Forgotten Islands: Monitoring Tourist Numbers and Managing Tourism Impacts on New Zealand's Subantarctic Islands.' Resources 6, no. 3: 38. 2017.

5. Guthrie-Smith, quoted in Taylor, 2006. 9.

6. Derek Lightbourne, personal communication.

7. Giselle Clarkson, personal communication.

8. Allen, 1997. 66.

9. Hiking New Zealand (www.hikingnewzealand.com)

10. Malone, 1854. 63.

11. 'Visiting New Zealand's little-known Campbell Islands.' Newshub, 5 January 2017.

BIBLIOGRAPHY

Books

Allen, Madelene Ferguson. *Wake of the* Invercauld: *Shipwrecked in the Sub-Antarctic: A Great-Granddaughter's Pilgrimage.* Exisle Publishing, 1997.

Austin, Alfred. *A Musterer's Sojourn on Campbell Island: the Diary of Alfred Austin, 1919–1921.* Dingwall, Paul and Gregory, Geoff (eds.). NZ Department of Conservation, 2004.

Braund, James (ed.). *Ferdinand Hochstetter and the Contribution of German-Speaking Scientists to New Zealand Natural History in the Nineteenth Century.* Germanica Pacifica series, volume 10. Peter Lang Publishing, 2012.

Carrick, Robert. *New Zealand's Lone Lands: Being Brief Notes of a Visit to the Outlying Islands of the Colony.* Government Printer, 1892.

Chipman, Elizabeth. *Women on the Ice: A History of Women in the Far South.* Melbourne University Press, 1986.

Cumpston, J.S. *Macquarie Island.* Australia Dept. of External Affairs, Antarctic Division, 1968.

Druett, Joan. *Island of the Lost: Shipwrecked at the Edge of the World.* Allen & Unwin, 2007.

—— *Lady Castaways.* Old Salt Press, 2015.

—— *Petticoat Whalers: Whaling Wives at Sea.* Collins Publishers NZ, 1991.

Egerton, Rachael; Jones, Kevin; Dingwall Paul (eds.). *In Care of the Southern Ocean: An Archaeological and Historical Survey of the Auckland Islands* (monograph). New Zealand Archaeological Association, 2009.

Eden, Allan. *Islands of Despair: Being an Account of a Survey Expedition to the Sub-Antarctic Islands of New Zealand.* Andrew Melrose, 1955.

Escott-Inman, H. *The Castaways of Disappointment Island.* Whitcombe and Tombs, 1946.

Esler, Lloyd. *Whaling and Sealing in Southern New Zealand.* Lloyd Esler, 2014.

Eunson, Keith. *The Wreck of the* General Grant. Reed, 1974.

Fairhead, James. *The Captain and 'the Cannibal': An Epic Story of Exploration, Kidnapping, and the Broadway Stage.* Yale University Press, 2015.

Fraser, Conon. *Beyond the Roaring Forties: New Zealand's Subantarctic Islands.* Government Printing Office Publishing, 1986.

—— *The Enderby Settlement: Britain's Whaling Venture on the Subantarctic Auckland Islands 1849–52.* Otago University Press, 2014.

Funnell, John. *Rescue Pilot: The Daring Adventures of a New Zealand Search and Rescue Pilot.* Penguin Random House NZ, 2016.

Kerr, Ian. *Campbell Island: A History.* Reed, 1976.

King, Michael. *Moriori: A People Rediscovered.* Viking, 1989.

Lawson, Will. *The Lady of the Heather.* Angus and Robertson, 1945.

McLaren, Fergus. *The Auckland Islands: Their Eventful History.* Reed, 1948.

McNab, Robert. *Murihiku: A History of the South Island of New Zealand and the Islands Adjacent and Lying to the South, from 1642 to 1835.* Whitcombe and Tombs, 1909.

Macdonald, Charlotte; Porter, Frances (eds.). *My Hand Will Write What My Heart Dictates: The Unsettled Lives of Women in Nineteenth-Century New Zealand As Revealed to Sisters, Family and Friends.* Auckland University Press with Bridget Williams Books, 1996.

Mackworth, William Augustus and Munce, William John. *Enderby Settlement Diaries: Records of a British Colony at the Auckland Islands 1849–1852.* Edited by P.R. Dingwall, C. Fraser, J.G. Gregory, C.J.R. Robertson. Wordsell Press and Wild Press, 1999.

Macgregor, Miriam. *Petticoat Pioneers: North Island Women of the Colonial Era*. Reed, 1973.

Malone, R.E. *Three Years' Cruise in the Australasian Colonies*. Bentley, 1854.

Morrell, Abby Jane. *Captain's Wife: Narrative of a Voyage in the Schooner* Antarctic *1829, 1830, 1831*. Edited with an introduction by Vincent McInerney. Naval Institute Press, 2012.

Peat, Neville. *Subantarctic New Zealand: A Rare Heritage*. Department of Conservation, 2003.

Raynal, F. *Wrecked on a Reef; or, Twenty Months Among the Auckland Isles*. Nelson, 1874.

Ridley, Glynis. *The Discovery of Jeanne Baret: A Story of Science, the High Seas, and the First Woman to Circumnavigate the Globe*. Broadway Books, 2011.

Redwood, Rosaline. *Forgotten Islands of the South Pacific: The Story of New Zealand's Southern Islands*. Reed, 1950.

Richardson, Ethel and Cass, Cynthia. *We Three Go South: the 1890 Diary of Ethel Richardson's Trip to the Sub-Antarctic*. Phantom House Books, 2014.

Russ, Rodney and Terauds, Aleks. *Galapagos of the Antarctic: Wild Islands South of New Zealand*. Heritage Expeditions, 2009.

Schalansky, Judith. *Atlas of Remote Islands: Fifty Islands I Have Never Set Foot On and Never Will*. Penguin Books, 2010.

Taylor, Rowley. *Straight Through From London: The Antipodes and Bounty Islands, New Zealand*. Heritage Expeditions, 2006.

Turbott, E.G. *Year Away: Wartime Coastwatching on the Auckland Islands, 1944*. Department of Conservation, 2002.

Vance, Matt. *Ocean Notorious*. Awa Press, 2016.

Wilkinson, Mike. *Our Far South*. Phantom House Books, 2012.

Yska, Redmer. *An Errand of Mercy: Captain Jacob Eckhoff and The Loss of The* Kakanui. Banshee Books, 2001.

Articles, reports and theses

Armstrong, Henry. 'Cruise of the Brig *Amherst*: Official report.' *NZ Government Gazette*, Southland Province, April 11, 1868. vol. 6, issue 9.

Bade, David. 'The changing imaginings and perceptions of the Auckland Islands: Placing the Auckland Islands into the Geography of Islands research and literature.' (Unpublished BA Hons. dissertation, University of Auckland, 2007.)

Carrick, Robert. 'Romantic Episodes: Southern New Zealand and its outlying islands.' *Otago Witness*, 10 November 1898.

Chapple, Geoff. 'Harvest of Souls.' *NZ Geographic*. July–August 2005.

Dawson, Elliot and Duerbeck, Hilmar. 'The German Transit of Venus Expedition at the Auckland Islands, 1874-1875.' The Hutton Foundation Special Papers No. 3. 2008.

Falla, R.A. 'A Vanished Township: Hardwicke, or Enderby Settlement.' *Preliminary Results of the Auckland Islands Expedition 1972-1973*. (ed. J. Valdwyn.)

Fotheringham, B. 'The Southern Whale Fishery Company.' PhD thesis, Scott Polar Research Institute, 1995.

Fowlds, George. 'The mystery lady of Campbell Island: who was she, princess or prisoner?' 1964. The National Library of NZ (photocopied booklet).

Jurisich, Mark. 'A postal history of Campbell Island/Motu Ihupuku (NZ).' August 2017 (Monograph. 4th edition).

Loveridge, Donald (Dr). 'The Settlement of the Auckland Islands in the 1840s and 1850s: The Maungahuka colony, the Enderby colony and the Crown.' Waitangi research paper, 1995.

Ludlow, Barbara. 'The enterprising Enderbys: Whaling for oil.' *Journal of the Greenwich Historical Society*, Vol. 3 nos. 4 & 5.

MacKenzie, Raewyn. 'Life on Campbell Island.' *NZ Geographic*. January–March 1989.

Manson, C. & C. 'Wairarapa Worthies, No.3: Granny Cripps, a hostess of the Nineties.' *Wellington Dominion*, 3 April 1954.

Mikaere, Buddy. 'Maungahuka: The nearest Māori settlement to the South Pole.' *Tu Tangata* magazine, nos. 31 and 32, 1986.

Pope, Lindsay. 'Wild splendour.' *NZ Geographic*. October–December 1990.

Price, Des. 'Auckland Islands settlement was doomed to fail.' *NZ Genealogist magazine*, Sep/Oct 1999.

Scadden, Ken. 'The Auckland Islands 1806–1900: Research in progress.' *Archifacts*. March 1988.

Shand, A. 'The occupation of the Chatham Islands by the Māoris in 1835: Part IV — Inter-tribal dissensions.' vol. 2, 1893. 74–86.

Warne, Kennedy. 'A Wing and a Snare, Part 2: Islands of Birds.' *NZ Geographic*. March–April 2003.

TV, radio and online

Dawson, Elliot W. 'The Auckland Islands/Motu Maha/Maungahuka/Subantarctic New Zealand: A working bibliography.' The Hutton Foundation New Zealand Special Papers No. 7. December 2012. Accessed via www.academia.edu.

'Invercauld: Catastrophe on the Auckland Islands.' *Intrepid NZ*. Series one, episode 2. TVNZ On Demand.

'Grafton: Perilous voyage to the mainland.' *Intrepid NZ*. Series one, episode 5. TVNZ On Demand.

Our Big Blue Backyard. Series 2, episode 5. TVNZ On Demand.

McCrystal, John. 'Shipwreck tales.' RadioLive. 2012–13.

'Our changing world: Exploring New Zealand's subantarctic islands.' Radio New Zealand, February 2014.

Australian Antarctic Division (www.antarctica.gov.au)

National Library of Australia (https://trove.nla.gov.au)

Early New Zealand Books, University of Auckland (www.enzb.auckland.ac.nz)

New Zealand Department of Conservation (www.doc.govt.nz)

New Zealand Electronic Text Collection, Victoria University of Wellington (nzetc.victoria.ac.nz)

Papers Past (https://paperspast.natlib.govt.nz)

The Rare Breeds Conservation Society of NZ (www.rarebreeds.co.nz)

Tasmania Parks & Wildlife Service (www.parks.tas.gov.au)

Te Ara, the Encyclopedia of New Zealand (https://teara.govt.nz)

The Yellow-Eyed Penguin Trust (www.yellow-eyedpenguin.org.nz)

'Wreck of the *General Grant*.' (www.wreckofthegeneralgrant.com)

PHOTOGRAPHIC CREDITS

INDEX